Volume 29, Number 2

differences

Black Marriage

Guest Editor
Ann duCille

Faith Ringgold, *Groovin' High* (1986). Acrylic on canvas, tie-dyed, pieced fabric border

Introduction: Black Marriage and Meaning from Antoney and Isabella to "Beyoncé and Her Husband"

Marriage has been a complicated concept in African American history. Chattel slavery, as a defining condition of blacks in the Americas, made everything abnormal, including the institution of marriage, not least because slaves were not allowed to marry legally. Historians like Lerone Bennett Jr. point out, however, that the earliest Africans in North America—"20 and odd Negroes" brought to Jamestown, Virginia, in 1619 and traded to the colonists—were treated as indentured servants, not as slaves. Two of them, known only as Antoney and Isabella (or Isabell), married some years later and in 1624 gave birth to a son, baptized William Tucker, believed to be the first black child born in the English colonies—that is, the first African American. Thus, as Bennett maintains, the black experience in North America began not with slavery but with marriage.

The issue of black marriage—the right of African Americans to partake of holy or civil wedlock and enjoy its legal privileges and protections—has been a greater force in u.s. history and the making (and breaking) of the nation and its laws and customs than we sometimes realize. The black slave Dred Scott, who unsuccessfully sued for freedom for himself and his family, lives in the annals of American history as the plaintiff in the infamous u.s. Supreme Court decision in *Dred Scott v. John Sandford* (1857) that declared the Missouri Compromise (1820) prohibiting slavery in the northern and western states and territories unconstitutional and decreed that no Negro, whether enslaved or free, was or could ever be a u.s. citizen with the right to sue in federal court or entitlement to any other civil liberties. What has received less attention than the political consequences of the ruling, however, is the fact that Scott had a wife, Harriet Robinson Scott, and that their marriage was at the heart of the notorious case, which she was instrumental in pushing forward through the courts.

Dred Scott and Harriet Robinson met and were allowed to marry in the 1830s while living with their respective masters in the free territories of Illinois and Wisconsin. In fact, it was Robinson's owner, Major Lawrence Taliaferro, an Army officer and justice of the peace, who married the two slaves in a civil ceremony and effectively gave away the bride to the groom's household so that the couple could live together as husband and wife. The fact that the Scotts had been legally married while living in free territory was a key component of their later suits for freedom, which reached the highest court in the land where, by a vote of seven to two, the justices made what many historians and legal scholars consider the Supreme Court's single worst decision: a landmark ruling that reeked of racism and proslavery sectional bias, propelling the nation closer to civil war.

Although not a named plaintiff in the case that reached the Supreme Court and little noted in the historical record, Harriet Scott, like her husband, had filed suit for freedom in the lower courts in the slave state of Missouri on the grounds of having been legally married and having lived freely in territories where slavery was prohibited. The fact that the Scotts and their supporters, including their lawyers, claimed wedlock as *prima facie* evidence of liberty and citizenship suggests precisely why it was that slaves were denied the right to marry. "Could one be truly married and be a slave?" Tera Hunter asks in *Bound in Wedlock: Slave and Free Black Marriage in the Nineteenth Century*. "Does marriage in itself imply certain rights of citizenship and confer social belonging?" (62). In answer, she quotes from the dissenting opinion of Justice Benjamin R. Curtis in *Scott v. Sandford*: "There can be no more effectual abandonment of the legal rights of a master over his slave, than by the consent of the master that the slave should enter into a contract of marriage, in a free state" (qtd. in Hunter 62). Each in its own way a "peculiar institution," slavery and marriage were incompatible, even for those bondmen and women who managed to wed on free soil.

Ultimately, the Scotts' wedding vows were not enough to win them freedom or citizenship, but their case and other freedom suits and citizenship claims based on matrimonial rights suggest the complications this other peculiar institution held and would continue to hold for African Americans, even, if not especially, after emancipation.

Even now, well into the twenty-first century, debates continue to rage over the status of the marriage contract and condition within African American communities. The union of Barack and Michelle Obama, for eight years the First Couple, is pointed to as a model marriage at the same time that many experts pronounce the death of the institution for African Americans and present alarming statistics to support their claims. Marriage rates are declining nationally across racial groups, but the drop is particularly dramatic among African Americans and, it is argued, especially consequential for black women, who studies show are at least three times more likely than their white female counterparts never to marry.

In a 2011 monograph with the provocative title *Is Marriage for White People? How the African American Marriage Decline Affects Everyone,* the Stanford University law professor Ralph Richard Banks asserts that for black women, "[B]eing unmarried has become the new normal, single the new black" (6). As Rebecca Wanzo, one of the contributors to this special issue, has wisely pointed out in another venue, facts and figures behind such claims have a built-in heterosexual presumption. "Statistics are not adjusted for women who do not want husbands," she writes, "either because they desire women or because they may sexually prefer men but remain single by choice" (2). Contemporary discussions about the dearth of eligible black men and the plight of the unmarried and unmarriageable black professional woman, in particular, not only erase lesbians and women with no need or desire for a husband; they also oversimplify a historical dynamic and current climate that are far more complex than mere numbers suggest.

The essays collected in this volume offer variations on the theme, concept, complications, contradictions, and complex history of black marriage. Contributors—who include historians, social scientists, literary theorists, and legal scholars—examine what the institution has meant and continues to mean in African American culture, from both historical and contemporary perspectives. Essays look back to scholarly, legal, and literary treatments of the marriage question, from the earliest days of blacks in the Americas to current concerns and new modes of investigation, including the critical interventions of black feminist scholars such as Tera Hunter and Hortense Spillers working to resurrect and restore to American history lost, erased, and overlooked black female figures like Harriet Robinson Scott. Topics treated in this special issue range from Beyoncé's music and marriage as played out sonically, socially, and autoethnographically in her visual album *Lemonade* and her husband Jay-Z's response in *4:44* to such timely intimate matters as interracial coupling and its new genre of advocacy literature; marriage equality and the good, the bad, and the perilous of *Obergefell v. Hodges* granting marriage rights to same-sex couples; the "marital alibis" of fallen black celebrity "love objects" like Michael Jackson and Bill Cosby; black female "oneness" and the crisis of coupling in the work of Audre Lorde and Toni Morrison; and the historical rise and fall of African American marriage rites and the right to marry.

We are particularly honored to open this issue with a conversation with the distinguished black feminist critic Hortense Spillers, the Gertrude Conaway Vanderbilt Professor of English at Vanderbilt University, whose work across four decades in the academy has been pivotal in reassessing the institutions of slavery, marriage, and family. We join the disciplines of historical, literary, and feminist studies in commemorating the thirtieth anniversary of the publication of Spillers's revolutionary essay "Mama's Baby, Papa's Maybe: An American Grammar Book" (1987), which has transformed how we read and write the African American past.

We are also pleased to include a special section on what might be called the present, if not the final, frontier in considerations of color and coupling: the question of marriage equality. Occasioned by and in response to Katherine Franke's provocative monograph *Wedlocked: The Perils of Marriage Equality* (2015), three distinguished social scientists and legal scholars, Mignon Moore, Kendall Thomas, and Patricia J. Williams, discuss and debate the cautionary tale Franke advances about what can be both gained and lost with the acquisition of certain civil rights and legal responsibilities. In *Wedlocked*, Franke, the Sulzbacher Professor of Law and Director of the Center for Gender and Sexuality Law at Columbia University, undertakes a probing comparative analysis of black and gay campaigns for the right to marry. Drawing on the experiences of former slaves, free to wed legally for the first time after the Civil War, Franke explores the social, cultural, and judicial complications inscribed within the institution of marriage as a highly regulated, inherently patriarchal construct, which, she argues, has profound implications for the LGBTQ community and for same-sex marriage. Williams, Moore, and Thomas respond here in equally probing and provocative essays that attend in particular to issues of history, race, gender, and the consequences of *not* having such rights, particularly for nonnormative communities. Thomas's reading of the 2018 film *Black Panther* carries the question of black marriage into the Afrofuturistic realm of Wakanda, closing this special issue and opening new avenues for thinking about black coupling and its relation to the state.

Marriage may not be for everyone, but it should be for anyone. As a nation with a nearly four-hundred-year history of denying the fundamental right to marry to those it others—and remembering, in particular, the transgendered—we still have miles to go to arrive at what Toni Morrison defines in *Beloved* as real freedom: a place where we can love anyone we choose, "not to need permission for desire" (162).

ANN DUCILLE, emerita professor of English at Wesleyan University, is currently a visiting member of faculty at the Pembroke Center for Research and Teaching on Women and the Center for the Study of Race and Ethnicity in America (CSREA) at Brown University. She is the author of *Technicolored: Reflections on Race in the Time of* TV (Duke University Press, 2018), *Skin Trade* (Harvard University Press, 1996), and *The Coupling Convention: Sex, Text, and Tradition in Black Women's Fiction* (Oxford University Press, 1993), as well as numerous articles in the fields of American and African American studies, popular culture, and feminist theory.

Works Cited

Banks, Ralph Richard. *Is Marriage for White People? How the African American Marriage Decline Affects Everyone.* New York: Dutton, 2011.

Franke, Katherine. *Wedlocked: The Perils of Marriage Equality.* New York: New York UP, 2015.

Hunter, Tera. *Bound in Wedlock: Slave and Free Black Marriage in the Nineteenth Century.* Cambridge, MA: Harvard UP, 2017.

Morrison, Toni. *Beloved.* New York: New American Library, 1987.

Wanzo, Rebecca. "Black Love Is Not a Fairytale." *Poroi* 7.2 (June 2011): 2–18. http://ir.uiowa.edu/poroi/vol7/iss2/5/.

HORTENSE SPILLERS
with ANN DUCILLE

Expostulations and Replies

*H*ortense Spillers, the Gertrude Conaway Vanderbilt Professor at Vanderbilt University and one of the undisputed deans of black feminist theory, has a significant presence in this special issue of *differences*, as she does in the broader realm of American and African American letters. A number of the contributors to this issue draw on and engage with her important body of scholarship. In light of this fact and in honor of the thirtieth anniversary of the publication of her masterful critical intervention "Mama's Baby, Papa's Maybe: An American Grammar Book," we thought it not only appropriate but also imperative to include her voice, her insights, and her current thinking on this special issue's theme, "black marriage," and on the state of the field that she has been so instrumental in developing. We sent Professor Spillers a set of eleven questions, hoping that she might address a few of them. Happily, she generously replied to all of them. As you will see, each response is its own deeply reasoned, richly textured, profoundly provocative, and poetically penned essay, which we are delighted to share with our readers.

Volume 29, Number 2 DOI 10.1215/10407391-6999746

© 2018 by Brown University and **d i f f e r e n c e s : A Journal of Feminist Cultural Studies**

Ann duCille: The original call for this special issue invited contributors to "revisit the subject of 'black marriage,' examining what the concept has meant and continues to mean in African American culture, broadly considered from both historical and contemporary perspectives." Your work, especially your pivotal 1987 essay "Mama's Baby, Papa's Maybe: An American Grammar Book," forces us to reconsider the terms—the "grammar"—of our history and our discourse, especially in thinking and writing about slavery. *Marriage* is certainly one of those terms and concepts "thrown into unrelieved crisis," as you suggest, by the facts and fictions, the ungendering, the dispossession, and the dislocation of desire born in and of the violence and violation of kidnap and captivity. I wonder, then, what you might say about the inherently fraught nature of our theme—about the question of "black marriage" and what you have spoken of as the coercive conjugality and "shadow families" that the "peculiar institution" produced.

Hortense Spillers: Even though the "peculiar institution" has exercised an unfathomable impact on the historical subjects most directly affected by the trans-Atlantic slave trade—which is to say, those African communities along the African littoral of the western Atlantic—it might also be said to have shifted the entire social calculus of intimate relations across all the demographies that participated in the world of slavery. In other words, I am now convinced that the "problem of slavery," as David Brion Davis named the phenomenon, actually produced no "winners," if we think of the latter as the place from which "freedom" is defined. If that is the case, then "marriage" and "family," as two of the practices that advanced the idea of a racialized perception of reality, will have to be reconsidered; the "shadow family," for example, or those families engendered in sexual congress between masters and enslaved women, disappears into the massive operations of the everyday world. Unless such families are isolated by historians, as in the case of Sally Hemings's children with Thomas Jefferson in the research of Annette Gordon-Reed, a lay audience gets the impression that contact between slave and free was limited. But I'm convinced that the practice of concubinage, or just plain sexual exploitation, was so common across the Atlantic world of the eighteenth and nineteenth centuries that we don't even have a name for it yet. The incontrovertible quiddity of these social and cultural phenomena was so insistent and pervasive that Frederick Douglass, as you will remember, called the fruit of these relationships "new people." My question is, to what extent did the presence of these children and their mothers, or the families that lived in the interstices of the institution of marriage, or in the shadows of the "official" family, transform what went on in the Big House? Do we still call the Big House relations between a husband and wife a *marriage*, and if so, what kind of marriage was it? Do we call the relations between husband and wife under those conditions love relations? What happens to our concepts of love and intimacy under those circumstances? The laws protect the rights of property and sexuality and legacy under slavery so that masters could have their cake and eat it, too; I suppose that this has always been the way of power, and power in this instance is no different. But I now believe that our "sentimental education" is inadequate as we have inherited it because it cannot explain how, on the one hand, the official family is "loved" while, on the other, the "shadow" family is disinherited for the most part, or not loved enough. I have to go for broke in this case because it has upset what I thought I knew about love and marriage, period. That is what I mean when I say that the whole social calculus comes under question when and where slavery prevails. This is one of the subjects with which I am attempting to come to grips at the moment.

AD: In the author's note to *Dessa Rose* (1986), Sherley Anne Williams writes, "I loved history as a child, until some clear-eyed young Negro pointed out, quite rightly, that there was no place in the American past I could go and be free" (5–6). "Mama's Baby" has had that kind of effect on generations of feminist scholars and critics. I mean, it is that kind of "clear-eyed" seismic disruption reminding us that there is no place in the African American past we can go and be "woman," "wife," "mother," "daughter." The intervention you make in "Mama's Baby" continues to reverberate throughout the critical enterprise of contemporary scholars and theorists. One feels its presence in the work of Saidiya Hartman and Farah Jasmine Griffin and Jennifer Morgan and Shelly Eversley (who interviewed you in 2006) and Christina Sharpe and Aliyyah Abdur-Rahman and Sharon Holland and Kevin Quashie, to name only a few of many scholars and theorists engaged in what you call "the retrieval of mutilated female bodies" ("Mama's" 68). A number of the contributors to this special issue cite "Mama's Baby" as formative and foundational. I know you have said that you simply wanted to "find a vocabulary" that would make black women part of a larger conversation that black people had historically initiated but were positioned outside of, as nothing more than "raw material"—the peasant under glass syndrome, I call it. Yet, at the same time that you wanted to center black women within feminist discourse, you also wanted to move the conversation beyond the "gender question." Do you have the sense that the conversation has moved in the ways you hoped? Is newer work taking up the challenges you put forth in your groundbreaking (I won't say "seminal") essay? Are we something more than raw material these days?

HS: The work that our generation carried out on gender and race relations in their intersectional configuration has been vividly advanced by brilliant scholarship that comes after; I do think that work on African American women quite specifically is no longer peripheral to feminist criticism, but rather, has assumed if not centrality then a vivid discursive presence in our broader exchanges. I cannot think of a single subject that feminist critique takes up today that can proceed without reference to the African American project right across the field of cultural criticism, from birth to death. In Saidiya Hartman's research, for example, the thematics of coercive entertainment and bondage has been so poignantly reread that what was inchoate in "Mama's Baby, Papa's Maybe" has become an ineluctable feature of our whole understanding of conditions of enslavement. The newer work, in my view, has fleshed out many of the hunches that we had before the turn of the century, and to that extent, the new scholarship has changed the tune. Let's say that the new has yielded a different pattern of drumming riffs!

AD: Although I refuse the paradox of "seminal," as you yourself have pointed out, men, too, are in "Mama's Baby." You in effect issue a warning in the essay that black men cannot afford to become white men—that is, to assume what Zora Neale Hurston calls the like-a-white-man ways of patriarchy or, as you say in the "Whatcha" interview, "to appropriate the gender prerogatives of white men." Because of their different history, a history shared with black women, you explain, "Men of the black diaspora are the only men who had the opportunity to understand something about the female that no other community had the opportunity to understand, and also vice versa" (Spillers et al. 304). There was a kind of African American communitarian androgyny, an ungendered humanity that your young self believed black culture was on the brink of creating. That ship has sailed, you seem to say, but has it sunk?

HS: This is a difficult question to negotiate because intervening patterns of living and experience have so interpolated themselves into our considerations that there is no direct route to an answer. For one thing, the field of cultural critique has so flowered and proliferated that certain assumptions that were in place in, say, 1987 are no longer where they were. If we have had to ask, not tongue-in-cheek, what is a "woman," how does gender work, we have also had to add "men" and "male" to the social calculus. I do not think that we have yet reached that "ungendered humanity" that you pose in your question, but in a circumlocutive way, we have approached it by way of interrogations advanced by LGBTQ/differently abled historical subjects whose inquiries have shattered our working assumptions; we now have to start from a different vantage—"women" and "men" in all the porosity of gender signature so that we "start" from a vantage of uncertainty or do not know where a path will lead until we reach it! At the same time, though, I suspect that the questions we posed about black males of the diaspora in 1987 have not entirely run their course because "queerness," for example, has not exhausted the realities of "difference," but simply highlighted them. What, for instance, is the black gay man's relationship to straight women, to women who are lesbians? Does the black gay man assume maleness in relationship to them, or can he afford to discover another style of attitude?

AD: You end "Mama's Baby" with a riff on the Sapphire stereotype that both excites and embarrasses me. You suggest, "'Sapphire' might rewrite after all a radically different text for female empowerment." I'm excited by the idea of claiming Sapphire as a figure of black female empowerment, but I'm ashamed of myself when I see some loud "angry black woman" figure in popular culture today and catch myself slipping into the head shaking and eye rolling my mother used to perform (between chuckles) watching Sapphire's antics on *Amos 'n' Andy* back in the 1950s and '60s. I think of the hypersexual madwoman personas the comedian Leslie Jones often assumes on *Saturday Night Live*, for example. Will you say more about claiming/reclaiming Sapphire, as a black female figure with the power to name?

HS: I must say that the way you put the matter in this question makes me have to think again about that "Sapphire" reclamation! I see your point about the uses to which certain black popular culture manifestations have been put. The hypersexual madwoman persona is a bit hard to take, I would admit! But here's a thought: I am now of the opinion that the behavior we associate with a plethora of black responses actually originates in the afterlife of slavery, to echo Saidiya Hartman, and that is to say, in the unfettered violence of force. To realize that does not alter the problematic of "Sapphire" and all the iterations of which "she" is capable, but it might open a breach that permits perspective. The problem here might be not the black comedienne who crosses a line to a discerning eye but the mechanisms that are chosen to frame the situations of employment that continue to rely on stereotypical, even archetypical, notions of what a black woman is, how she behaves. If Sapphire was, in the first place, a parody; if this character never really existed anywhere; if all the time, she was Amos's and Andy's twin in the sense that they were all produced from the same ovum, then we are, as Nicole Fleetwood might say, having to contend with the problem of frames of seeing: the problem of public relations and who "they" say black people are. To my mind, one of the ongoing crises of black reality is how we are seen, and this has to do with the realm of rumor, or the practices and institutions of public relations. And those relations are undergoing glacial change. I would dare predict that the day might well come when sNL will be forced, at the level of televisual unconscious, let's call it, to "think" something else for a Leslie Jones that is not minstrelsy updated. If that in fact occurs, then "Sapphire" will not have gone anywhere, will not have had to have gone anywhere, except Madame Tussaud's! Again, though, "Sapphire" signifies a female who talks back, and it seems to me that we do not want to lose that after all. We have seen what happens when historical subjects who are women do not talk back! The outcome of the 2016 presidential election tells us exactly what that looks like! An enormous white elephant, stalking the hallways of our would-be quiet!

AD: "'Peaches' and 'Brown Sugar,' 'Sapphire' and 'Earth Mother,' 'Aunty,' 'Granny,'" and so on. Are there other names for black females as "marked women" that you would add to this list today? This does, of course, relate to the preceding question. I wonder what you make of some of the dominant representations of "black womanhood" today (if that's what they are). I think certainly of Beyoncé, of the debates about her feminism, and, of course, of bell hooks's famously calling her a "terrorist." Not that I imagine you have a lot of time for television, but if you do (on occasion) tune into shows like *Scandal* or *How to Get Away with Murder* on ABC or *Empire* on Fox or *Insecure* on HBO, I would love to hear what you make of their black female leads, Olivia Pope (Kerry Washington), Annalise Keating (Viola Davis), Cookie Lyon (Taraji P. Henson), and/or Issa Rae as Issa Dee, or their creators, such as Shonda Rhimes.

HS: I should, but I customarily do not follow the new television series; from time to time, I've dipped into *Scandal*, but to be frank, the *writing* of this programming seems to come from the same hands: the kinetic and discursive gestures, the lines of narrative emplotment, the camera angles, the way the scenes are set, and so on are all predictable and so repetitive that it is as if we are watching different versions of the very same story. I am pleased to see more black faces on the screen because the achievement announces the goal of diversity in programming, and that's a good thing, but I want better stories rather than black actors repeating the same old, same old. The stories as types do not, to my mind, challenge our imaginative and intellectual powers, but cross terrain with which we are already overfamiliar; I would like to see this narrative and imagistic overdetermination demolished so that we might begin to plunge down into the depths of human feeling and response rather than dwell on the comfortable surfaces. The black female lead tends to look exactly like the white one, I think, and where does that leave us?

AD: Along those same lines, "Mama's Baby" has always provoked and unsettled me. Every time I turn to it, I discover something new I didn't see before or didn't grasp. It hasn't aged; it has only become more salient, more powerful. It's like an onion whose layers I keep peeling, finding more and more pulp, more and more sustenance. I cannot imagine it as anything more, but is there something you would add (or subtract) thirty years later? A postscript, perhaps?

HS: Actually, there is a kind of postscript to "Mama's Baby" offered in the penultimate section of "'All the Things You Could Be by Now, If Sigmund Freud's Wife Was Your Mother.'" In that section of the latter essay, which anticipates your question, above, I attempt to take up the problematic of missing and absent fathers. As I see it, those two positions are to be differentiated: Missing fathers are fathers who have been subtracted, or extirpated, from the field of social play, as I believe many African fathers this side of the Middle Passage were, in fact; they are removed on behalf of convenience to a protocol of degradation so that greater harm can be inflicted or harm visited on the body of a community with impunity. We know all the reasons why such fathers would not have been welcome on the social scene. My conviction is that this removal occurred systematically and with all the willful violence of a genocidal intention. Absent fathers, by contrast, might "choose" to disappear, though we might never know why they do. My own paternal grandfather, for example, as my father told his children the story, was not known to his infant son. I will never forget that my father, who died at ninety years old in 1995, having been born in 1905, said very simply and elegantly, "I never knew my father," in heartbreaking periodicity—a rending break in human and social procedure. I often wonder about that grandfather and what happened to him, why he left Miss Allee, my father's mother, and her beautiful little boy, Curtis, who was actually raised by his maternal Uncle Benny, who lived with his and Aunt Beulah's large family in the big city, Memphis. I feel pathos for the absent father in this case, but if it makes any sense, I also thoroughly dislike him and imagine that if I ever met him along a roadway somewhere, I might be moved to smack him upside his fat head! Look at what you left, I might say! In any case, the Moynihan Report does not sufficiently discriminate between these postures of black father-hood and simply elides them, though they might well overlap. The Report wants to make the problematic of fatherhood the culprit, when, to my mind, the picture is infinitely more complicated than that. What I never admitted, because I did not want to agree with Moynihan's conclusions and do not agree now, is that the missing and/or absent father *is* problematic, but not for the reasons that the Report supposes. The absent/missing father engenders a crisis for the woman who is the mother and the one who bears the children and for the children of the union, not because it looks bad to the world! And not because it makes the women/mothers stronger than they normally would be. That whole analysis, to my mind, is mistaken because it takes "itself" as paradigmatic, which I regard as an error. What I am trying to do in that part of the essay, then, is to articulate the crisis of authority as it changes hands from one generation to the next. If this transfer happens without a father figure, what are the implications of that failure for *intramural* relations, or lateral relations, as well as vertical ones? I didn't know enough in 1987 to position the question in this way without "blaming" black women. I know slightly more now than I did then and firmly believe that on the "other side" of the Middle Passage, where we are located, African Oedipus was never solved and that it is our business to solve it, not so much by learning the names of the African peoples from whom we've come—because that *is* the crisis!—wherein answering it would dissolve something of the riddle. This is the Skip Gates protocol, and it is a useful one. But what I'm talking about is a heuristic device, a way to satisfy a hermeneutic demand, to find a way to break the thrall of silence of the African past. The "father" is there, on the African side of the Middle Passage, and "he" transfers his authority through mothers and fathers on *this* side. The whole point of "All the Things" was an attempt to find a way to erect a scaffold of narrative and analysis that would set up this problem—not to answer it, because we cannot, or cannot easily answer it, but to plausibly respond to the sheer complexity of a conundrum that might *stand in for* a solution.

AD: Speaking of "'All the Things You Could Be by Now, If Sigmund Freud's Wife Was Your Mother': Psychoanalysis and Race" (1996), Rebecca Wanzo, one of the contributors to this issue, has pointed to that piece as another of your gripping, awe-inspiring essays. It, too, represents a foundational intervention in the field that links race, African American culture, and psychoanalytic theory. In an interview with Tim Haslett in 1998, you elaborate on the point you make in the essay about "interior intersubjectivity" and the distinction you draw between the "one" and the "individual," even though, as you said, the positions overlap. "The individual of black culture exists strictly by virtue of the 'masses,'" you wrote in 1996, "which is the only image of social formation that traditional analysis recognizes" ("'All'" 395). Rebecca Wanzo wonders whether you have more to say about this distinction between the "one" and the "individual" today. What, if anything, would you add or change in your analysis? Has African American culture found a place for the "one"? Has psychoanalysis secured a place in African American discourse?

HS: I think I'm supposed to believe that psychoanalytic theory has secured a place for the "one" in African American discourse, but I actually think we've abandoned the search and have come to concentrate instead on the strategems of black popular culture. In short, it seems to me that we have been arrested in a stage of "presentism" that is obsessed with hip hop and its mechanisms, television, the movies, and social media. We have been overcome by the toxic fumes of celebrity and need an exorcism! To mix metaphors, forgive me, we are playing in a single groove these days, and doing so is immeasurably impoverishing. I believe it is time for us to look up and see wider and deeper, to take on more of the world of ideas and stop surrendering to the constraints of the ever more narrowly girdled academy, bunkered down over its own navel, so to speak. The analysis must not only return to these abandoned topics but renew its faith in its own vocation, its own possibilities.

AD: To state the obvious, you are one of the founding "mothers" of the academic field we now call "black feminist theory." I place *mother* in quotation marks not just because of the ways in which you have problematized female gender, motherhood, and maternity but also because I remember how the late Barbara Christian blanched at the term and the maternal metaphor in "Conference Call," an "intergenerational polylogue" between eminent and emergent women's studies scholars, published in *differences* 2.3 in 1990. Barbara wrote at the time that thinking in terms of feminist generations of scholars reminded her of her "marginal position as a feminist academic of color" who for much of her university life had wondered whether she would have any intellectual "children" at all. "Would there be any young women (men were even more unlikely), whether black, colored, or white," she wrote, "who would freely choose a low-status mother and focus on intersections of race, class, gender in Afro-American women's literature, in fact in any literature written by people of color?" (57). She went on to say that, because of a growing interest in African American women's literature, she was becoming an academic mother to more and different kinds of children than she ever would have imagined, even as many of her white counterparts were already academic grandmothers. You are at the forefront of a field you helped build that now has generations, and your own intellectual offspring are legion. I know you talk a little about your history in the academy in your department profile, but, at the risk of turning you into that pillar of salt like Lot's wife, may I prevail upon you to look back for a moment and say more about your literary life—about how it feels to build a field—and then turn forward again to comment on the state of feminist studies and black feminist theory in the academy today?

hs: I could be wrong about this, but my sense is that black feminist theory, writ large, has assumed a centrality in the humanities academy today precisely because it has eschewed certain postmodernist persuasions and occasions; we never quite believed the prevailing views of postmodernists without putting questions back at them, or changing words, as Cheryl Wall might say, with them. As for my own role in this outcome, I have never quite believed it! Not that I have not appreciated how some colleagues have made use of my work! I'm surprised by it, frankly, and very grateful that I have apparently not been wasting my time. But to tell the truth, I'm trying to consolidate my career at this late date, to go further and deeper into territory that I have only started to explore. I really meant to write fiction, as Marianne Hirsch said at some point that I did in a sense! But I also wanted to write criticism and theory. I wanted to do both, like Robert Penn Warren did, and was told that no one else could do that, which I still do not quite believe. In any case, I'm still climbing, even if I'm in the "last days of knees," as I call it! Feminist studies and black feminist theory, as both have been absorbed into the now wider interdisciplinary aims of the humanistic academy, must today reassert themselves and their inimitable passion for the truth because it is absolutely shocking to me how incomplete our victories actually are. I keep going back to the u.s. presidential election of 2016 and the appalling upshot. How in God's name is it possible that such an outcome could have fructified for all that women must know by now? I hesitate to mention the obvious here—that 53 percent of white women voters cast their lot with the current occupant of the White House. To my mind, this means that whatever we did has hardly been enough. It is unbelievable to me that we seem to have come full circle and that we are compelled now to start all over again in light of this incredible revanchist movement that is afoot across the Western world complex. We must now find our way through massive complications that we did not anticipate between the 1970s and the turn of the century. How in the world did we get here? And what is the next iteration and installment? If there is no next, then we will have betrayed everything we thought and said we believed so long ago!

AD: You are about to receive a well-deserved Lifetime Achievement Award from the Caribbean Philosophical Association. In announcing the award, Neil Roberts, the president of the association, remarked: "Spillers is a foremost intellectual troubadour whose writings and teaching for over 40 years have set the terms of discussion for a range of conversations in black studies, gender theory, critical theory, literature and humanities more broadly" ("Hortense"). I love his use of the word "troubadour" because it captures both the spirit of movement that accompanies your speech acts and (to borrow from Longfellow) the deep-voice neighboring oceans of your intellectual performance—that is, the thinking voice we read on the printed page and the speaking voice we hear in the open air. I'm not sure it's fair that you get to be prophet, poet, and performer—and brilliant and beautiful—but with that rich, full, oceanic speaking voice, it is no surprise that you were once a radio disc jockey with aspirations of becoming Hortense "Walter Cronkite" Spillers, TV newscaster. Even without television, you are still a model to multitudes. Other than Cronkite (who also rocked my youthful newshound's world), who are your models? I have read that it was William Blake who first turned your head from radio and TV broadcasting to literary studies, but I would love to know who else has inspired you.

HS: Being called an "intellectual troubadour" is one of the finest things anyone has ever said about me! I am thrilled that the Caribbean Philosophical Association came up with the description and highly honored to have received a lifetime achievement award from them as well as one from *Callaloo*, conferred at Oxford University in November 2016. When I think of role models, there are faces that crowd the mind from my childhood. These faces sprint across the retina of memory from old high school and college yearbooks that my sister and brothers brought home from Tuskegee and Tennessee State University in the 1940s and '50s, women and men so beautiful and elegant and dignified that it is as if they were never real but somehow figments of my imagination. They were astounding studies in new-world Africanity whose graciousness no one could ever have doubted, to my mind, to say nothing of attempted to repress and destroy. Then there are the church people, a photo on one of my kitchen walls that shows my parents when they were young—my tall father, arrow straight, looking like Julius

Nyerere, and my lovely, stern mother with piercing eyes and excellent posture, and my own generation of the young in all the hopefulness of untried glorious beauty, going out to greet and meet the world. Those picture galleries inhabit my mind, and while it would take me days to write about them in their overwhelming uprightness of conviction and the sheer romance of getting on with the business of living, I can at least say that without them, I am not imaginable even to myself. They occupy my mental life—majorettes, principals, football coaches, cheerleaders, football players, hall of famers, preachers, teachers, postmen, maids, deacons, ushers, mothers, high-school speakers, judges, doctors, lawyers, orators, drunks, loud talkers, braggarts, the high, the humble, the proper-talking, the grammar-breaking, the humor, the way with words, the grain of the voice and all the seductiveness that accompanied it—all of it, my first and natal humanity. Everything that I wanted to be started right there in my reality and imaginary on Deadrick Avenue in Memphis, Tennessee. I wanted to be *that* because it was brilliant and superior and soaring to my young mind, at least as I have remembered it! And overlaying it all were those fabulous sepia-toned photographs that graced the pages of the weekly *Pittsburgh Courier.* These influences grabbed me long before Blake and Cronkite entered! I was not afraid of them because I felt like somebody long before I knew their names. For the record, Spillers comes from the great massive sure-enough of black American being, I do believe!

AD: We have all been reading you for a long time. Even if I just go back to "Interstices: A Small Drama of Words" (1984), one of the first pieces of yours I read, it has been nearly thirty-five years. No "small drama," it was your big, bold, brilliant play with words and wit that caught me, from "interstices" forward. That, and the opening linguistic joke about sexual discourse as the speech act of intercourse—that is, "what you talk about when you make love" (73). But the piece itself was/is no laughing matter. It was an icebreaker. It broke the silence about black female sexuality. You called black women "the beached whales of the sexual universe, unvoiced, unseen, not doing, awaiting *their* verb" (74). Wow! It was a manifesto. At the time, it made me determined not to be a beached whale; all these years later it still moves and inspires me. I would welcome any thoughts you have about the piece today or any comments you would like to make about "sexuality as discourse."

HS: "Interstices" was the beginning of something that has lasted for me over the years; I cannot quite decipher how I got there, but the essay does demarcate a nodal point that was engendered by my attendance as a member of the first class of the School of Criticism and Theory, convened on the campus of the University of California, Irvine, in the summer of 1976. To say the least, this experience was mind blowing with inspirational instruction from the likes of Hayden White, Hazard Adams, René Girard, Murray Krieger, Ralph Freedman, Fredric Jameson, Edward Said, Frank Kermode, and so on. I first heard of someones by the names of Michel Foucault and Jacques Derrida, Émile Benveniste, Ferdinand de Saussure, and Louis Althusser that summer, and it was all so new. Fair to say that I left there with a sense of things that must have been comparable to someone on the threshold of a new world! I believe my whole sense of things radically shifted as this intellectual horizon blossomed before me. I don't think I knew that sexuality had a "discourse" until then, and the "discovery" from there led to ways of reading and writing that were explosive for me. I do think, by the way, that black women still have yet to come into self-revelation as sexual beings because the world, as they encounter it, remains backward with regard to female sexuality. My hunch is that the only desire that comes close to satisfaction is still signed by the male, even though the fragility of his ego frustrates him as a subject of sexuality as well. We will not admit it in a circumstance that, because it is oversexualized, is not sexual at all. Big surprise thirty years later. And perhaps this might explain why our society is so deeply alienated and fearful and so driven by resentment and conservative, benighted aims. In that regard, black women are not "interstitial" alone! We've got plenty of company! I did not quite know that in 1983, when the essay was penned.

AD: Finally, you say in the "Whatcha" interview that you wrote "Mama's Baby" with a feeling of both hopelessness and urgency because you were trying to explain what seemed to you at the time unexplainable—"to bring the language of a postmodern academy to a very old problem [. . .] that historians had been writing about for at least fifty years"—and to make that move in a way that "respected history" but that approached it anew because, as you say, "the language of the historian was not telling me what I needed to know": "what it is like in the *interstitial* spaces" (Spiller et al. 308). There it is again, that word that first grabbed me: "interstices," or a form thereof. Part of what you were feeling then, in the late 1970s and early 1980s, and what I think you are saying about the outsider situation, writing in the wake of and theoretically and conceptually in response to the Gloria (Akasha) Hull, Patricia Bell Scott, and Barbara Smith collection, *All the Blacks Are Men, All the Women Are White, but Some of Us Are Brave* (1982), is that you could no longer bear being shoved aside and pushed through the cracks. You can't talk about American slavery without talking about black women, you say; nor can you talk about black men without talking about black women—but that is not where the discourse was in the mid-1980s, practically or theoretically. "I mean, we really are invisible people," you said (Spillers et al. 308). You set out to change all that, to insist both on being the story and on getting to say what the story means. I want to ask you what you feel about the state of the story now. Where is your "hopelessness" meter—a tough question in these times, I know, but I ask it more in terms of the work than the world, although it's hard if not impossible to separate one from the other. Another way of approaching the question might be through the discourse of Afro-pessimism, which takes as its starting point your concept of "captive flesh" and the theft of the black body. In other words, it claims you. Do you claim it? But before you address this two-pronged question, I must presume to answer for you—that is, to give a portion of the answer to part one from the outside that you cannot from inside. You changed everything, and in that regard, I owe you both gratitude and apology. The gratitude is obvious, I hope; the apology stems from the fact that it is too easy to take for granted the way we are and forget the way we were. I've written words—including words about slavery—that your work made possible, and I didn't necessarily at every moment see that or acknowledge that indebtedness. So this issue is in its own way a tribute, a kind of overdue Hortensean praisesong.

hs: It will appear that my "hopelessness meter," from my response to some of your questions, is going off—loud—all over the place, but I am really not a pessimist, of the Afro or any other sort, and continue to believe that as long as we are conscious of what is happening to us, we have a chance. There are no excuses now. We do not know everything, but we know enough, from the dangerously shifting biomass and the massive damage we do to our planet and its ecological systems daily, down to diet and health. But where's the determination to handle what we do know? I am cheered by the Parkland, Florida, kids and those satellite images of Saturday's March on Washington ("Never Again") that found their way to me in a hotel room in Amsterdam over the weekend. Here we are once more. At a beginning, and perhaps we will find the wherewithal to rise in joy to meet it, despite our knees! As feminists, our work is, as usual, cut out for us.

HORTENSE SPILLERS is the Gertrude Conaway Vanderbilt Professor at Vanderbilt University. Her publications include *Black, White, and in Color: Essays on American Literature and Culture* (University of Chicago Press, 2003) and "Mama's Baby, Papa's Maybe: An American Grammar Book" (1987), along with numerous articles in the fields of American and African

American literature and black feminist theory. She edited *Comparative American Identities: Race, Sex, and Nationality in the Modern Text* (Routledge, 1991) and coedited, with Marjorie Pryse, *Conjuring: Black Women, Fiction, and Literary Tradition* (Indiana University Press, 1985). She is currently at work on two related research projects: the first focuses on the idea of black culture and women; the second on early republican formations, as well as three smaller, related projects on William Faulkner's Thomas Sutpen from *Absalom, Absalom!*; DuBoisian "double consciousness," "statelessness," and the early modern black subject; and Richard Wright, James Baldwin, and Ralph Ellison at midcentury.

ANN DUCILLE, emerita professor of English at Wesleyan University, is currently a visiting member of the faculty at the Pembroke Center for Research and Teaching on Women and the Center for the Study of Race and Ethnicity in America (CSREA) at Brown University. She is the author of *Technicolored: Reflections on Race in the Time of TV* (Duke University Press, 2018), *Skin Trade* (Harvard University Press, 1996), and *The Coupling Convention: Sex, Text, and Tradition in Black Women's Fiction* (Oxford University Press, 1993), as well as numerous articles in the fields of American and African American studies, popular culture, and feminist theory.

Works Cited

Christian, Barbara, Ann duCille, Sharon Marcus, Elaine Marks, Nancy K. Miller, Sylvia Schaffer, and Joan W. Scott. "Conference Call." *differences* 2.3 (1990): 52–108.

"Hortense Spillers to Receive Lifetime Achievement Award." *Vanderbilt News* 17 Feb. 2017. https://news.vanderbilt.edu/2017/02/17/hortense-spillers-to-receive-lifetime-achievement-award/.

Spillers, Hortense. "'All the Things You Could Be by Now, If Sigmund Freud's Wife Was Your Mother': Psychoanalysis and Race." *Black, White, and in Color: Essays on American Literature and Culture.* Chicago: U of Chicago P, 2003.

——————. "Interstices: A Small Drama of Words." *Pleasure and Danger: Exploring Female Sexuality.* Ed. Carole Vance. New York: Routledge, 1984.

——————. "Interview with Hortense Spillers." By Tim Haslett. *Black Cultural Studies Web Site Collective.* 4 Feb. 1998. http://www.blackculturalstudies.net/spillers/spillers_intvw.html.

——————. "Mama's Baby, Papa's Maybe: An American Grammar Book." *Diacritics* 17.2 (1987): 64–81.

Spillers, Hortense, et al. "'Whatcha Gonna Do?': Revisiting 'Mama's Baby, Papa's Maybe: An American Grammar Book': A Conversation with Hortense Spillers, Saidiya Hartman, Farah Jasmine Griffin, Shelly Eversley, and Jennifer L. Morgan." *Women's Studies Quarterly* 35.1–2 (2007): 299–309.

Williams, Sherley Anne. *Dessa Rose.* 1986. New York: William Morrow, 2018.

Blacks of the Marrying Kind: Marriage Rites and the Right to Marry in the Time of Slavery

There was a time when marriage was so uncommon among Negroes that almost every Negro infant in the United States was born out of wedlock. Few masters encouraged even unofficial marriages among their slaves. Thus most of the children of slaves—and probably a considerable proportion of those of the relatively few free Negroes—were born out of wedlock.
—Bernard

Exercising the civil right to marry [. . .] was as important to the newly freed black population as exercising another civil right [. . .] Negro suffrage [. . .]. To vote and to marry, then, were two civil responsibilities that nineteenth-century black people elected to perform; they were twin indexes for measuring how black people collectively valued their civil liberties.
—Tate

Historicizing the "Black Marriage" Contract

"*M*arriage," much like "family," has been a contested term in African American history. As Tera Hunter writes in her recent monumental study, *Bound in Wedlock: Slave and Free Black Marriage in the Nineteenth Century*, "The state of the slave family and the meaning of marriage within it have been enduring sources of controversy in discussions of the value of black life in American society" (17). At the heart of the debate over the meaning of marriage and the nature of intimate slave life lie not only African American history itself but also American and African American literature and historiography—that is, not just the lived experiences of black Americans but how and by whom those experiences have been written. This essay tracks the broad sweep and temporal turns of that literature.

On the face of it, African American history would seem to be grounded in chattel slavery, arguably the defining condition of the "black experience" in the New World. In recent years, however, a more complex portrait of the black diasporic past has begun to emerge, as historians like

Hunter have reinterpreted earlier findings and turned to new sources and different modes of investigation. At the same time, a number of contemporary black feminist critics and cultural theorists—Hortense Spillers, Saidiya Hartman, and Christina Sharpe among them—have called attention to both the gender and "ungendering" of slavery, questioning the very terms and terminology, the "grammar," in Spillers's framework, through which we have attempted to comprehend the trade in human flesh and what these theorists explode as slavery's "undecipherable markings" and reverberating "afterlife" or "wake" (Hartman, *Lose* 6; Sharpe, *In the Wake* 13–21; Spillers, "Mama's" 65–67). These insights and methodologies compel us to reexamine historical treatments of the black marriage question alongside newer considerations of slavery and its consequences.

At least since the early twentieth century, scholars have attempted to assess the immediate and long-term effects of 250 years of bondage on the intimate lives and familial relations of African Americans. Some experts maintain that the systematic enslavement of Africans completely undermined and effectively destroyed the institutions of marriage and family as well as the morale and mores of bondmen and bondwomen, reducing black men to mindless, childlike Sambos and absentee fathers and black women to, on the one hand, Jezebels and white men's concubines and, on the other, mammies and matriarchs. Other scholarly camps insist that slaves found creative ways to be together, care for each other, and build enduring marital relationships and family networks, in spite of the forced separations and other hardships and horrors of the plantation system. Still others point out that not all African Americans were enslaved and that free black men and women formed stable marriages, fashioned traditional nuclear and extended families, and established thriving black communities in cities such as Boston, New York, Philadelphia, Baltimore, Richmond, and New Orleans. Nor were free blacks as few in number or as far removed from the "norms" of mainstream colonial and early American marriage and family patterns as the esteemed white feminist sociologist Jessie Bernard suggests in the passage from *Marriage and Family among Negroes* (1966) that appears as an epigraph to this essay.

According to the first federal census in 1790, there were just over 59,000 nonwhite free persons living in the sixteen United States; by the 1860 census that number had climbed to nearly 500,000, still only about 1.5 percent of the total population. But a purely statistical analysis does not address the extent to which free blacks embraced the American Dream and attempted to pursue the trappings of so-called normal life, including marriage, home, and family. This was especially true in colonial New England, where Puritan moral strictures against premarital and extramarital sexual relations—for blacks as well as whites, enslaved as well as free—superseded the structural, economic, and judicial considerations that later would lead to the enactment of slave codes throughout the antebellum South that denied bondmen and bondwomen the legal standing to enter into marriage contracts.

In *The Negro in Colonial New England* (1942), one of the more important historical studies of its time, Lorenzo Johnston Greene argues that because the family was the fundamental unit of Puritan society and the primary vehicle for preserving and perpetuating Puritan ideals, "marriage was rigidly controlled" and the regulations governing intimate relations applied to everyone—"black as well as white persons, slaves as well as freemen" (191–92). Unlike their Southern counterparts, Greene asserts, "New England slaves were compelled to marry in the manner prescribed for the general population," and their marriages "were duly solemnized and recorded in the same manner as those of white persons" (192–93).

Whether required or desired and at the time more a civil matter than a religious rite, wedlock was an institution to which the known record suggests many early African Americans were deeply committed, in some instances laboring long and hard to purchase partners and other family members out of bondage. But even understanding the custom, convenience, and in some circumstances—along the frontier, for example—the necessity of purchasing mail-order brides, it is hard to imagine a "marriage" built on a foundation where one partner has had to buy another out of bondage. The colonial-era slave known as Venture Smith (Broteer Furro) reportedly bought and paid for precisely such a marriage. Born the son of a West African prince circa 1729, according to the narrative he dictated and had published, kidnapped around age eight and enslaved in New York and Connecticut, Smith was a defiant and ambitious captive who, by his own account, resisted the terms of his bondage and negotiated with more than one master for the right to retain a portion of his earnings from hiring himself out to other farmers and from fishing, planting, chopping wood, and performing other odd jobs on his own time. Through his industry and entrepreneurship, he was able to purchase first his freedom, then that of his two oldest sons, Solomon and Cuff, and eventually—through their labor as well as his—his then pregnant wife Meg and their daughter Hannah. At the time of Smith's death in 1805, he was a free man of considerable wealth and property. But, as the concluding words of his narrative purport, the greatest consolation of his old age was not the hundred acres he owned or the three habitable dwellings, but Meg, "the wife of my youth, whom I married for love, and bought with my money" (Smith).

Venture Smith married Meg, a slave on his first master's estate, when they were both about twenty-two, by his reckoning. He tells us nothing about their courtship or the nature of their union, but he clearly considered himself married for life and father to all the children Meg bore, even though they were separated for some time when he was sold away. Smith's long-term commitment to the wife of his youth (a phrase we will encounter again a hundred years later in the title of Charles Chesnutt's short story, "The Wife of His Youth") is not the typical portrait of tenuous coupling in the time of slavery. His narrative and other firsthand accounts from the earliest African Americans, both free and enslaved, add to our understanding of the multiple meanings of "marriage among Negroes." Smith's life was certainly not without hardship, but one wonders how different his story might have been had the slave ship carrying him landed in Virginia or the Carolinas in 1739 instead of in Rhode Island.

Popularly defined as a social union, a legal contract, and a religious rite, with a built-in heterosexual presumption, the institution of marriage would become practically and ideologically incompatible with the institution of slavery as it evolved into the basis of the Southern economy in the eighteenth and nineteenth centuries, but that was not initially the case in colonial New England. Even as the slave trade thrived in northern port cities like Boston, Massachusetts; New London, Connecticut; and Providence, Newport, and Bristol, Rhode Island, the earliest Africans in New England hovered in a tenuous status between indentured servitude and indefinite bondage. "Though in general regarded as property," Greene writes, "slaves in some instances were recognized as persons. As such, they were accorded certain legal rights commonly associated with freemen" (177). They could inherit, purchase and own property, enter into contracts, give testimony, and even bring lawsuits against white colonists as well as black.[1] Greene cites several court cases, including one from 1663 in which a black woman testified in a paternity suit (*Taylor v. White*) and another famously unfortunate instance in which a slave named Wonn bore such convincing witness against a white woman named Bridget Oliver (later Bishop) for sorcery that his testimony contributed to her later becoming the first victim hanged during the Salem Witch Trials of 1692 (180–81).[2]

Under the influence of Puritan morality and the primacy of the white patriarchal family, "Negro servants," as Puritans preferred to call their black slaves, counted among their civil liberties not just the right but also the responsibility and sometimes even the requirement to marry, in keeping with Puritan dictates rather than with whatever social customs and coupling conventions they had known in Africa. But as slavery became entrenched in the South and claimed as the region's own "peculiar institution,"[3] black bondmen and bondwomen increasingly were figured not as persons but as private property—"chattels personal"—in local and state statutes known collectively as slave codes; as such, they had no legal entitlement to the liberties and privileges of civil society. As Hunter points out, it is no accident that the "legal principles used to justify the denial of marriage rights for slaves," established during the colonial era (in the South more so than in the North, I would add), "emerged along with the codification of slavery" as central to the South's plantation economy and worked in every way to support that system (64).[4] Slaves could and clearly did continue to form intimate social unions, but unlike the slaves of Puritan New England, as chattel they could not enter into legal agreements, including marriage contracts. Even where enslaved men and women did form meaningful conjugal relationships, their status as personal property meant that their unions had no legal standing and were subject to disruption and dissolution at the will and whim of the masters who owned them.

Of the many prohibitions laid out in the American slave codes, the edict against marriage may seem to some the most peculiar. After all, from New England Puritans to Southern politicians, slavery's most ardent proponents and apologists maintained that bringing heathens out of the jungles of the Dark Continent into the enlightenment of Western civilization was an act of Christian charity, a humanitarian mission that bettered the Africans' condition and saved them from themselves. The prominent Puritan minister Cotton Mather, himself a slave owner, had preached as much in the seventeenth century to those he hailed as the "Miserable Children of Adam and Noah"; additionally, in a thirty-five-page pamphlet dated 1706, he called upon "all you that have Negroes in your House" to be "the Happy Instruments of Converting, the *Blackest* Instances of *Blindness* and *Baseness*, into admirable *Candidates* of Eternal Blessedness."[5] Over a century later in 1837, the South Carolina statesman John C. Calhoun famously advanced the same kind of save-the-heathen argument on the floor of the Senate: "Never before has the black race of Central Africa, from the dawn of history to the present day, attained a condition so civilized and so improved, not only physically, but morally and intellectually. It came among us in a low, degraded, and savage condition, and in the course of a few generations, it has grown up under the fostering care of our institutions [read: slavery and Christianity], as reviled as they have been, to its present comparatively civilized condition" (Crallé 630).

In Calhoun's view and that of like-minded nineteenth-century citizens of the South, Africans were savages who benefited from the paternal "care of our institutions." But if civilizing and Christianizing the black pagan justified enslaving the race, what, then, was the rationale for excluding the enslaved population from partaking of the most fundamental elements of Western civilization and Christian doctrine? Unlike in Mather's day, when matrimony was a civil matter, by the eighteenth century and certainly by Calhoun's era, marriage had become a religious rite as well as a civil liberty. Why make Christians out of heathens and then force them to live in sin, without benefit of the marriage sacrament?

Abolitionists like the Reverend William Goodell in his antislavery treatise, *The American Slave Code in Theory and Practice* (1853), and the former slave Frederick Douglas in his autobiography, *Narrative of the Life of Frederick Douglass* (1845), locate the answer in the self-serving social logic of the system on which the South's economy depended. The slaves' right to legally binding marriages would have interfered with the owners' property rights, including entitlement to any and all offspring born of slave women, even or perhaps especially those the masters and other white men fathered, since, by the doctrine of *partus sequitur ventrem*, first enacted in the colonies in 1662, a female slave's issue inherited the condition of the mother rather than the father, as had been the custom in English common law. Goodell by specific references—and Douglass by implication—traces *partus* to its Roman roots and its prior more modern application to animals, that is, to the principle that by law a calf is born the property of the cow's owner rather than the stud bull's. Quoting Southern jurists on the subject, Goodell critiques the fact that *partus sequitur ventrem* not only placed slaves on "the same level with *brute* animals," but it also displaced the patriarch and codified the condition of slave as matrilineally inheritable in perpetuity (26–27). Douglass in *Narrative* also pulls no punches in describing the application of this law to black female humans as the planters' transparent scheme "to administer to their own lusts, and make a gratification of their wicked desires profitable as well as pleasurable; for by this cunning arrangement," he writes, "the slaveholder, in cases not a few, sustains to his slaves the double relation of master and father" (13–14).

Hortense Spillers reads both Goodell and Douglass as regarding *partus* as slavery's "fundamental degradation," supposing "descent and identity through the female line as comparable to a brute animality." It is, of course, the dehumanizing southern law and custom, which Goodell and Douglass both take pains to critique, that place "the mother and mother dispossessed," in Spillers's words, "*out* of the traditional symbolics of female gender" (80). Spillers rightly directs our critical attention to *partus* as the moment when and the means by which slavery becomes institutionalized as matrilineal by the "ungendering" of the female and dispossession of the mother, neither of which particularly concerns these two male abolitionists, preoccupied as they are with condemning slavery as a breach of Natural or Father Law, symbolized, in their view—and that of generations of male historians to come—by the fact of its matrifocality.

Further exploring such points of law in *The American Slave Code*, Goodell argues that the genius governing the South's version of chattel slavery was its ability to rationalize the irrational based on "a single fundamental axiom," from which "all parts of the system are logically and scientifically educed": "The slave has no rights." And because the slave has no rights and is not ranked among sentient beings, "he, or she, cannot have the rights of a husband, a wife" (106–7). The slave codes and local laws and customs are clear on this point, Goodell argues, citing various summary judgments to that effect, including the findings of a jurist he identifies as Judge Jay: "A *necessary consequence* of slavery is the absence of the marriage relation. No slave can commit bigamy, because the law knows no more of the marriage of slaves than of the marriage of brutes" (qtd. in Goodell 113). The Judge notes that slaves might go through the motions of marrying each other in religious rites or secular rituals such as jumping the broom, but "so far as legal rights and obligations are concerned, it is an idle ceremony."

Goodell goes on to argue that the legal and structural obstacles slaves faced in attempting to maintain traditional matrimonial relations also necessarily inhibited their efforts to form and sustain nuclear families. While they were expected, encouraged, and often forced to bear children, the courts held that they had no parental rights. On this point, Goodell again cites the findings of Judge Jay: "*Of course*, these laws do not recognize the *parental* relation, as belonging to slaves. A slave has no more legal authority over his child than a cow has over her calf" (113). The remarkable but unremarked grammatical slippage from "his child" to "her calf" that masculinizes the slave even as it dehumanizes, erases, and, as Spillers would say, "ungenders" the black mother, is as striking as it is disturbing.

This, of course, is not Goodell's point. Throughout his study, he quotes legislative decrees, case law, and religious tracts in documenting the degree to which the state, the courts, and, perhaps most peculiarly, the church were complicit in sustaining the illogical social logic of slavery, even where and when doing so flew in the face of the founding principles of the republic, the rule of law, and the canons of Christianity. He attends in particular to the insidious ways in which chattel slavery contaminated everything it touched, even and perhaps especially the Southern Christian church, which even went so far as to provide biblical exegesis for the enslavement of Africans as the alleged descendants of Ham, Noah's youngest son, cursed to be the lowest of servants unto his brethren—according to Genesis 9:18–27—for the sin of looking upon his father's nakedness. The Africans' dark skin was supposedly a sign of God's punishment for sins that in some interpretations exceeded merely gazing upon the naked, inebriated Noah to include violating him in some sexual manner.

Despite Goodell's blanket indictment of the church, religious leaders were not of one mind about the matrimonial state of grace of the enslaved. Many clergymen and some slaveholders believed that bondmen and bondwomen should be united in holy wedlock, according to the laws of God, even if the laws of man did not recognize their unions. Some white ministers performed marriage ceremonies between slaves and between black couples in which one partner was enslaved and the other free. These unions usually had the sanction of the planters, since slaves generally could not marry without their masters' consent. It was often to the slaveholder's advantage to "encourage African-Americans to marry, to adopt Western Christian notions of marriage rather than so-called heathen practices from their past," Hunter explained in an interview on National Public Radio, in part because promoting marriage (even if it had no legal standing or permanence) and some semblance of family life "made economic sense. It mollified the slaves. It kept them reasonably content. It gave them incentives to remain on their plantations, as opposed to running away" ("Slave").

The notion that slaves were in any manner "reasonably content" has to be carefully contextualized within the terms and conditions of their confinement, which Hunter certainly does in *Bound in Wedlock*. John Blassingame explores this pivotal point in his 1972 study, *The Slave Community: Plantation Life in the Antebellum South*, pointing out that although some slaveholders encouraged monogamy for religious reasons, far more did so as a form of control, believing that a black man "who loved his wife and children was less likely to be rebellious or to run away than would a 'single' slave" (151). It is also worth noting, I would add, that marriage, such as it was, increased the masters' property holdings, since they would own whatever progeny these unions produced. A Louisiana freedman reported that his former master chose mates for his slaves according to his own design and "would never allow the men to be single after they were eighteen, nor the women after they were fifteen" (Albert 107).

Goodell, like other antislavery activists, used such practices as well as the laws and language of the plantation system to indict the system. The charge that slavery, with the church's blessing, delegitimized marriage and customarily broke family bonds was at the heart of the abolitionists' impeachment of the institution. It was also at the heart of numerous slave narratives and other literary and historical texts. Douglass, for example, begins *Narrative* by detailing how he was separated from his mother and the extent to which such partings of child from parent were standard practice. "My mother and I were separated when I was but an infant—before I knew her as my mother," he writes in chapter 1. "It is a common custom, in the part of Maryland from which I ran away, to part children from their mothers at a very early age. Frequently, before the child has reached its twelfth month, its mother is taken from it, and hired out on some farm a considerable distance off, and the child is placed under the care of an old woman, too old for field labor" (13). Of his father, Douglass says he knew only that he was a white man and rumored to be his master. There was no question of marriage between his parents, of course, since his father was a white man of means and his mother was enslaved, but Douglass does make it clear that the presence on the plantation of mulatto offspring like him was "a constant offense" to white mistresses, who were forced to confront on a daily basis the living proof of their husbands' infidelity.

Troubling "Marriage," "Love," and "Sex" in the Time of Slavery

Douglass's writings demonstrate how little wedding vows meant to the planter class, an indictment in which I believe we must include white women as well as men.[6] How does a white mother watch the black unmothered—raped perhaps by her own slaveholder husband and bereft of the misbegotten brown baby chattel but not its milk—wet nurse her own white infant and continue to breathe that fouled air? Straying from a wife's bed to the slave quarters, especially during pregnancy when the white missus was sexually unavailable, was such accepted custom among Southern gentlemen that the latter terms of a wife's lying in were known as "gander months" (D'Emilio and Freedman 95). There is some speculation and considerable circumstantial evidence that as many as three of the suspiciously light-skinned mulatto offspring of Margaret Garner—the inspiration for Toni Morrison's historical masterwork *Beloved*—including the daughter Garner killed rather than return to slavery, were products of her master's gandering through his wife's three pregnancies (Taylor; Weisenburger). That possibility lends another layer of meaning to the young slave mother's desperate act of infanticide to spare her girl child what she had endured.

While the plantation mistress was certainly in some sense likewise the victim of the patriarchal system to which she was wedded, she was also in many instances the victimizer, either as the silent/silenced codependent enabler or as the abuser, physically, emotionally, and in some cases sexually assaulting, tormenting, and terrorizing the enslaved, including—worst of all—children. In her at times painfully illuminating biography, *Sojourner Truth: A Life, A Symbol*, Nell Irvin Painter writes of her subject as the young girl then known as Isabella: "The sexual abuse came from her mistress Sally Dumont, and Truth could tell about it only obliquely, in scattered pages in her *Narrative*" (16). As Painter also points out, "master-slave sex was a standard part of the abolitionist bill of indictment against the slave South. [. . .] Less easily acknowledged, then and now, is the fact that there are women who violate children" (16).

Other forms of abuse are fairly well documented in slave narratives. Truth, for example, readily acknowledges being beaten by both master and mistress. For the most part, however, the interiority of sexual injury—especially in its same-sex proportions—is less well written, often only hinted at obliquely, as in Truth's *Narrative*, or relayed metaphorically. The rape of male slaves is almost entirely unwritten. According to Maurice Wallace in *Constructing the Black Masculine*, "the sodomitic threat was as real during slavery as the heterosexual rape of women" (88). One of few scholars even to raise the issue of male rape, Wallace points to a passage in *Beloved*—a painful moment of rememory, in which the men of a coffle or chain gang are made to kneel in the grass to receive "breakfast" from the guards—as a rare representation of the male slave's sexual violation. Sometimes called "buck breaking" or "buck busting," the rape of male slaves was much more than a threat. Oral and anal sodomy was, by some accounts, a ritualistic instrument of submission, designed to debase, emasculate, and control male slaves, especially those who dared to resist. In a single sentence, Morrison captures the submissive posture and ritualistic brutality of this particular homo-abnormative power play, as well as the horrifying fact that the chained and kneeling captive's only means of resistance meant his almost certain death. "Occasionally a kneeling man chose a gunshot in his head as the price, maybe, of taking a bit of foreskin with him to Jesus" (qtd. in Wallace 88).

"Slavery was rape," Ned and Constance Sublette rightly assert in *The American Slave Coast*, their recent history of the peculiar institution as a breeding industry that necessarily depended on rape and reproduction for increase and profit (36). They argue that because slaves were property with no right to refuse intercourse of any kind, with or without the threat of force, the sex act could never be consensual. As readily as we may theorize slavery's inherent sexually coercive condition today, neither archive nor narrative offers much in the way of material evidence or personal testimony as explicit as Morrison's fictional rendition, not because such violations were rare but because the system suborned silence about its sins of the flesh, whether hetero- or homosexual. "'Delicacy' and 'modesty,'" Gabrielle Foreman has argued, "allowed for and even demanded that narrators systematically come short of the 'truth,'" that they "maneuver in the field" of what Foreman calls the "undertell" (77), the unsayable necessarily left unsaid in keeping with the dictates of Victorian propriety.

Contemporary scholars like Foreman, Wallace, Aliyyah Abdur-Rahman, and Shatema Threadcraft are among those theorists working to expose some of the most deeply concealed traumas and intimate terrors of slavery's queered consumption of black bodies—what Abdur-Rahman calls the "metaphorics of sexuality" and "sexual transgressivity" (3–5). "Queer" in this context, as Abdur-Rahman explains in *Against the Closet*, does not refer solely to "sexual or identity practices and politics," but takes on a larger, more historically profound meaning that is played out in the dominant culture's "specific linkage of homosexuality and blackness," stemming from the notion among Europeans that Africans were hyperlibidinous sexual savages, doomed, as the descendants of Ham, to "generational enslavement precisely for the historical crimes of incest and homosexuality" (6, 27). Reduced to a basic absurdity, "racial blackness," Abdur-Rahman concludes, "was believed (throughout slavery and since) to evince, and to engender in others, an entire range of sexual perversities" (27). This kind of imagining, I would add, allowed white civil society to project its deepest, darkest, most "wicked desires"—both hetero and homo-abnormative—onto the always already aberrant Negro, turning the at-your-service slave population into vessels for rape, sodomy, bestiality, and breeding, bodies used and abused as sexual playthings often in ways too terrible to tell.

There is a lot to say and lot that has been said about what Harriet Jacobs reveals and conceals or "undertells" in her autobiographical narrative, *Incidents in the Life of a Slave Girl, Written by Herself* (1861), including speculation about the sexual jousting between and among master, mistress, and slave that amounts to, in Abdur-Rahman's reading, a "virtual ménage à trois" (46) and, in Foreman's, sexual assaults that the slave girl, a mere child fighting off a grown Goliath, perhaps did not always escape (77–78).[7] While Foreman raises the all too painful possibility that Jacobs did not always manage to outsmart and fend off her attacker like her alter ego Linda Brent, both Wallace and Abdur-Rahman, in addition to probing the Flints' sexual predilections, direct our critical attention to a largely unremarked moment near the end of *Incidents* where Jacobs pauses in telling her own tale to comment on the torment of a slave named Luke, whose cruel, crippled owner seemed particularly to enjoy inflicting punishment on the half-naked body of the black whipping boy he required to wait on him wearing nothing but a shirt.

It is clear that Jacobs means to make the white man in question the symbol of slavery's sexual perversions and systemic violence and degradation, writing that Luke's young slave master "became prey to the vices growing out of the 'particular institution'" and eventually was "deprived of the use of his legs, by excessive dissipation" (192). Both Wallace and Abdur-Rahman read Jacobs's coded language—her references to "vices," "excessive dissipation," "freaks of despotism"—as metaphors for venereal disease (the crippling illness) and homosexuality (the "freaks [. . .] of a nature too filthy to be repeated"). But here again, as with "queer," "homosexuality" is not necessarily referenced as identity, as we understand it today, not as sexual orientation, that is, but as sensual gratification taken to hedonistic extremes, along with drunkenness and debauchery: too much wine, women, and dong.

Wallace puts it more politely in his provocative reading of the scene, pointing out that Jacobs portrays Luke's palsied young master as showing "all of the worst symptoms of sexual deviancy according to then popular discourses of illness and health." Palsy in one "once vigorous and virile" was understood to be a consequence of the "sexual perversions including masturbation and sodomy" in which Luke—"made to kneel beside the couch [and] not allowed to wear anything but his shirt" (Jacobs, qtd. in Wallace 89)—was forced to participate and which Jacobs, for the sake of decorum, could not name. Nor, of course, could she name her own sexual violation, assuming that, as Foreman proposes, there is more to Jacobs's story than she is able to tell. Wallace also offers a compelling reading of the sexual undertell in Douglass's autobiographical narratives, beginning, as Douglass does, with the unspeakably brutal, bloody flaying of a half-naked

Aunt Hester, which Douglass unmasks as motivated by sexual jealously and where he, too, obliquely alludes to other "outrages, deep, dark, and nameless" (Douglass qtd. in Wallace 90).

The omnipresence of abuse, physical, sexual, and emotional, and the tendency, if not the tradition, of undertelling intimate details of slave life necessarily complicate any attempt to assess the ways in which terms like *sex*, *love*, and *marriage* mean historically. As Painter asserts in her biography of Truth, "romantic love has been a luxury for the leisure classes." Truth's marriage, she writes, "seems to have conformed to the working-class model of people attached to one another without the gloss of what middle-class people prize as love" (18). As a young girl of perhaps sixteen or seventeen, Truth (then Isabella) appears to have had a brief love affair with a slave named Robert from a neighboring farm (who Painter suggests may have fathered the first of Truth's five children), "the sole romance of Truth's entire life," Painter writes, only vaguely alluded to in *Narrative*. The relationship, such as it may have been, ended abruptly when Robert's master, who "did not want his slave having children off his premises," beat Robert "within an inch of his life" for disobeying his orders, breaking the slave's spirit and forcing him to marry a woman from his owner's farm, ultimately driving him into an early grave.

Yet, even as the narratives of nineteenth-century figures like Douglass, Jacobs, and Truth raise questions about the nature of (in)human interaction among slaves and their masters and mistresses, other early black writers and abolitionists took pains to show how important the institution of marriage was to the black population denied entitlement to its protections. The runaway slave William Wells Brown, credited with publishing the first African American novel, *Clotel; or, the President's Daughter* (1853), which posits the title character as the progeny of Thomas Jefferson, invokes the marriage rite and the right to marry as emblems of freedom and humanity.[8] He begins his tale of slavery's woes by indicting both the plantation system and the church for desecrating the institution of marriage by "depriving [slaves] of all the higher and holier enjoyments of this relation." "The marriage relation, the oldest and most sacred institution given to man by his Creator, is unknown and unrecognized in the slave laws of the United States," Brown writes on page one. "Would that we could say that the moral and religious teachings in the slave states were better than the laws; but, alas! we cannot" (37). In the same fashion as Goodell, he goes on to quote directly from various religious teachings and ecclesiastical pronouncements that sanction nonmarital sexual relations among the slaves, even as he insists that for the captives themselves, who "show a willingness to obey the com-mands of God on this subject," marriage is "a sacred obligation" and what he describes as—in keeping with the sentimental and romantic traditions from which he is borrowing—the font of love between a man and a woman (38).

There is a certain historical irony built into Brown's apotheosis of marriage as the seat of heterosexual love and the quintessential signifier of freedom and citizenship for African Americans, especially articulated at precisely the same moment that middle-class white women, beleaguered by what they viewed as the dominant/submissive character and legal limita-tions of patriarchal wedlock (married white women could not own property, for example), were mounting a critique of the marital relation as a site of inequality, oppression, and "civil death." Indeed, the hierarchical power dynamic of male-female relations, the subordination of a woman's will to her husband, and the strictly defined gender roles and separate spheres within white, middle-class marriage would become key concerns of the nineteenth-century woman's rights movement, as early feminist activists, especially those also involved in abolition, increasingly likened the slaves' inhuman condition to what many of them characterized as their own "domestic slavery."

Nor were all black women of the era—many of whom were or had been literally owned as property—as starry-eyed about romantic love or as uncritically enamored of the marital relation as Brown appeared to be on paper, despite his own troubled first marriage.[9] Sojourner Truth, a staunch advocate of both civil and women's rights, conditionally opposed universal *male* suffrage and the Fifteenth Amendment giving only black men the right to vote because she was scornful of the personal power imbalance political inequality would breed. "If colored men get their rights and not colored women theirs," she famously said, "the colored men will be masters over the women, and it will be just as bad as it was before." According to the transcript of her remarks printed in the *New York World* on May 10, 1867, Truth went on to make the point that a single woman's earnings were her own, "but if a colored wife goes out to do a little washing," her husband first quizzes her about where she has been and then takes all her money. "The man claims her money, body, and everything for himself," she reportedly said. "It's not right" (qtd. in Foner and Branham 464).

Truth's skepticism was a shared concern among black women activists, but that is not to suggest that African American women were com-pletely disdainful of or resistant to marriage as an important element of civil society. In fact, mindful of slave mothers like Margaret Garner (about whom Frances Ellen Watkins Harper wrote the poem "The Slave Mother, a Tale of the Ohio"),[10] who owned neither their bodies nor those they bore, what many black women wanted was entitlement to the husband, children, and home from which some white women sought relief. Even many diehard woman's rights activists, from writers and public intellectuals like Harper and Pauline Hopkins, to the antilynching crusader Ida B. Wells-Barnett and the writer and educator Anna Julia Cooper, reimagined black marriage as a partnership between equals, jointly committed to uplifting the race, and warned women of the dangers of accepting less. Cooper, for example, protests in *A Voice from the South* (1892) that "the colored woman too often finds herself hampered and shamed" by the conservative attitudes of black men who believe a woman's proper place is in the home (134–35). Enlarging upon this theme, Harper in "The Two Offers" (1859), credited as the first published short story by an African American, dramatizes the consequences of marrying a sweet-talking charmer, "vain and superficial in character," who "looked upon marriage not as a divine sacrament for the soul's development and human progression, but as the title deed that gave him possession of the woman he thought he loved" (64). Harper's message is clear: a single life of service to mankind (or to the race) is better than marriage to a man for whom a wife is a possession to be used, abused, and discarded like any other object owned.

But the other part of the message these nineteenth-century writers and activists conveyed in their work is the sense that patriarchy at its worst was white. Although this perception would change in the twentieth century, as black women writers increasingly indict their brothers, in both fiction and exposition, for taking on the characteristics of white patriarchy, these early feminists repeatedly challenged black men to do better and be better than their Caucasian counterparts, as they imagined a new world order and attempted to write it into being. After subjecting their main characters Iola Leroy and Sappho Clark (Mabelle Beaubean) to the gendered terrors of slavery—including concubinage, rape, forced impregnation and reproduction at the hands of white men—Harper and Hopkins redeem and reward the mulatta heroines of their respective novels, *Iola Leroy* (1892) and *Contending Forces* (1900), with happily-ever-after marriages to progressive black patriarchs who do not require piety, purity, deference, or domesticity in a wife. As imagined, these male characters represent what the black feminist critic Claudia Tate calls the "revised text of husband," race men who have been divested of Victorian gender codes and operate outside what I call the "discourse of deference" that required wives to submit to their husbands' authority (duCille, *Coupling* 42–43, 49–50; Tate 119–24).[11]

It is also clear, however, from both the historical and the literary records, that for nineteenth-century black women, the legal entitlement to marry also meant the freedom to choose whom to love—although "love," too, as Nell Painter suggests, is not a term we can use uncritically in the context of slavery and its consequences. Jacobs personalizes the term and the issue of romantic love and marriage in *Incidents*. Writing as Linda Brent, she begins chapter 7 of her autobiographical narrative with the haunting questions: "Why does the slave ever love? Why allow the tendrils of the heart to twine around objects which may at any moment be wrenched away by the hand of violence?" (37). The master's word and will were law, and Jacobs's owner, who, as we know, had his own sexual designs on her, would not allow her to marry the free-born colored carpenter whom she says she adored "with all the ardor of a young girl's first love," even though, as she notes plaintively, their union would have had no legal standing anyway: "But when I reflected that I was a slave, and that the laws gave no sanction to the marriage of such, my heart sank within me" (37).

Hearts still may sink at reading these and other firsthand accounts of the slave past. Yet, however heartrending this difficult history of lives lost, desire denied, and families torn asunder and however long-lived its legacy, it is not a linear or one-dimensional past, readily codified and contained by adjectives like "tragic" and "pathological," to invoke the terms later used by social scientists to describe black familial and intimate relations. Strict and stringent as slave codes clearly were, they were not full impediments to courtship and marriage among bondmen and bondwomen in the antebellum South or, for that matter, between blacks and whites, as well as Native Americans, in all regions of the country. Interracial coupling was also strictly forbidden by slave codes, and intermarriage between blacks and whites was criminalized by other statutory antimiscegenation laws from the mid-seventeenth century until such state regulations were finally declared unconstitutional by the u.s. Supreme Court in *Loving v. Virginia* in 1967; however, the rapid rise of a mulatto population in early America indicates how little force these prohibitions actually had. The laws of the land and the customs of the country are one thing; the will and wherewithal of a people are another.

Indeed, Eugene Genovese argues convincingly in his comprehensive study *Roll, Jordan, Roll: The World the Slaves Made* that a generation of scholars was misled about marriage and family life among bondmen and bondwomen because they looked too closely at slave laws and not closely enough at slave lives—at how the enslaved actually lived and coupled in the quarters (450–51). Substantiating Genovese's point, the songs, sermons, lectures, letters, poems, stories, memoirs, and other writings collected in Frances Smith Foster's edited anthology, *Love and Marriage in Early African America*, along with the counternarrative to conjugal pathology she constructs in her companion monograph, *'Til Death or Distance Do Us Part: Love and Marriage in African America*, offer compelling evidence of the importance of marital and family relations in the everyday lives of early African Americans, both free and enslaved.

Other recent studies of slavery and marriage—including most notably Hunter's historical monograph, *Bound in Wedlock*, and Katherine Franke's comparative analysis of black and gay struggles for marriage rights, *Wedlocked: The Perils of Marriage Equality*—deploy a wide variety of public and private sources to complicate the wedding portraits Genovese and others have painted. This newer work and other texts such as Brenda Stevenson's *Life in Black and White: Family and Community in the Slave South*, Emily West's *Chains of Love: Slave Couples in Antebellum South Carolina*, and Jennifer L. Morgan's *Laboring Women: Reproduction and Gender in New World Slavery*, along with Jacqueline Jones's landmark 1985 study, *Labor of Love, Labor of Sorrow: Black Women, Work, and the Family, from Slavery to the Present*, use Works Progress Administration narratives, Freedmen's Bureau records, diaries, autobiographies, plantation, court, and census records to detail the efforts of bondmen and bondwomen to be together, even in so-called "abroad" or "cross-plantation" marriages where husband and wife lived and worked on different estates. But, as many of these investigations point out, "marriage" for enslaved men and women was not a standardized relationship that all slaves experienced in the same way. Rather, it took different forms at different historical moments and in different locations and circumstances and often deviated from the traditional European and Anglo-American models, which, of course, had variations of their own. Foster adds the important detail that for most early Americans across racial groups, marriage was "a malleable and diverse institution," which included common-law couplings and other consensual unions. She concludes, perhaps somewhat quixotically, that early African Americans married, in whatever manner, because they wanted what most human beings want: "to love and be loved, to have and to hold, to combine one's destinies and resources with someone one holds dear" (*'Til Death* 70).

Like men and women throughout history, free and enslaved African Americans of the antebellum era no doubt married, partnered, and coupled for a variety of reasons, including the Western ideal of romantic love. Undoubtedly, however, less venerated incentives such as security, convenience, companionship, economics, and, all too often, coercion drove the nuptials and other forms of intimate pairings, or what Franke calls "marriage-like arrangements." Such arrangements included "sweethearting" or "taking up," which Franke defines as "an open-ended and nonexclusive type of relationship" that was separate and distinct from both marriage and "living together," both of which implied a certain level of commitment and monogamy, as well as outside recognition of the pair as a couple and quite often the master's permission (80–81).

Hunter likewise adds a note of realism to any romantic speculations about love in the time of slavery. "For all the love and affection that fugitive writers emphasize in their narratives," she writes, "some slaves looked past sentiment and went straight to the pragmatism of living in a hard-edged world." They didn't do the courtship dance, in other words, or dillydally with the "niceties" of a normalcy that was in no way theirs. "If they agreed to marriage," she explains, "it was for them merely instrumental, a practical surrender to the need for companionship, domestic help, or a way of escaping from frustrating isolation." Furthermore, the slaveholders' utter disregard for their chattel's marriage vows—and their own—made it harder for some slaves to take seriously bonds they knew could be broken at any time (*Bound* 44–45). Not only were children and couples separated from each other and sold off, but also for breeding purposes—that is, to increase his "herd" and holdings—a planter might force male and female chattel deemed good stock to mate and multiply, regardless of their marital status.

As Leon F. Litwack writes in his Pulitzer Prize–winning study, *Been in the Storm So Long: The Aftermath of Slavery*, "On some plantations, 'marriages' were forced upon men and women who had spouses in other places from whom they had been separated by sale" (234). Exploring this point, he quotes from the painful recollections of Stephen Jordon, the same former Louisiana slave I referenced earlier, who was sold away from his wife and children and given a second mate who also had a spouse back on her former plantation: "We were put in the same cabin, but both of us cried, me for my old wife and she for her old husband," Jordon laments. He goes on to explain that he and the woman his master gave him lived together not as wife and husband but as mother and son, since she was much older. Although he was the not-so-secret son of his former master, he was nevertheless a favorite of his old mistress, who had allowed him to be reared along with her own children, his half-siblings, who shared their lessons with him. On his new plantation, he used his literacy to write out passes for himself and other slaves in the same situation, so that they could go and see their former spouses. When that strategy no longer worked, he ran away but was caught and sold even farther from his beloved. Eventually, he and his first wife both remarried, "during the long years of our enforced and hopeless separation," he says (qtd. in Litwack 234–35).[12]

Rooted in such hard, horrible facts, African American history has rarely been conceived of in terms of love stories and marriage plots. Yet, according to the black historian Lerone Bennett, Jr., African American experience began with a love story. As he wrote in a special issue of *Ebony* magazine in 1981, it all began with "the love story of two of the first Black immigrants to English America, Antoney and Isabell, who brought what might have been a shipboard romance to a significant conclusion by marrying in Virginia in 1623 or 1624." The couple had a son, William, who, Bennett notes, "was probably the first Black child born in English America" (32).[13] Referencing Antoney and Isabell and millions of unnamed couples like them, Bennett concludes that love—or what he identifies specifically as "Black love"—"is perhaps the only reason Black people survived in this land" (36). And "Black love," he asserts, "is a product of a particular history [. . .] born, not on the plantation, not in Harlem, but in Africa, where there were particular, *non-European* and *stable* marriages and mating patterns" (32).

Antoney and Isabell, or Isabella, as Bennett identifies her in *Before the Mayflower: A History of Black America*, were among the "20 and odd Negroes" brought to Jamestown, Virginia, in 1619 aboard a Dutch man-of-war and traded to the colonists by a crew who had divested a Spanish ship of its payload. Although these twenty or so Africans were surely human cargo, involuntarily brought to the Americas by way of the transatlantic slave trade, their status in colonial Jamestown appears to have been akin to that of indentured servants rather than slaves per se. Yet, inasmuch as these "20 and odd Negroes" were utterly without choice in their kidnap and transport to Virginia, their circumstance, and no doubt their state of being and body, was fundamentally different from that of the white indentured servant. The fact that at least two of these putatively free Negroes eventually married each other and produced black offspring gives flesh and blood to Bennett's argument that black history in America actually begins not with slavery but with marriage.

At the same time, however, Bennett's uplifting but perhaps implausible notion of "Black love" is rooted in romantic fantasy that may contradict rather than complement historical fact. "Antoney, who had no surname, fell in love with Isabella and married her," the historian mansplains in *Before the Mayflower* (29). What a fabulous flight of fancy it is to imagine two young black no-surname captives, cruelly kidnapped from the only world they knew, falling for each other amid the terror of sailing the high seas of the slave trade's Middle Passage in what the poet Robert Hayden describes as a "voyage through death / to life upon these shores" (1501–5). But Antoney and Isabella almost certainly had surnames, African names, that history does not know. Unfortunately, little is known about this first African American couple and the nature of their union, whether it was a true love match (whatever love means, as England's Prince Charles famously mused), born of a shipboard romance, as Bennett speculates, or a marriage of convenience, as settlers, servants, and slaves commonly entered into in an alien and alienating new world, or even a be-fruitful-and-multiply master-planned mating, which indeed promptly produced livestock.

If we give any credence to Spillers's brilliant argument in her momentous essay, "Mama's Baby, Papa's Maybe: An American Grammar Book," we have far more reason than Prince Charles to question the meaning—and perhaps even the possibility—of love in the context of slavery and its consequences. After raising the questions she says we cannot "politely ask"—"whether the captive female and/or her sexual oppressor derived 'pleasure' from their seductions and couplings" and whether "pleasure" is even possible for the not free—Spillers suggests that we could "go so far as to entertain the very real possibility that 'sexuality,' as a term of implied relationship and desire, is dubiously appropriate, manageable, or accurate to *any* of the familial arrangements under a system of enslavement," for the captive or the captor and their issue (my emphasis). "Under these arrangements," she concludes, "the customary lexis of sexuality, including 'reproduction,' 'motherhood,' 'pleasure,' and 'desire' are thrown into unrelieved crisis" (76). In other words, were the conditions of captivity, even or perhaps especially in the semblance of lovemaking with a putative beloved (not to mention in the throes of rape and confines of concubinage), so unspeakably horrific that even the terms of art and endearment, the "grammar," we deploy in our attempts to undress and redress the naked truths of our ancestors—to know and name in human terms the always already dehumanized—are woefully inadequate and dubiously *in*appropriate? How and through what language can we know and name the flesh's untellable?

We do know from the Jamestown Muster of 1624/25, a census of sorts ordered by King James himself, that, along with "40 barrels of corn, four pistols and three swine," Antoney and Isabella are listed as "Negro servants" in the household of Captain William Tucker: "Antoney Negro and

Isabell Negro and William theire child" (O'Neill). Tucker was a sea captain turned Virginia planter who presumably allowed the couple to marry. Their son, born January 3, 1624, is believed to have been baptized William Tucker, presumably in honor of the captain, but the record is unclear on this point. There is a clan of African American Tuckers in and around Hampton, Virginia, whose oral history and family lore, passed from generation to generation for nearly four hundred years, has led them to believe themselves descendants of this first black child born on these shores. Unless DNA does for them what it has done for the black descendants of Thomas Jefferson and Sally Hemings, however, the rest of Lerone Bennett's "black love story" is lost to history, like the many thousands gone with the wind and what Sharpe would call the "wake" of the Middle Passage (25–62)

Marriage, Home, and Family
from Motherland to Father Lost

Nevertheless, Bennett and other scholars are right to direct our critical attention to Africa and to this first known African American couple in assessing the meaning of marriage in early black history. While it is all too easy to generalize broadly and romantically about Africa, it is fairly safe to say that Antoney and Isabella, like Venture Smith and the majority of Africans kidnapped and brought to the Americas, were taken from villages and communities where marriage was a fundamental, sacred institution, uniting not only a particular man and woman but also their extended families and kinship networks—what Europeans dubbed "clans" and "tribes"—into civic societies. Theirs was a motherland in which marital unions, and the extended families they produced, formed the basis of a well-organized social, economic, and political existence.

Whatever the particular courtship rituals, matrimonial practices, and lineage patterns of a given region, weddings were generally celebratory communal events, occasions for feast and festival. In some African societies—among the Yoruba of southwestern Nigeria, for instance—a daughter, once married, as well as whatever children she went on to bear, became part of her husband's family for life. Because women were considered valued, productive, and ideally fertile members of the community, in many regions the groom's kinfolk were expected to bestow gifts upon the bride's family as a sign of respect and a way of acknowledging and honoring the loss of a daughter's contributions to her kin group's wealth and well-being. Europeans, misreading this practice as an inversion of the Western dowry, labeled it "bride price" or "bride wealth," terms that do not capture the full spirit of the custom in the African context. This is not to suggest that marriage in pre- and even postcolonial Africa was a romantic rather than economic arrangement.[14] As in Europe, wedlock in African societies had many different ways and means, modes and motivations; however, here, too, a single man in possession of a good fortune was expected to be in want of a wife, and his parents, his extended family network, and even his village or community would make sure he found an appropriate mate.

Christian missionaries and other Europeans also made much of the fact that polygamy was practiced across much of the African continent, although it was more common among the wealthy and the royal, who could better afford to support multiple wives and large numbers of children. Polygamy was important because children were important—considered the wealth of the nation. In enlightened Western societies, a king like Henry VIII might divorce or behead a barren wife, or two or six, in pursuit of a male heir. Conversely, in what these same civilized societies considered "primitive" cultures, a man of means and property did not have to do away with a first wife in order to take a second and third to assure himself both progeny and productivity, although he might need to secure a first wife's blessing. (Venture Smith explains in his narrative that his mother took him and two siblings and left his father, intent on returning to "her own country," because her husband had taken a third bride without her consent as the first and eldest wife, "contrary to the custom generally observed among my countrymen.")

Since the North American plantation system denied slaves' unions the benefit of sacred or civil sanction even as it promoted and profited from routinized rape, concubinage, and serial conjugality, or bigamy of sorts, there is deep hypocrisy in the Western critique of polygamy as practiced by some West African societies. Africanists and other experts in the field have noted that, viewed within their own cultural context rather than through Western eyes, traditional African marriage practices, including polygamy, and extended family lifestyles may have held some practical benefits for women and children, such as greater economic security and emotional support, while also providing a degree of relief from the arduous labor of subsisting in what were most often agrarian societies. More hands made lighter the workload in both home and field; widows and orphans, as well as the elderly and the infirmed, could be cared for communally, rather than cast adrift, institutionalized, or sheltered and shouldered as a burden by a single individual or household.

The more immediately relevant point, however, is that, by and large, African Americans originally came from cultures in which the institution of marriage was more than a social union, a legal contract, or a religious rite; marriage and family functioned as the source, the seat—the end-all be-all—of public as well as private life. A young woman might leave her family and village to wed a chosen partner (as Smith's mother apparently did), but rather than striking out on their own, married couples and their kin groups often lived together in family compounds, with extended familial networks forming clans and tribes, headed by chiefs and councils of elders or rulers who sometimes bore the titles of king or prince. Seats of power, governmental rule, and political economies were internal to the kin groups, so that the private was simultaneously public and vice versa, all emanating from and reducible to marital and familial ties.

Revisionary Scholarship and Married Life upon These Shores

For some time, though, conventional wisdom held that what happened in Africa stayed in Africa. Prevailing scholarship maintained that the shock of capture, the disorientation of detachment from the known world, and the mental and physical trauma of the Middle Passage and life in captivity rendered African slaves moronic and malleable and all but erased cultural memory. The mid-twentieth century gave rise to the first wave of revisionist scholarship in which historians such as Kenneth Stampp and Stanley Elkins, writing against the grain of earlier interpretations that painted slavery as a benign, paternal institution, sought to expose the brutal, dehumanizing effects of the system and their destabilizing impact on marital and family relations. Often heavily dependent on the records and observations of planters rather than the testimonies of slaves themselves, this historiography, coupled with the earlier work of the influential black sociologist E. Franklin Frazier, played a major part in giving black marriages a bad rap that has been hard to shake. It identified not only slavery but also the role of black women in plantation society as the root causes of dysmorphic gender relations and dysfunctional family structures that continued to plague the African American community even after emancipation.

In contrast to theories of African cultural retention advanced by scholars such as Carter G. Woodson and Melville Herskovits, Frazier's landmark study, *The Negro Family in the United States* (1939), argues that the

African way of life, with its well-defined patriarchal family structure, was lost in translation from old world to new. With the sexual practices, taboos, and restraints of their own culture largely lost, generations of demoralized (in the most literal sense of the word) blacks were locked into a dehumanizing plantation existence characterized by transitory conjugal relationships, tenuous family ties, rampant promiscuity, and pervasive illegitimacy, as well as unspeakable sexual and sexualized violence that, as I have suggested, until relatively recently was little spoken of or written about in the mainstream literature. What was claimed by Frazier and others was the notion that biology supposedly bound mother to child and generated a degree of "respect" among owners for the black female role within the plantation economy; the male slave, by contrast, the argument goes, experienced little or no filial connection to either sexual partners or offspring and enjoyed no particular regard from the master class.

This rendering of the black past paid little attention to the fact that, far from commanding any measure of "respect," the female slave was not only ungendered, as Spillers argues, but also supersexed as a breeder, more often regarded as a walking womb rather than as a wife, as a mother, or even as a woman. Most of this modern historiography focused instead on the plight of the male captive, who, divested of his rightful place as head of the household, provider, and protector, supposedly became a bit player in the fortunes of the black family. Forced separations and the loss of male authority gave rise to what Frazier calls a "Negro matriarchate," an inverted familial structure in which the mother—often left to fend for herself and her children—ruled the cabin and the slave community. "As a rule, the Negro woman as wife or mother was the mistress of her cabin," Frazier claims, "and, *save for the interference of master or overseer*, her wishes in regard to *mating and family matters* were paramount. Neither economic necessity nor tradition had instilled in her the spirit of subordination to masculine authority. Emancipation only tended to confirm in many cases the spirit of self-sufficiency which slavery had taught" (125; my emphasis).

Frazier's analysis makes the female slave's lack of "subordination to masculine authority" an offense and the slave woman's lot superior to the man's. Strength and perseverance in the face of brutality are not the same as power and control. Frazier's disavowal of the cultural survival argument notwithstanding, self-sufficiency as a black female virtue rather than as an "emasculating" vice dates back to Africa, where there were matrilineal as well as patrilineal societies and a long tradition of female independence and entrepreneurship. Even in male-dominated countries and cultures, African women were not figured as frail, helpless, shrinking violets and second-class citizens as in Europe and Anglo-America. Rather, women in precolonial Africa often had well-defined roles that were critical to the domestic and political economies of their villages and societies.

While, again, the continent is too large and variegated for broad generalizations, from her research, especially among the Yoruba in Nigeria and Benin, the distinguished anthropologist Niara Sudarkasa has concluded that, with the exception of the "highly Islamized societies" of the sub-Saharan regions, women were "more conspicuous in 'high places'" in precolonial Africa than in any other part of the world. "They were queen-mothers; queen-sisters; princesses, chiefs, and holders of other offices in towns and villages," she writes, as well as "occasional warriors" and, in the well-known case of the Lovedu (or Lobedu) people, even "the supreme monarch." Furthermore, Sudarkasa concludes, "[I]t was almost invariably the case that African women were conspicuous in the economic life of their societies, being involved in farming, trade, or craft production" (91).

More to my immediate point, the "interference of the master or the overseer" in the life and liberty of slave women was not the small thing Frazier implies. Since black women did not own their own bodies or the right to mother the children those bodies bore, how then could they control "mating" and other "family matters"? Frazier, again, was far more concerned with the black male's loss of authority than with the black woman's vulnerability to rape and forced reproduction. The larger problem, in his view, is that what he saw as a pattern of female dominance continued—and, for certain segments of the black population, even exploded—after emancipation.

Those families that had attained "a fair degree of organization during slavery"—that is, those in which "the authority of the father was firmly established" and "the woman in the role of mother and wife fitted into the pattern of the patriarchal household"—made the transition from slavery to freedom, Frazier claims, "without much disturbance to the routine of living" (106). But for the masses of black men and women with histories of only nominal marriage relations, the loose ties that had held them together in slavery were easily broken in the chaos of emancipation (106). In Frazier's estimation, their tenuous ties to women and children and no custom of patriarchal obligation made it easier for men to leave the plantation environ. Historically, however, even when freedmen stayed behind and sought to solemnize their slave unions—as men and women did by the tens of thousands—the past posed certain challenges to happily ever after for many couples. Under slavery, they may have had more than one partner. Who in such instances was to be the lawful spouse? What claims did a long-ago slave husband or wife have on the here-and-now heart of a sold-off, escaped, or otherwise long-lost lover?

Charles Chesnutt dramatizes exactly this conundrum in his short story "The Wife of His Youth," published in the *Atlantic* in 1898. Just as he is preparing to host a ball at which he plans to propose to a lovely, refined quadroon, much younger than he but of similar social standing and even lighter complexion, the elegant, eminently eligible Mr. Ryder, the free-born "dean" of a certain northern city's elite Blue Vein Society (bourgeois blacks so light-hued that their blue veins show through their pale skin), is approached by a toothless, dark-skinned former slave named 'Liza Jane, looking for her beloved Sam Taylor, the free-born husband she helped escape her master's secret plot to enslave him, despite his freeman status, twenty-five years earlier. She has come to Mr. Ryder's door, she explains, because she "heerd" he "wuz a big man" and hoped he might know something of the "merlatter man" she is looking for (11). From the story she relates of her old plantation life, of being sold down the river for helping Sam escape, and of her quarter-century search for her long-lost husband, Ryder realizes that he does know the man she is looking for but keeps that knowledge to himself. Instead, he alerts his guest to the fruitlessness and perhaps foolishness of her search for a man who may well have married another woman. "Your slave marriage would not have prevented him," he explains, "for you never lived with him after the war, and without that your marriage doesn't count" (15). He may have "outgrown you, and climbed up in the world where he wouldn't care to have you find him," he warns. 'Liza Jane is unperturbed and resolute in her belief in Sam's fidelity. He was good to me but not much good for anybody or anything else, she tells Ryder, "fer he wuz one er de triflin'es han's on de plantation." He wouldn't work, she adds in the dialect in which all her lines are written, wholly in keeping with the way many nineteenth-century writers mark color and class distinctions within the race. She expects to have to support him when she finds the "merlatter" spouse she is sure she would recognize "'mong a hund'ed men," despite the passage of time (15–16). Making no promises or revelations, Ryder sends the toothless colored crone on her way, taking her address as a courtesy in case he happens to hear tell of her mulatto.

Called upon to give a toast that night at the ball he is hosting in honor of Mrs. Dixon, the lovely young widow he hopes to marry, Mr. Ryder praises woman's "fidelity and devotion to those she loves" and then as an example recounts for his fellow Blue Veins the story 'Liza Jane had told him earlier, adding a few details of his own about a husband who, soon after his escape, learned that his wife had been sold away. All efforts to find her having failed, suppose that young man moved on, Ryder offers. "Suppose that he was young, and she much older than he; that he was light, and she was black, that their marriage was a slave marriage, and legally binding only if they chose to make it so after the war." Ryder continues for some time, offering several more suppositions before finally asking his guests what such a man should do or, rather, "what ought he to do, in such a crisis of a lifetime?" (21–23). Having listened "with parted lips and streaming eyes," Mrs. Dixon, Ryder's own beloved intended, is the first to speak. "He should have acknowledged her," she says, her words echoed and affirmed by the entire assemblage. Thanking his guests for the response he expected, Mr. Ryder leaves the ballroom briefly and returns with 'Liza Jane, whom he introduces to the group as "the wife of my youth."

In this racialized riff on the marriage plot and the happily-ever-after ending, the protagonist, who could so easily have pulled the wool over 'Liza Jane's unseeing eyes, remained silent, and claimed his own happy ending with the love of his life, ultimately chooses duty over desire, obligation over opportunity, and embracing the slave past as part of the present, even though it means giving up the future he imagined. But there is so much more to plumb in this rich short story, not least its piercing commentary on class, colorism, and economic stratification within the black community, so often treated as a monolith. What strikes me is, of course, Chesnutt's representation of the ways in which slave marriages, already fraught, became still more complicated after emancipation.

While marriages between slaves had no legal standing in the antebellum South, during the Civil War, both the Union and the Confederacy realized that the containment of a splintering slave population could not be left to the planters alone, and the marital and familial unit became at once a national problem and the principal medium through which each side began its attempt to negotiate the terms and conditions under which African Americans would live within a postwar social order, whether under the Confederate flag or the Stars and Stripes. As Hunter writes: "The debate on both sides of the war illuminated how important the denial of legal marriage was to sustaining slavery and how integral the promulgation of marital rights was to emancipation" (167). Both camps, neither of which had seen black relationships in the same light as white, recognized the need to reshape African American households after the dominant nuclear family model.

Moreover, in the face of heavy losses, Abraham Lincoln and the Union army, initially reluctant to enlist black soldiers, began to see the benefit of putting black bodies in uniforms, not only those in the seceded territories and therefore putatively freed by the Emancipation Proclamation but also and perhaps especially those bondmen in the four slaveholding states still within the Union (Delaware, Maryland, Kentucky, and Missouri) and therefore ironically not covered by the Proclamation. The fact that they were promised not only their freedom but also that of their wives and children enticed thousands of slaves to run away from their masters and join the Union army. But this massive recruitment of male slaves in some cases made marriage a kind of "bounty" on the heads of wives and children left behind at the mercy of masters and other Southerners angered by the fact that their loyalty to the Union had been rewarded by the conscription of their slaves and by the outrageous idea of blacks being granted "marriage rights" or civil liberties of any kind (Franke 14–15, 23–50).

"If the nation-states were to formally recognize slave marriages," Hunter explains, "they would need to enfranchise black soldiers and government workers as husbands and heads of households, making them miniature sovereigns on par with whites." But as she also points out, there was no role the powers that be could imagine for black females positioned as they were so far outside the category of woman, leaving them "expendable compared with their men" (167–68). Much as Sojourner Truth predicted, then, without attention to women's rights, so-called freedom would be no better for the black female than slavery. Hunter seems to concur. "As the idea of marriage as the undoing of slavery and as a way to preserve the nation-state took hold," she writes, "it also meant the further inscription of masculine conceptions of freedom and citizenship" (167).

The Civil War brought many twists and turns in the fates and fortunes of black people in public and private spheres, but it was after emancipation that the institution of marriage underwent a sea change, certainly for former slaves but also, ultimately, for all Americans, as wedlock and other intimate relationships increasingly became subject to state and federal oversight and regulation.[15] In fact, the degree of policing and coital interference that accompanied the former slaves' acquisition of marriage rights—along with the political and practical perils of privileging marriage as the ideal adult relationship—inspired Franke to use this nineteenth-century instance of marriage apotheosis and government intervention not only as a case study but also as a cautionary tale for gays and lesbians involved in the contemporary marriage equality movement.

Franke explores the pitfalls and complications that attend marriage as both a legal contract and a patriarchal institution, as well as the dangers that inhere when marriage becomes the medium for marking citizenship, normalcy, and admission to the body politic, if not the category "human," especially for the nonnormative. As Franke argues in the introduction to *Wedlocked*, "[T]he deeply gendered nature of marriage renders the 'freedom to marry' a radically different experience for men than for women," while the nature of the institution itself—with its "complicated and durable values and preferences"—raises "complex questions of justice and equality" (2). In other words, be careful what you wish for. With all due respect to Janis Joplin, "freedom" isn't just another word for nothing left to lose.

Many of the same southern states that for so long had denied slaves the right to marry quickly passed legislation requiring freed men and women to register their slave marriages, with stiff penalties for couples who failed to comply, as the intimate relations of African Americans were subjected to federal as well as state surveillance through the Freedmen's Bureau and other government agencies and emissaries. Bernard was among the first scholars to point out that these laws were actually a form of social control, a way for the states to impose order on the masses of newly freed men and women roaming the countryside, "many with equivocal family status" (11). The historian Herbert Gutman has argued, however, that neither forced socialization nor the influence of northern missionaries and Freedmen's Bureau officials accounts for the high marriage rate following emancipation. In his view, the all-deliberate speed with which former slaves registered their unions indicates their "widespread approval of legal marriage" and their desire to secure its protections for themselves and their families (417).

There is no doubt that, along with male suffrage, the right to marry was a newfound civil liberty many former slaves freely and even joyfully exercised. Jones has written of the pride black couples took in the legitimacy of their unions, which she argues was reflected even in the colorful, more elaborate apparel many freed people donned that replaced the drab, homespun garments of their slave days. "When a freedman walked alongside his well-dressed wife," Jones writes in *Labor of Love*, "both partners dramatized the legitimacy of their relationship and his role as family provider" (69). Of course, this observation contains within it the very problematic that will come to haunt black marriage and become the subject of black feminist critique in the twentieth century: the debilitating misogyny and patriarchal pride of ownership that would treat a wife as a possession to be dominated and controlled.[16]

But it is also true that laws and legislative decrees requiring marriage registration and other forced forms of solemnizing unions between one man and one woman—including the automatic conversion of cohabitation into wedlock—wreaked havoc among the African American population, compelling freed men and women who had had multiple partners during slavery to make difficult choices, like Chesnutt's protagonist, or face charges ranging from fornication and adultery to bigamy and desertion. And although women were not exempt from such charges, it was primarily black men who faced legal action, perhaps, Franke speculates, as yet another means of disenfranchising black males: convictions for bigamy or desertion would prevent them from voting (139).

Frazier presents desertion, in particular, as a major threat to marital relations following emancipation, as the failure to find wage labor to support their families deprived black men of their masculine roles, as in slavery, and drove them to take to the open road in search of work. "Without the assistance of a husband or the father of their children," Frazier writes, the women left behind "were forced to return to the plow or the white man's kitchen in order to make a livelihood for their families" (126). Not only did they assume the man's role as wage earners and heads of households, but instead of pining away in celibacy, they often pursued sexual liaisons "more or less of a casual nature," according to Frazier, leaving them knocked up and, "as in slavery, surrounded by children depending upon [them] for support and parental affection" (107). Moreover, "their ranks were swelled by other women who, in seeking sex gratification outside of marriage, found themselves in a similar situation" (126). (There is no comment about the sexual gratification men sought outside of marriage or its effect on the black community.) With no real sanction against premarital sex and little stigma attached to out-of-wedlock birth, the result was an epidemic of what Frazier describes as "unfettered motherhood" and the development of a black family structure in which "the woman has played the dominant role" (107).

Frazier's analysis in *The Negro Family* is more comprehensive and nuanced than this reductive rendering of it. But for all the charts and tables, facts and figures that swelled his tome to nearly seven hundred pages, the portrait of the disintegrating black family and the not only dominant but domineering black matriarch looms larger than anything he has to say about strong black men who, like Venture Smith, worked long hours in fields or factories or small enterprises to buy themselves and their families out of slavery or to support their households after emancipation, in some instances acquiring wealth, property, and respectability en route to joining free blacks as W. E. B. Du Bois's "Talented Tenth" and the middle-class subjects of Frazier's later study *The Black Bourgeoisie* (1957). Almost overnight, Frazier's theory of the structural instability of the colored masses and the rise of the Negro matriarchate became the dominant understanding of gender, marital, and family relations in the u.s. Even into the 1960s and 1970s, scholarly and lay communities alike followed Frazier's lead, accepting largely uncritically the claim that the black women ruled the roost in slavery and in freedom and indiscriminately populated the country with hordes of mostly fatherless children.

Citing Frazier in an article that appeared in special issues of *Ebony* in 1960 and again in 1963, Lerone Bennett asserts that black women's independent spirit "grew out of the slave social system which devaluated the role of the Negro male. Negro women, as a result, have been as free, powerful and expressive vis-à-vis their men as any group of women in history. On the slave plantation, they ruled their cabins, their children and sometimes their men." In fact, men of the plantation were so dependent on women, he concludes—this time quoting the historian Maurice R. Davis (*Negroes in American Society*, 1949)—"that they regarded freedom from female domination as one of the gains from emancipation" ("Negro" 38).[17]

Given the masculinist bent of most scholarship in the 1940s, it may not be so surprising that a learned professor like Maurice Davis would take such a swipe at black women in print. It is surprising, however, that Bennett, who would go on to prattle about the beautiful love song black men and women created, despite slavery, would repeat such a reckless charge in the nation's leading black publication in the 1960s. Fingering bondwomen as the oppressors of black men—as one of the tyrannies of slavery—scapegoats the victim and reduces black women to ball-busting fishwives who emasculate their men and drive them from the home. The claim activates the "Sapphire" stereotype, named for the sharp-tongued, overbearing black female character in *Amos 'n' Andy,* the radio and television show of the 1930s, '40s, and '50s, which even after production ceased in 1953 continued to air on television in syndicated reruns until 1966.

As the perpetually angry wife of George "Kingfish" Stevens, Sapphire made an art form of belittling her ne'er-do-well husband and his get-rich-quick schemes. The Sapphire figure has become a staple of popular culture—from Aunt Esther on *Sanford and Son* and the surly maid Florence on *The Jeffersons* to Leslie Jones's various horny dominatrix personas on *Saturday Night Live* and a host of would-be angry black women played by men in drag, such as Martin Lawrence's Big Mama and Tyler Perry's Medea, who tread a fine line between Sapphire and another enduring caricature of black womanhood, Mammy. As a signifier, Sapphire is by some reckonings one answer to why black marriages fail and why black men prefer white women. Sapphire, however, was invented, written, and originally played by white men. Spillers ends "Mama's Baby" by theorizing not only a different reading of the Sapphire stereotype but also a different footing for the figure—"the *insurgent* ground as female social subject"—"with the potential to name," in which instance "Sapphire might rewrite after all a radically different text for a female empowerment" (80).

What a coup it would be to imagine Sapphire not as the husband-battering battle-axe of white male mythology but as a symbol of black female empowerment, unleashed not only to tell her own story but also to name what the story means. Frazier may not have invented the Sapphire stereotype, but his analysis in *The Negro Family* legitimized and institutionalized the image of the domineering black female by providing an intellectual basis for it in slavery.[18] As Spillers writes, "[T]he African-American female's 'dominance' and 'strength' come to be interpreted by later generations—both black and white, oddly enough—as a 'pathology,' as an instrument of castration" (74). Frazier's thesis was taken up by scholars and politicians and rewritten as fact in both historical discourse and public policy, from hugely influential, much taught, and widely cited texts such as Kenneth Stampp's *The Peculiar Institution* (1956) and Stanley Elkins's *Slavery* (1959) to the commanding, if controversial, *Moynihan Report* (1965).[19] These and other texts like them institutionalized Frazier's theories about the unfortunate fall of the father and rise of the mother—often using the same language and similar examples—that place the slave woman in control over domestic "activities" and "responsibilities," while reducing the black male to little more than a sperm donor. Or, as Stampp puts it, "the male slave's only crucial function within the family was that of siring offspring" (343), while Elkins likewise asserts that "the very etiquette of plantation life removed even the honorific attributes of fatherhood from the Negro male" (130). Elkins goes on to add a controversial theory of the slave personality to the mix that likens African captives to Jewish victims of Nazi concentration camps, so dependent on Massa and so infantilized and stupefied by the shock, awe, and isolation of a closed plantation system that the men, in particular, became the childlike Sambos of Southern lore.

Part of what is elided in claims that make the slave woman H.N.I.C.—politely, "Head Negro in Charge"—and the man, in Stampp's words, "at most his wife's assistant," often thought of as her "possession (Mary's

Tom)" (344), is the historical fact that while the "mother-child dyad" at times may have been, in Hunter's words, "the most basic family unit" (19), "mother" is a misnomer that did not convey maternal birth rights, since parental and other forms of power and control rested with the owner, not the owned. Nor were the domestic "responsibilities" or "activities" over which bondwomen had domain matters of privilege or choice. More often than not, the slave "mother" worked in either the fields or the big house—sometimes both—at least from sunup to sundown and then cleaned the cabin, prepared the food, made and mended the clothes, took care of the children (not necessarily her own), the elderly, the infirmed, and the men (again, not necessarily related to her). What heading the household meant for such women was "double duty, not power parity," Christie Farnham has observed, adding that even husbands in abroad marriages, who saw their wives only occasionally, did not wash their own dirty clothes. On the weekends, the roads between plantations reportedly were littered with men carrying bags of laundry to their wives to wash (79–80). Such service to multiple masters and support of her family might have made the slave woman heroic. Instead, it made her a liability for generations to come in the minds of critics unable to sanction anything other than the conventional, male-headed household or to appreciate the distinction Hunter makes between the matrifocality that emerged out of the plantation system, in part because husbands and wives were often separated by sale and abroad marriages, and the reigning stereotype of the matriarchy (19), a relation of power slave women did not possess.

Murdering Moynihan and the "Myth of the Black Matriarchy"

The work of Frazier, Stampp, and Elkins, and of others who walked in their intellectual footsteps, played a significant role in constructing "black marriage" as a troubled category unto itself and in locating its difficulty in the topsy-turvy gender hierarchies and marital relations and the unstable family structure supposedly seeded in slavery. Confusing strength with dominance, each of these immensely influential studies, and others like them, largely elided a critique of the actual power relations in force when it came to examining the black woman's role within the peculiar institution of chattel slavery. Yet, while much of this revisionist scholarship has been thoroughly critiqued and in some cases outright debunked, perhaps no single study of black marriage and family life has generated more controversy and criticism than *The Negro Family: A Case for National Action*, a report on the

"Negro problem" issued by the U.S. Department of Labor in 1965, more or less as the marching orders of the Johnson Administration's War on Poverty.

Compiled by Daniel Patrick Moynihan, at the time assistant secretary of labor, later a U.S. senator from New York (succeeded by Hillary Rodham Clinton in 2001), the *Moynihan Report*, as the document became known, attempted to identify the root causes of the poverty plaguing much of black America and what Moynihan and others saw as the widening gap between increasingly separate and unequal black inner-city and white suburban nations. A trained sociologist himself, he drew heavily on the work of Frazier, Elkins, and the black psychologist Kenneth Clark, who had written about the self-perpetuating pathology of the inner city in his own study, *Dark Ghetto: Dilemmas of Social Power*, also published in 1965. Not surprisingly, given his sources, Moynihan concluded that, while there was "no one Negro problem," at the heart of what ailed black America was the instability of the family resulting from the inversion of marital roles, a holdover from slavery. "It was by destroying the Negro family under slavery that white America broke the will of the Negro people," Moynihan asserts in the report's particularly controversial fourth chapter, "The Tangle of Pathology," which links black poverty, unemployment, illegitimacy, delinquency, crime, and other social and economic ills to the increasingly matriarchal character of the black community and "the reversed roles of husband and wife."[20]

Indeed, treating opinion as empirical fact, a section labeled "Matriarchy" in bold print marshals the claims of various male scholars and civil rights leaders in identifying the African American community as a matriarchal society dominated by angry black women so embittered by the failures and inadequacies of their men that they "perpetuate the mother-centered pattern" by alienating the male from the family and "by taking a greater interest in their daughters than their sons." No actual evidence is offered to substantiate these charges, perhaps because both history and literature more readily present examples of black women working multiple jobs to educate and support *all* of their children, while any number of narratives—including those by male authors like James Baldwin—suggest, if anything, favorite son or "manchild" favoritism, which is certainly the case with Baldwin's semi-autobiographical novel *Go Tell It on the Mountain* (1953), where the character Florence Grimes bitterly resents the preferential treatment her younger brother Gabriel received from their mother.

While most liberal discourse of the 1960s tended to present the descendants of slaves as helpless victims of forces beyond their control, the *Moynihan Report* had the unfortunate effect of seeming to include black women, as wives and mothers, among the oppressive forces working against black men and, hence, the black community. Repeatedly represented as more educated, more gainfully employed and employable, and otherwise better off than their men, black women emerged from the report and the modern historiography of slavery confirmed not merely as matriarchs but also as emasculating Sapphires and bitter, man-hating mothers who drive away their mates and psychologically damage their sons. The best way to save boys and men from the destructive effects of female domination, Moynihan concluded, was to encourage black males to enlist in the "utterly masculine world" of the armed forces, "a world away from women, a world run by strong men of unquestioned authority," and even more optimistically colorblind for the era, "a world where the categories 'Negro' and 'white' do not exist"—the one place where "black men were truly treated as equals."

As suggested by its subtitle, the main objective of *The Negro Family: A Case for National Action* was a call to arms to save the black community from the consequences of alleged female dominance. What it called up instead was outrage, on the one hand, and a second wave of revisionist scholarship, on the other, as intellectuals of various stripes rushed to rebut many of the report's claims. One of the first and most pithy counternarratives came from Angela Davis in "Reflections on the Black Woman's Role in the Community of Slaves," published in the *Black Scholar* in 1971.

Writing from a cell in the Marin County Jail, Angela Davis labeled the idea of a black matriarchate a myth consecrated by the *Moynihan Report* with Washington's blessing. "In the most fundamental sense, the slave system did not—and could not—engender and recognize a matriarchal family structure," she wrote, because "inherent in the very concept of the matriarchy is 'power,'" which did not rest in the hands of either slave women or men (4). The black woman worked alongside the black man in resisting their shared oppression, Davis insists, and was forced by the system that enslaved her "to leave behind the shadowy realm of female passivity," but she stood beside, not ahead or above, her black male counterpart (14). Challenging by name Frazier as well as Moynihan, "et al.," Davis calls for a more complex analysis that would "debunk the myth of the matriarchate" and "attempt to illuminate the historical matrix of [the black woman's] oppression" and "her varied, and often heroic, responses to the slaveholder's domination" (4).

Although not all of their efforts offer the more complex portraits of bondwomen that Davis called for, a slew of historians published major studies of slavery in the 1970s and 1980s explicitly aimed at debunking

Frazier and Moynihan and revising Stampp and Elkins. The distinguished African American historian John Blassingame, who was among the first scholars to take slave narratives and other firsthand testimony seriously as primary sources, deftly explodes Elkins's Sambo thesis in his 1972 monograph, *The Slave Community*, without actually mentioning Elkins's name (except in an appended essay on sources). Revising Frazier, dismissing Elkins, and discrediting Stampp's argument as too hyperbolic to trust "even when it is [. . .] relatively accurate," George P. Rawick argues in *From Sundown to Sunup: The Making of the Black Community* (1972) that, far from living in "cultural chaos," as Stampp claims, the "Afro-American family under slavery was part of a distinct, viable black culture, adapted to slavery and deprivation" (74, 79).

Such critiques notwithstanding, it was, arguably, Herbert Gutman's previously mentioned monograph, *The Black Family in Slavery and Freedom*, and Eugene Genovese's *Roll, Jordan, Roll* that quickly became the gold standards of revisionist histories of slavery when they appeared in 1976. Gutman takes great pains to disprove the claim that slavery inverted the roles of husband and wife by documenting the existence of double-headed households and long-term marriages among captives as well as freepersons. Genovese similarly maintains that "slaves created impressive norms of family life, including as much of a nuclear family norm as conditions permitted," and "entered the postwar social system with a remarkably stable base"—meaning black men were in place and in charge of black families that resembled the white model. Moynihan and the others got it wrong, he says, because they read history in reverse, looking backward from the modern urban ghetto and assuming "a historical continuity" (451–52).

There's No Place Like Home in Historiography . . .

. . . By which I mean that we should never be comfortable with what we think we know about the past. Genovese may be correct that Moynihan and the others got it wrong, but that does not mean that he and Gutman and other latter-day revisionists got it all right. The very nature of the research enterprise, of historical inquiry, is perpetual discovery. No interpretation is or should ever be beyond critique. Accordingly, a number of subsequent studies have called into question some of the data and assumptions that underpin both *The Black Family* and *Roll, Jordan, Roll*, as well as other touchstone texts of the time. For example, Deborah Gray White warns in her own pivotal monograph, *Ar'n't I a Woman?* (1985), that "statistics on long-lived marriages must be approached with caution. The length of a slave marriage does not necessarily indicate how voluntary it was, [or] the circumstances under which it occurred" (150). Farnham argues that the term "double-headed," as employed by Gutman, is misleading because it "avoids the issue of serial monogamy" and "obscures the fact that many men were not the biological fathers of all the children present in the family" (73).

Both White and Farnham laud scholars like Gutman and Genovese for their efforts to retrieve the black family from claims of extinction and to reinstall the absented black male within its midst. Too often, however, these efforts, in Farnham's words, "have had the unfortunate effect of trivializing the importance of the female-headed household," which even the most progressive mainstream scholarship of the 1970s and '80s continued to represent as aberrant and transitory (73). White adds that many of these revisionist texts are so intent on "negating Samboism" and reasserting male authority that they diminish and demean the role of female slaves by "putting black women in their proper 'feminine' place" and "imposing the Victorian model of domesticity and maternity on the pattern of black female slave life" (21–22).

In this regard, Genovese's claim that "slaves created impressive *norms* of family life, including as much of a *nuclear family norm* as conditions permitted" may provide a degree of insight into why it has been so difficult for historians to tell the story of intimacy and marriage in the time of slavery. "Social norms" are popularly and sociologically defined as the accepted rules and standards of behavior by which a society lives. The "conditions permitted" in this instance were captivity, concubinage, rape, sodomy, and other forms of sexual violation and physical and psychic violence. Even in the South, where it was claimed as "our peculiar institution"—that is, particular to our normal way of life—slavery made everything *ab*normal, for white as well as black. The would-be marital and nuclear family norms held out by historians and social scientists as models of civil southern society were, after all, characterized by serial infidelity, rape, incest, concubinage, miscegenation, and generations of mixed-race offspring whose white patresfamilias owned their black mothers and enslaved their own brown progeny, whom they just as conventionally disavowed.

This, then, is what has made the work of Hortense Spillers so critical to the study and the writing of American slavery: the degree to which her intervention in "Mama's Baby" has exploded any notion of "norms" and "thrown into unrelieved crisis," as she says, "the customary lexis" and traditional methodologies through which generations of scholars attempted to codify and comprehend the complexities of "marriage and the family among Negroes," to invoke Jessie Bernard's construction from the 1960s.

Ironically, forty-five years ago, Blassingame, who mistakenly judged Harriet Jacobs's narrative as inauthentic, was criticized in some quarters not for that misreading but for his use of what his detractors called "nontraditional" sources, for turning to diaries, letters, interviews, testimonies, and personal narratives of captivity, escape, survival, and deliverance—in other words, for trusting the voices of slaves as authors of their own experience, not simply as objects of investigation or "raw material" (Spillers et al. 300).

Today, through the work of Spillers and a new generation of feminist scholars, in particular, several of whom I have drawn on in this essay and many more I have not, our approach to and understanding of slavery and its afterlives—what we know and do not know, including the authenticity of *Incidents in the Life of a Slave Girl* and the multiple meanings of *marriage* and *family*—are broadened and deepened by the use of exactly such nontraditional sources. Turning to these and other voices and venues has engendered the invention and intervention of creative new methodologies and archaeologies of discovery, called upon when the archives are not enough, where the historical record is silent, or when it lies, dissembles, or dispossesses.

In her tour-de-force strain against the limits and silences of the archive, "Venus in Two Acts," Saidiya Hartman asks: "How can narrative embody life in words and at the same time respect what we cannot know? How does one listen for the groans and cries, the undecipherable songs, the crackle of fire in the cane fields, the laments for the dead, and the shouts of victory, and then assign words to all of it? Is it possible to construct a story" she muses, quoting Stephen Best, "from 'the locus of impossible speech' or resurrect lives from the ruins?" (3). Her answer in "Venus" is an inventive methodology she calls "critical fabulation," a play with and rearrangement or even displacement of "the received or authorized account," which allows us to envision what might have been, not in an effort "to *give voice* to the slave," she says, "but rather to imagine what cannot be verified" (11–12). Critical fabulation allows the scholar to read between the lines of ships' logs and court records, as Hartman does brilliantly in "Venus" and elsewhere in her oeuvre, to trace the paths of the historically othered in order to fill in some of the interstitial spaces and faces left blank by silence and slow time, whitewashed, erased, muffled, muted, and obliterated by what most often has been male-authored and -authorized accounts, official documents, and sanctioned celebrations of masculine heroics. In other words, critical fabulations are grounded in the archive, even as they move beyond its absences and erasures in order to retrieve and rematerialize that which and those whom history has disappeared.

Deeply rooted in history while challenging its "fact" and figurations, silences and secrets, critical fabulations are by no means fantasy. As much as we may wish to join Lerone Bennett in contemplating shipboard romances between star-crossed captives who gave birth to "black love," coupling in the time and terror of slavery was much more complicated than any such quixotic reading allows. It is, of course, impossible to know precisely what marriage meant to the earliest African Americans or even to capture the many different meanings the institution has held and continues to hold for their descendants. But along with the insights we gain from new scholarship like Hunter's historical monograph and Hartman's critical fabulations, the genre of the neoslave narrative or what I might presume to call "literary fabulations"—novels such as Gayl Jones's *Corregidora*, Barbara Chase-Riboud's *Sally Hemings*, Sherley Anne Williams's *Dessa Rose*, and Toni Morrison's *Beloved*—"resurrect lives from the ruins" and allow us to envision the interior lineaments, forbidden loves, crossed paths, unspeakable injuries, and impossible choices of characters brought to life on the printed page, out of a past we can only imagine.

The genre of fiction affords the creative writer the kind of poetic license and provocative play with the past and present with which William Wells Brown so boldly inaugurated the African American novel tradition with the publication of *Clotel; or, the President's Daughter.* Reams have been written by and about Thomas Jefferson, the president in Brown's title, not so, of course, for Sally Hemings, the subject of its backstory. While it does not speak her name—Jefferson's colored concubine is called Currer in the novel—for nearly two centuries, *Clotel* was arguably the only literary *or* historical text to approach the story of Sally Hemings or to acknowledge the existence of such a black female figure.

Anticipating the coming rise of historical novels that explore the intimate lives of black female protagonists, in 1975 Gayl Jones published *Corregidora*, which chronicles the trauma and sexual terror of four generations of black women literally and figuratively owned by an unspeakably cruel slaveholder, whose legacy of incest and sexual abuse haunts the narrative's blues singer heroine, Ursa Corregidora, and her troubled marriage. As its title suggests, *Sally Hemings*, far more frankly than *Clotel*, fictionalizes in pulsating prose the intimate relationship between Thomas Jefferson and the slave girl who was not only his mistress and the probable mother of progeny he did not acknowledge but also his dead wife's half sister. *Dessa Rose*, which tells the story of a pregnant slave girl condemned to death and the white plantation mistress who gives shelter to her and other runaways, is likewise drawn from real people and actual historical events: two separate characters and cases Williams first read about in Angela Davis's "Reflections."[21] And Morrison's Pulitzer Prize–winning literary fabulation, *Beloved*, which, as previously noted, was inspired by the all too terribly true story of Margaret Garner, revolves around a mother forever haunted by the horrors of history and the visage of the daughter she sacrificed to spare her the living death of slavery.

On the significance of such narrative fabulations to the particular issue of "black marriage" that is the theme of this special issue, it seems only fitting that Spillers should have the last word. In a meditation on the emerging discourse of Afro-pessimism, which looks to the deadly, dehumanizing condition of slavery as the indelibly defining mark of racial blackness, Jared Sexton invokes Spillers's reading of a pivotal passage from Chase-Riboud's novel. A furious Sally Hemings, in "an explosion of insulted motherhood," contemplates clubbing Jefferson to death with a poker for his callous disavowal of their four sons, for having "renounced his sons from the day of their birth!" (276). As with Morrison's kneeling, coffled slaves, to strike her master, to beat him senseless with an iron poker, would surely mean her own death, but in that moment of rage and recognition of her own nothingness and theirs, Sally Hemings, as Chase-Riboud portrays her, would willingly die to claim her own humanity.

Saluting what the author captures so forcefully in this literary fabulation, Spillers proclaims: "What our writers have paid imaginative witness to is the fact that there is no human loneliness and alone-ness remotely comparable to that of the enslaved beyond the reach and scope of love and freedom. The day that the enslaved decides to act out the threat of death that hangs over her, by risking her life, is the first day of wisdom. And whether or not one survives is perhaps less important than the recognition that, unless one is free, love cannot and will not matter" (qtd. in Sexton). This, then, is the question and the crisis of interpretation that necessarily hangs over any consideration of coupling and marriage in the time of slavery: not whether there was love, but the far more complex, incalculable, and impossibly disquieting quandary that in the coffin of social death, where there can be no consent and all is consequence, how did it, how could it matter?

ANN DUCILLE, emerita professor of English at Wesleyan University, is currently a visiting member of the faculty at the Pembroke Center for Research and Teaching on Women and the Center for the Study of Race and Ethnicity in America (CSREA) at Brown University. She is the author of *Technicolored: Reflections on Race in the Time of TV* (Duke University Press, 2018), *Skin Trade* (Harvard University Press, 1996), and *The Coupling Convention: Sex, Text, and Tradition in Black Women's Fiction* (Oxford University Press, 1993), as well as numerous articles in the fields of American and African American studies, popular culture, and feminist theory.

Notes

1   As Nell Irvin Painter details in her stunning biography, *Sojourner Truth: A Life, A Symbol*, one of the lesser-known facts about Truth is that in 1828, with the aid of Quaker friends and lawyers, she successfully sued for the return of her youngest son, Peter, who at five or six had been illegally sold into Southern slavery just as New York state's emancipation act, prohibiting such sales, went into effect. "Peter was only one of thousands of black New Yorkers illegally sold into perpetual bondage in the South," Painter explains, as slick, profit-minded northern slaveholders attempted to circumvent the new state law. Truth—or Isabella, as she was then known—won the case and also rescued her son, later prevailing in another lawsuit against a white couple who accused her of trying to poison them (32–35, 58).

2   Although Greene implies that Wonn's (perhaps a variant of "Juan") testimony helped condemn Goody Oliver to death, the widow was actually tried twice for witchcraft, once while married to her abusive second husband Thomas Oliver, when she was apparently acquitted, and the second, more famous instance in 1692, by which time she was married to her third husband and known as Goody Bishop. This time she was convicted and hanged, and it does seem that Wonn's inflammatory and unforgettable accusations from the earlier trial were instrumental in the 1692 verdict. See also, among other sources, Rosenthal 82.

3   Although chattel slavery came to be identified as the South's own "peculiar institution"—so called because it was particular to or characteristic of the Southern states—Massachusetts was actually the first British colony to legalize slavery in 1641, two decades before Maryland became the first Southern colony to do so. For an insightful study of slavery in New England and its importance to the area's domestic economy, see Melish.

4   Hunter also points out that the codification of slavery as law as well as custom was written on the backs of black women, beginning with statutes passed by the Virginia Assembly in 1643, which categorized "African women as 'tithable' labor," and 1662, which recognized the doctrine of *partus sequitur ventrem*, meaning that henceforth and forevermore the offspring of Africans, like those of cattle, would follow the condition of the mother, contrary to the rule of paternal descent that had characterized English common law (65).

5   See Mather, "Negro" and "Rules."

6   Several significant studies use diaries, letters, and plantation records to shed light on the interior lives of white women in the Old South, including, in addition to Fox Genovese's *Within the Plantation Household*, Anne Firor Scott's *The Southern Lady: From Pedestal to Politics 1830 to 1930*, Catherine Clinton's *The Plantation Mistress: Woman's World in the Old South*, and Laura

F. Edwards's *Scarlet Doesn't Live Here Anymore: Southern Women in the Civil War Era.*

7   Abdur-Rahman cites both Hortense Spillers and Karen Sánchez-Eppler in concluding that Mrs. Flint's actions in "visiting" Linda Brent nightly, whispering sweet nothings in her ear in her husband's voice, and cruelly forcing Linda to relate the details of Dr. Flint's sexual harassment amount to sexual abuse—what Sánchez-Eppler labels "erotic domination"—and make the mistress a "sexual culprit" along with the master. See Abdur-Rahman 43–45. See also Sánchez-Eppler 95–97; and Spillers, "Mama's" 474.

8   In making Clotel and her younger sister, Althesa, Jefferson's offspring, Brown extrapolated from a rumor that the third president had fathered several children by his slave girl concubine Sally Hemings and that one of his daughters had been sold on the auction block. For a discussion of *Clotel* and the Jefferson-Hemings "rumor," which the muckraking journalist James Thomson Callender first exposed in print in 1802, as well as an analysis of the DNA evidence that seemingly turned rumor and historical fiction into historical fact in 1998, see my essay, "Where in the World Is William Wells Brown?" See also Brodie; and Gordon-Reed.

9   Brown's marriage to Elizabeth Schooner, the free black woman he met and wed not long after his escape from slavery in 1834, was troubled by his travels and her restlessness and infidelity. Brown's antislavery activism frequently took him away from home, and his wife's affections wandered elsewhere, leading to a separation in the latter 1840s and a scandal when Mrs. Brown, who had

left husband, home, and family, reportedly for another man, returned with a child presumably not her husband's and demanded support, publically denouncing her estranged spouse to his fellow abolitionists when he did not meet her demands, thus threatening his career. Brown was exonerated after an investigation and offered sympathy for his "great forbearance" as the aggrieved party—or so the story goes, one side of it anyway. Who knows the truth of women's lives, especially when they are married to powerful men? The first Mrs. Brown died in 1851 or 1852, having spent the last years of her life trying to retrieve the daughters she supposedly abandoned. In 1860, Brown married Anna Elizabeth Gray. See Cashin's annotated edition of Clotel xi–xii, xiv; see also Sterling, ed. 144–47.

10   Not to be confused with Harper's earlier poem, "The Slave Mother" (1854).

11   See also Carby 143–44.

12   Fascinated by the brief excerpt in Litwack, I traced Jordon's story to its origins, where I learned more of his harrowing account in *The House of Bondage*, true stories of slavery collected by a former slave and serialized in the *Southwestern Christian Advocate* before being published in book form by Oxford University Press in 1890. See Albert 101–19.

13   See also Bennett's study *Before the Mayflower* 28–29; and Foster, '*Til Death or Distance Do Us Part* 1–3.

14   Some of these courtship and marriage rites and rituals remain in practice today, as I first learned long ago from a Yoruba boyfriend.

15   When it comes to government interference, one might think of

Richard and Mildred Jeter Loving, legally married in Washington, DC, in 1958 but ripped from their marital bed by local law enforcement shortly thereafter and arrested because he was Caucasian and she was "colored" (African and Native American), and their marriage violated Virginia's Racial Integrity Act of 1924, which prohibited intermarriage between whites and nonwhites. The couple pled guilty to "cohabitating as man and wife, against the peace and dignity of the Commonwealth" and were given a one-year sentence, suspended on the condition that they leave the state, ultimately leading to the landmark Supreme Court case *Loving v. Virginia* in 1967.

16   Elizabeth Fox-Genovese points out in *Within the Plantation Household* that even in slavery black women had a fondness for fancy, colorful clothing and accessories, which led some fine Southern ladies to complain that their slave girls were more interested in how they kept themselves than in how they kept the household. Love of colorful fabric and finery may have been a holdover from Africa, but it was an affront to white sensibilities. Fox-Genovese notes a 1740 South Carolina law that restricted slaves to wearing cheap, homespun clothes. "After emancipation," she adds, "to the despair of many whites, freedwomen enthusiastically took to carrying parasols and wearing veils," which so offended the refined sensibilities of white gentlewomen that many of them ceased sporting these items themselves (219–22).

17   The quotation comes from Maurice Davis, *Negroes in American Society* 207. Davis draws heavily on Frazier in a chapter on the Negro family.

18   Anastasia Curwood argues that Frazier viewed the Negro matriarchate as a temporary phenomenon and was actually far more troubled by the rise of middle-class working women and educated black female professionals whose failure to defer to male authority posed a real threat to natural dominant/submissive gender hierarchies and therefore to the ultimate stability of the African American community. See Curwood, "Fresh." See also her original and insightful study of race, class, and marriage, *Stormy Weather.*

19   To be fair, I should point out that George Rawick, who is excessively careful and respectful in critiquing Frazier, even referring to him as "Professor," maintains that many scholars who claim to base their arguments on Frazier's research ignore his many "qualifications" and his insistence that there are "many different types of black families" (Rawick 92).

20   This and all subsequent quotations are from the electronic version of the report provided by the Department of Labor.

21   As noted, *Dessa Rose* expands Williams's earlier short story, "Meditations on History." In her author's note, Williams specifies that the novel is based on two historical events, the first of which she read of in Angela Davis's "Reflections": in 1829, a pregnant captive led a slave revolt; in tracing Davis to her source, Williams came upon the second incident from 1830 in which a white woman was reported to have given aid and comfort to runaway slaves on her remote plantation (5–6). Little more than historical footnotes, these two figures, who did not meet in fact, are brought together in Williams's fiction.

Works Cited

Abdur-Rahman, Aliyyah. *Against the Closet: Black Political Longing and the Erotics of Race.* Durham: Duke UP, 2012.

Albert, Octavia V. Rogers. *The House of Bondage.* 1890. New York: Cosimo Classics, 2005.

Bennett, Lerone, Jr. *Before the Mayflower: A History of Black America.* New York: Penguin, 1982.

——————. "The Negro Woman: Crumbling Matriarchate Poses New Problems." *Ebony* (Aug. 1960): 38–46.

——————. "The Roots of Black Love." *Ebony* (Aug. 1981): 31–36.

Bernard, Jessie. *Marriage and the Family among Negroes.* Englewood Cliffs: Prentice-Hall, 1966.

Blassingame, John W. *The Slave Community: Plantation Life in the Antebellum South.* Rev. ed. New York: Oxford UP, 1976.

Brodie, Fawn. *Thomas Jefferson: An Intimate History.* New York: Norton, 1974.

Brown, William Wells. *Clotel; or, the President's Daughter: A Narrative of Slave Life in the United States.* London: Patridge & Oakley, 1853. Rpt. New York: Macmillan, 1975.

——————. *Clotel; or, the President's Daughter: A New Edition with Primary Documents.* Ed. Joan E. Cashin. Armonk: Sharp, 1996.

Carby, Hazel. *Reconstructing Womanhood: The Emergence of the Afro-American Woman Novelist.* New York: Oxford UP, 1987.

Chase-Riboud, Barbara. *Sally Hemings: A Novel.* 1979. Chicago: Chicago Review, 2009.

Chesnutt, Charles W. *The Wife of His Youth and Other Stories of the Color Line.* 1899. Ann Arbor: U of Michigan P, 1994.

Cooper, Anna Julia. *A Voice from the South.* 1892. Ed. Henry Louis Gates Jr. New York: Oxford UP, 1988.

Crallé, Richard Kenner, ed. *Speeches of John C. Calhoun, Delivered in the House of Representatives, and in the Senate of the United States.* Vol. 2. New York: Appleton, 1883. http://books.google.com/books?id=6Etx__aVlYYC&printsec=frontcover#v=onepage&q&f=false.

Curwood, Anastasia C. "A Fresh Look at E. Franklin Frazier's Sexual Politics in 'The Negro in the United States.'" *Du Bois Review* 5.2 (2008): 325–37.

——————. *Stormy Weather: Middle-Class African American Marriages between the Two World Wars.* Chapel Hill: U of North Carolina P, 2010.

Davis, Angela. "Reflections on the Black Woman's Role in the Community of Slaves." *Black Scholar* (Nov./Dec. 1971): 2–15.

Davis, Maurice. *Negroes in American Society.* New York: Whittlesey, 1949.

D'Emilio, John, and Estelle B. Freedman. *Intimate Matters: A History of Sexuality in America.* Rev. ed. Chicago: U of Chicago P, 1997.

Douglass, Frederick. *Narrative of the Life of Frederick Douglass.* New York: Norton, 1997.

duCille, Ann. *The Coupling Convention: Sex, Text, and Tradition in Black Women's Fiction.* New York: Oxford UP, 1993.

——————. "Marriage, Family, and Other 'Peculiar Institutions' in African-American Literary History." *American Literary History* 21.3 (Fall 2009): 604–17.

——————. "Where in the World Is William Wells Brown? Jefferson, Hemings, and the DNA of American Literary History." *American Literary History* 12.3 (Fall 2000): 443–62.

Elkins, Stanley M. *Slavery: A Problem in American Institutional and Intellectual Life.* 3rd ed. Chicago: U of Chicago P, 1976.

Farnham, Christie. "Sapphire? The Issue of Dominance in the Slave Family, 1830 to 1865." *"To Toil the Livelong Day": American Women at Work, 1780–1980.* Ed. Carol Groneman and Mary Beth Norton. Ithaca: Cornell UP, 1987. 68–84.

Foner, Philip S., and Robert Branham, eds. *Lift Every Voice: African American Oratory, 1787–1901.* Rev. ed. Tuscaloosa: U of Alabama P, 1997.

Foreman, P. Gabrielle. "Manifest in Signs: The Politics of Sex and Representation in *Incidents in the Life of a Slave Girl.*" *Harriet Jacobs and* Incidents in the Life of a Slave Girl. Ed. Deborah M. Garfield and Rafia Zafar. New York: Cambridge UP, 1996. 76–99.

Foster, Frances Smith. *Love and Marriage in Early African America.* Hanover: UP of New England, 2008.

——————. *'Til Death or Distance Do Us Part: Love and Marriage in African America.* New York: Oxford UP, 2010.

Fox-Genovese, Elizabeth. *Within the Plantation Household: Black and White Women of the Old South.* Chapel Hill: U of North Carolina P, 1988.

Franke, Katherine. *Wedlocked: The Perils of Marriage Equality.* New York: New York UP, 2017.

Frazier, E. Franklin. *The Negro Family in the United States.* Chicago: U of Chicago P, 1939.

Genovese, Eugene. *Roll, Jordan, Roll: The World the Slaves Made.* New York: Vintage, 1976.

Goodell, William. *The American Slave Code in Theory and Practice: Its Distinctive Features Shown by Its Statues, Judicial Decisions, and Illustrative Facts.* New York: American and Foreign Anti-Slavery Society, 1853.

Gordon-Reed, Annette. *Thomas Jefferson and Sally Hemings: An American Controversy.* Charlottesville: U of Virginia P, 1997.

Greene, Lorenzo Johnston. *The Negro in Colonial New England.* Rev. ed. New York: Antheneum, 1969.

Gutman, Herbert G. *The Black Family in Slavery and Freedom, 1750–1925.* New York: Vintage, 1976.

Harper, Frances Ellen Watkins. "The Two Offers." *Afro-American Women Writers, 1746–1933: An Anthology and Critical Guide.* Ed. Ann Allen Shockley. New York: New American Library, 1989.

Hartman, Saidiya. *Lose Your Mother: A Journey along the Atlantic Slave Route.* New York: Farrar, Straus and Giroux, 2007.

——————. "Venus in Two Acts." *Small Axe* 12.2 (2008): 1–14.

Hayden, Robert, "Middle Passage." *The Norton Anthology of African American Literature.* Ed. Henry Louis Gates Jr. and Nellie Y. McKay. New York: Norton, 1997. 1501–5.

Hunter, Tera W. *Bound in Wedlock: Slave and Free Black Marriage in the Nineteenth Century.* Cambridge, MA: Harvard UP, 2017.

——————. "Slave Marriages, Families Were Often Shattered by Auction Block." Interview with Michel Martin. *Tell Me More* 11 Feb. 2010. Transcript. https://www.npr.org/templates /story/story.php?storyId=123608207.

Jacobs, Harriet. *Incidents in the Life of a Slave Girl, Written by Herself.* 1861. Ed. Jean Fagan Yellin. Cambridge, MA: Harvard UP, 1987.

Jones, Jacqueline. *Labor of Love, Labor of Sorrow: Black Women, Work, and the Family from Slavery to the Present.* New York: Vintage, 1985.

Litwack, Leon F. *Been in the Storm So Long: The Aftermath of Slavery.* New York: Vintage, 1979.

Mather, Cotton. "The Negro Christianized. An Essay to Excite and Assist That Good Work, the Instruction of Negro-Servants in Christianity." 1706. *DigitalCommons@University of Nebraska–Lincoln.* https://digitalcommons.unl.edu/cgi/viewcontent.cgi?article=1028&context =etas (accessed 20 March 2018).

——————. "Rules for the Society of Negroes." 1693. *Library of Congress.* https://www.loc .gov/resource/rbpe.03302600/ (accessed 20 Mar. 2018).

Melish, Joanne Pope. *Disowning Slavery: Gradual Emancipation and "Race" in New England, 1780–1860.* Ithaca: Cornell UP, 1998.

Morgan, Jennifer L. *Laboring Women: Reproduction and Gender in New World Slavery.* Philadelphia: U of Pennsylvania P, 2004.

Moynihan, Daniel Patrick. *The Negro Family: A Case for National Action.* Washington, DC: Dept. of Labor. Office of Policy Planning and Research, 1965. http://www.dol.gov/oasam /programs/history/moynchapter4.htm.

O'Neill, Helen. "Personal Historian Finds Her Deep Roots." *Los Angeles Times* 22 Feb. 1998. http://articles.latimes.com/1998/feb/22/news/mn-21720.

Painter, Nell Irvin. *Sojourner Truth: A Life, A Symbol.* New York: Norton, 1997.

Rawick, George P. *From Sundown to Sunup: The Making of the Black Community.* Westport: Greenwood, 1972.

Rosenthal, Bernard. *Salem Story: Reading the Witch Trials of 1692.* New York: Cambridge UP, 1995.

Sánchez-Eppler, Karen. *Touching Liberty: Abolition, Feminism, and the Politics of the Body.* Berkeley: U of California P, 1993.

Sexton, Jared. "Afro-Pessimism: The Unclear Word." *Rhizomes: Cultural Studies in Emerging Knowledge* 29 (2016). http://www.rhizomes.net/issue29/sexton.html.

Sharpe, Christina. *In the Wake: On Blackness and Being.* Durham: Duke UP, 2016.

Smith, Venture. *A Narrative of the Life and Adventures of Venture, a Native of Africa: But Resident above Sixty Years in the United States of America. Related by Himself.* New London: C. Holt, 1798. http://docsouth.unc.edu/neh/venture/venture.html (accessed 12 March 2018).

Spillers, Hortense. "Mama's Baby, Papa's Maybe: An American Grammar Book." *Diacritics* 17.2 (1987): 64–81.

Spillers, Hortense, et al. "'Whatcha Gonna Do?' Revisiting 'Mama's Baby, Papa's Maybe: An American Grammar Book': A Conversation with Hortense Spillers, Saidiya Hartman, Farah Jasmine Griffin, Shelly Eversley, and Jennifer L. Morgan." *Women's Studies Quarterly* 35.1–2 (2007): 299–309.

Stampp, Kenneth. *The Peculiar Institution: Slavery in the Ante-Bellum South.* New York: Knopf, 1956.

Sterling, Dorothy, ed. *We Are Your Sisters: Black Women in the Nineteenth Century.* New York: Norton, 1997.

Sublette, Ned, and Constance Sublette. *The American Slave Coast: A History of the Slave-Breeding Industry.* Chicago: Chicago Review, 2016.

Sudarkasa, Niara. "'The Status of Women' in Indigenous African Societies." *Feminist Studies* 12.1 (1986): 91–103. http://www.jstor.org.ezproxy.wesleyan.edu/stable/pdf/3177985.pdf.

Tate, Claudia. "Allegories of Black Female Desire; or, Rereading Nineteenth-Century Sentimental Narratives of Black Female Authority." *Changing Our Own Words: Essays on Criticism, Theory, and Writing by Black Women.* Ed. Cheryl Wall. New Brunswick: Rutgers UP, 1989. 98–126.

Taylor, Nikki M. *Driven toward Madness: The Fugitive Slave Margaret Garner and Tragedy on the Ohio.* Athens: Ohio UP, 2016.

Threadcraft, Shatema. *Intimate Justice: The Black Female and the Body Politic.* New York: Oxford UP, 2016.

Wallace, Maurice O. *Constructing the Black Masculine: Identity and Ideality in African American Men's Literature and Culture, 1775–1995.* Durham: Duke UP, 2002.

Weisenburger, Steven. *Modern Medea: A Family Story of Slavery and Child-Murder from the Old South.* New York: Hill and Wang, 1999.

White, Deborah Gray. *Ar'n't I a Woman? Female Slaves in the Plantation South.* New York: Norton, 1985.

Williams, Sherley Anne. *Dessa Rose.* New York: William Morrow, 1986.

—————————. "Meditations on History." *Midnight Birds: Stories of Contemporary Black Women Writers.* Ed. Mary Helen Washington. Garden City: Anchor, 1980. 200–248.

To Be (a) One:
Notes on Coupling and Black Female Audacity

*I*n the exploration of what it is to be human, coupling is ever a problem: coupling disturbs or at least complicates the conceptualization of being, the philosophical deliberation of the one. This troubling is amplified for the black female subject, whose access to ideological oneness is rendered impossible in the logics of antiblackness and patriarchy. Indeed, philosophical thinking often excludes the specificity of black femaleness, such that the question of a black female one never quite appears in the discursive frame—except, that is, in the thinking of black feminists. Such an expression of black female oneness lives as the first-half title of Gloria (now Akasha) T. Hull, Barbara Smith, and Patricia Bell Scott's 1982 anthology, *All the Women Are White, All the Blacks Are Men, but Some of Us Are Brave.* Tucked within this aphorism—we could call it a poem, really—is an immaculate philosophy:[1] Notice, for example, how the calculus here side-steps naming black women specifically and instead signifies black femaleness as a common yet distinctive human characteristic, "brave." In this assessment, black femaleness is a habitat of being, a manner of being alive that eclipses the social logics of identity. The entire equation stands as a philosophical assertion, an

Volume 29, Number 2   DOI 10.1215/10407391-6999774

"ontology of relations" where being ("brave") is figured through difference.[2] And yet in this intersubjective calculation, black femaleness is not the mark of difference—not the pathology of otherness; rather, difference is a factor in conceptualizing what is inviolable about black female being. Indeed, the title phrasing imagines black female righteousness, a capacity of oneness, akin to the Combahee River Collective's determination, "Black women are inherently valuable."[3]

"All the women are white, all the blacks are men, but some of us are brave." Inspired by this, I want to explore a black female oneness, a philosophy of audaciousness, through relationality and difference. Specifically, I want to revisit the matter of marriage, which, for all its modern trappings, is really a social rendering of ideas about being, relationality, and oneness.[4]

On one level, black women don't figure easily into the discursive landscape of marriage because black femaleness exists outside the norms of domesticity. Moreover, as Ann duCille notes in a comprehensive review essay, "[M]arriage and family [became] peculiar institutions under two hundred and fifty years of chattel slavery," which further exiled black women from the ideals of the marriage convention ("Marriage" 605). Of course, duCille's *The Coupling Convention*, along with Claudia Tate's *Domestic Allegories of Political Desire* and Hazel Carby's *Reconstructing Womanhood*, reimagined marriage and domesticity vis-à-vis black femaleness. In fact, these three works constitute a formidable intellectual foundation about the "shifting representations and meanings of marriage, sexuality, and black womanhood" (duCille, *Coupling* 10), especially because they forgo the recuperation of marriage in the name of nationalism or authenticity and instead take account of the representational malleability of what marriage means.

It is in the spirit of this thinking that I want to explore the idea of a "black feminine ego," to study oneness—that transcendent human subjectivity of relation—through three figures of black female audaciousness: Lorde, Sula, Beyoncé.[5]

One: Lorde

Let's start with Audre Lorde, whose work centralizes difference as an ontological dynamic; that is, unlike the difference of black exceptionalism (or cultural exception), difference for Lorde was of and in her black female self, the audacious, self-centered core on which she scaffolded being. It is Lorde's intelligence we can use to think about the ideological limits of and possibilities for black female relation.

Lorde's thinking about difference and black femaleness travels through familiar domestic terrain, as is the case in her 1984 conversation with James Baldwin, "Revolutionary Hope." The conversation begins with Lorde's call for grappling with gender difference, not forgoing it in the name of racial solidarity since "[w]hen we deal with sameness only, we develop weapons that we use against each other when the differences become apparent" (Baldwin and Lorde 245). Central to their discussion—and disagreement—is the idea of the black family, especially the idiom of the black heterosexual companionate unit that haunts the imagining of freedom. Family becomes an impasse here because Baldwin wants to privilege the black man's burden as a failed man: "But don't you realize that in this republic the only real crime is to be a Black man." He continues:

> *A Black man has a prick, they hack it off. A Black man is a nigger when he tries to be a model for his children and he tries to protect his woman. That is a principal crime in this republic. And every Black man knows it. And every Black woman pays for it. And every Black child. How can you be so sentimental as to blame the Black man for a situation which has nothing to do with him? (250)*

Lorde interrupts Baldwin's litany—"the only crime is to be Black. I realize the only crime is to be Black, and that includes me too" (250)—and then offers her own catalog of the specific horrors visited upon black women by a racist sexist state and by black men who feel authorized to manifest their frustration against the women in their lives:

> *Do you know what happens to a woman who gives birth, who puts that child out there and has to go out and hook to feed it? Do you know what happens to a woman who goes crazy and beats her kids across the room because she's so full of frustration and anger? Do you know what that is? Do you know what happens to a lesbian who sees her woman and her child beaten on the street while six other guys are holding her? Do you know what that feels like? (251)*

Lorde and Baldwin's dialogue reflects the limits of domesticity as a basis for conceptualizing black freedom, especially in the ways that the domestic authorizes a normative tragedy of black maleness and reifies black women and children as objects of communal recuperation. Baldwin tries to settle their disagreement by proclaiming this a "family quarrel," which is different from a "public quarrel" (247), a point that calls to mind the arguments

Roderick Ferguson and Candace Jenkins have made about the idealization of publicness and black family heteronormativity. Notable, too, is how a black male–black female idiom runs up against the lived intimacies of Baldwin's and Lorde's queer personal realities. In some ways, neither Lorde nor Baldwin could easily be the signifier in this conversation about black liberation, though Lorde does dare to imagine a black lesbian possibility in the discursive example above.[6]

Throughout Lorde's work, the trouble of domesticity impacts her thinking about marriage—and coupling—as well as how she navigates being a mother. Indeed, motherhood and, to a lesser extent, relationships are important to Lorde's philosophical imagining of difference. As Alexis De Veaux explores in the indispensable *Warrior Poet: A Biography of Audre Lorde*, Lorde was not interested in a conventional notion of marriage or relationship: not with Ed Rollins, whom she married and with whom she had two children; not with the two women—Frances Clayton and Gloria Joseph— with whom she had long-term relationships; and not with or through the many shorter or more occasional sexual and/or emotional connections she had with other women.[7] De Veaux cites an unpublished poem where Lorde seems to define her overarching conceptualization of coupling:

> *We are not twins*
> *And I shall make my judgement*
> *Upon you*
> *Heavy as my hand on your thighs*
> *Heavy as my heart beating on your stomach*
> *Heavy as difference between us. (98)*

This verse riff recognizes embrace as a feature of differentiation, and it echoes Lorde's stance in her conversation with Baldwin that the aim is not the surpassing of difference but the capacity to bear its hefty weight, to be ethically capable of difference. Lorde refuses to erase herself, her black and female and lesbian self, from the plane of relation, a kind of self-centering gesture that runs counter to the logic of female subjectivity. Her consideration of coupling articulates an essential caveat of black female relationality, summarized efficiently in a journal entry: "we do not have to give up ourselves to get each other" (De Veaux 298). This ideation of a self-centered subjectivity proved even more crucial to Lorde's thinking about motherhood, given how regularly she grounded her identity in being a mother. "She did not imagine her life or work without [her children] Beth and Jonathan but saw self-preservation as an imperative," De Veaux surmises, noting that

Lorde, in her journal, wrote: "I will help them but I cannot sacrifice myself to them" (161).

Motherhood is a relationality, which Lorde's essay "Man Child: A Black Lesbian Feminist's Response" notes in its tagline, "Not only of a relationship, but of relating."[8] The distinction here shifts motherhood away from being for the other, a notion that is expressed clearly in Lorde's insistence, "We can learn to mother ourselves" (*Sister* 173). In Lorde's estimation, mothering is not conceived as displacement of a woman's being, but is instead a praxis that informs, sustains, and materializes a woman's capacity to be engaged in (her own) becoming. It is poet and scholar Alexis Pauline Gumbs who best mobilizes this insight of Lorde's thinking. As Lyndon K. Gill confirms, "[T]hrough Gumbs we come to recognize Lorde's concept of 'mothering' as a paradigm through which to describe our relationship (when we are at our best) to each other as human beings, our relationship to ourselves, and perhaps our relationship to the living, breathing natural world through which we move—in essence, our 'mother love' relationship to our existence" (173–74). This ideation of mothering is akin to oneness, an ethical orientation to being in the world that figures through the one rather than the two.[9]

Lorde was a theorist of black female being and, as such, was also a theorist of difference. And it is in conceptualizing difference that Lorde contends with the assumption of racial homogeneity. Hers was not a facile allegiance to a black female authenticity, but was instead a self-authorized understanding of being. In a journal entry from 1975–76, Lorde writes,

> *I have a right to be black. I have a right to be different and I have a right to survive. I have a right to join with other different human beings who are also black. Blackness doesn't mean we are one lump of chocolate poured on the face of eternity. Until each of us can love herself & himself fully, in all our contradictions, we will never survive as a people in this land because we will never survive as individuals. (De Veaux 159)*

This is part of Lorde's rejection of an "easy blackness" (203, 242) and also characterizes the way that difference functions not as a mark of her otherness but as a feature of her rightness of being. Said another way, for Lorde difference is ontological, and it generates from her black woman right to self-definition.[10]

The notion of a self-centered subjectivity might seem antithetical to an understanding of human dependency. But oneness is not incompatible with relation; rather, oneness is a relation, a habitat that facilitates one's being to the all that is around, beyond, within it—a capacious and transcendent inhabiting. My use of relation as a framework for Lorde's philosophical thinking is inspired by Martin Buber's case in *I and Thou*, where Buber argues for encounter as a superlatively open orientation to the world. That is, the person who has an I-Thou orientation is capable of meeting every other person or object as if each is worthy, full of thrill and surprise, capable of producing transformation. Importantly, the facility of I-Thou is not about two coming together, but instead resides in the preparedness of the one to meet the other one. I-Thou is a capacity of oneness, what Buber describes as "the genuinely reciprocal meeting in the fullness of life between *one active existence* and another" (*Eclipse* 46; my emphasis). I am compelled by this one of "active existence" in trying to understanding black female relationality.[11]

　　　Relation is the capacity of unfurling, of becoming more and more in/through the tension with another. In arguing for a black female relation, I am trying to articulate a justification for engaging relationality through how it informs oneness rather than through thinking about togetherness. I am interested in the integrity and essentiality of the one who is called into relation, how the one takes up the charge of the call, how the one envisions this taking-up, and how the one is instantiated as a one by whatever she becomes through the call to relation. For any marginalized subject, to be conceptualized via twoness is as perilous as it is inevitable; in this regard, oneness offers a way to imagine relational being where "relationality is *not* the social, but the figure for what sociality appears to misname" (Khalip 166). What necessitates Lorde's idiom of self-centeredness are the very locations of black femaleness as abject, as the nonideal human subject—the "brave" of the equation in the anthology's title. This recentering ensures that the ideological pursuit of a human ideal doesn't reify the logics that would erase black femaleness from that pursuit. I am struck, always, by the repetition of self-centeredness as an essential component of black female relationality: from Lucille Clifton's invitational untitled poem that begins "come celebrate with me" to June Jordan's closing line "we are the ones we have been waiting for" to ntozake shange's choral "I found God in myself and I loved her / I loved her fiercely" to Nikki Giovanni's "I am so perfect so divine so ethereal so surreal / I cannot be comprehended / except by my permission" to Jamila Woods's song "Holy," which states "I am holy by my own." These are audacious inhabitances of self as immanence that make possible the transcendence of surrender and relation.[12]

In every relation is a world, one of space and contact and unknowing and obliteration; in every relation is a world. What if that worldiness was of one who is black and female?

We can read Lorde's self-centeredness in this light, as an articulation of black female oneness—as a right to that oneness. De Veaux suggests that "self-centeredness kept Lorde alive well beyond medical expectations for someone with liver cancer. She could justify being self-centered: she had terminal cancer; what life she had left was hers alone to live and define" (357). It is not surprising, then, that the sharpest assertion of a subjectivity of oneness comes in *The Cancer Journals* (1980), a composite of journal entries and reflections including the well-known essay "The Transformation of Silence into Language and Action."[13] From *Cancer*'s initial sentence, the speaker Lorde constructs is full of existential awareness: "Each woman responds to the crisis that breast cancer brings to her life out of a whole pattern, which is the design of who she is and how her life has been lived" (7). A quick gloss of the opening page recognizes how the reflection moves from the singular idiom "each woman" to the relative case of "some women" to the first person: "I am a post-mastectomy woman who believes our feelings need voice in order to be recognized, respected, and of use" (7). This trajectory establishes the speaker as a subject of philosophical and relational reckoning.

In the third journal entry, Lorde consolidates the idiom of self-centeredness: "I feel so unequal to what I always handled before, the abominations outside that echo the pain within. And yes I am completely self-referenced right now because it is the only translation I can trust, and I do believe not until every woman traces her weave back strand by bloody self-referenced strand, will we begin to alter the whole pattern" (9). This emphasis accelerates the era's assertion that the personal is political and establishes an unyielding black female singularity. In fact, the claim here reflects Lorde's investment in outsiderness, the subjectivity of exceptional exemption as summarized in an October 1979 entry: "I am defined as other in every group I'm a part of. The outsider, both strength and weakness" (11).

In *The Cancer Journals*, autobiographical study is the basis of theoretical investigation.[14] As such, Lorde's construction of a subjectivity of exceptional exemption gains clarity in an entry written in the immediate aftermath of the mastectomy:

> *March 25, 1978*
> *The idea of knowing, rather than believing, trusting, or even understanding has always been considered heretical. But I would*

willingly pay whatever price in pain was needed, to savor the
weight of completion; to be utterly filled, not with conviction nor
with faith, but with experience–knowledge, direct and different
from all other certainties. (23)

The entry bristles with an Old Testament solemnity as Lorde argues for the
supremacy of knowledge that comes through experience, the direct knowing that is as sweetly intense as the pain the speaker references and was
enduring. In this regard, Lorde situates herself with the biblical Eve, she
whose yearning to know was a deeply felt fall into ungrace.[15]

This philosophical declaration collates true knowing with
embodiment, a thesis that reassures Lorde's celebration of self-centeredness
earlier in the book. (Embodied knowing can only be sustained through self-
awareness, and indeed, she later writes, "This is work I must do alone" [24].)
But a full comprehension of the intelligence here requires looking at another
iconic statement from *Cancer* as the speaker reflects on leaving the hospital:

In that critical period, the family women enhanced that answer
[to the question of death]. They were macro members in the life
dance, seeking an answering rhythm within my sinews, my syn-
apses, my very bones. In the ghost of my right breast, these were
the micro members from within. There was an answering rhythm
in the ghost of those dreams which would have to go in favor of
those which I had some chance of effecting.
[. . .]
For instance, I will never be a doctor. I will never be a deep-sea
diver. I may possibly take a doctorate in etymology, but I will
never bear any more children. I will never learn ballet, nor
become a great actress, although I might learn to ride a bike and
travel to the moon. But I will never be a millionaire nor increase
my life insurance. I am who the world and I have never seen
before. *(47–48; my emphasis)*

Notice, first, that the passage begins with an image of a cohort of women
(friends, lovers, her daughter) fused to her body–metabolized as her removed
breast. And after that beautifully random catalog of possibilities, the speaker
declares herself–singular but also composed of many women–as totality
and impossibility: "I am who the world and I have never seen before." This
definitive expression of exceptionalism functions in at least three ways:
literally, since later in the journal the speaker wonders, "Where were the

dykes who had had mastectomies" (50); epistemologically, since it describes an understanding of how knowing happens; and ontologically, since it is, centrally, a declaration of being, a revision of God's statement of immanence to Moses ("I am that I am"). In Lorde's writing, black femaleness is the position of thought.[16]

"I am who the world and I have never seen before": this is the idea of a black-female one, an idiom of certainty that dissolves into brilliant and terrifying uncertainty. It is a subjectivity that is at once of immanence and of transcendence, an audacious subject position for a black female human.

For Lorde, oneness is of relationality, the "being singular plural," "the moment when one consents not to be a single being."[17]

One: Sula

"The two of them together would make one Jude" (83): this clean line from Toni Morrison's 1973 novel *Sula* summarizes the troubled calculus of black marriage, especially since, in this moment, Nel and Jude are to be married, though the coupling impulse is less a rush of love and desire and more energized by the social and economic anxiety of racism. Jude is twenty and works as a waiter in the town's hotel, but he longs to be a construction worker on the new road being built through Medallion:

> *Along with a few other young black men, Jude had gone down to the shack where they were hiring. Three old colored men had already been hired, but not for the road work, just to do the picking up, food bringing and other small errands. These old men were close to feeble, not good for much else, and everybody was pleased they were taken on; still it was a shame to see those white men laughing with the grandfather but shying away from the young black men who could tear that road up. The men like Jude could do real work. (81)*

The narrative here identifies, through Jude's black male longing, the hunger to be successful in the patriarchal language of American masculinity (notice, for example, how the narrator adopts the expressive idiom "tear that road up," as if the moment slips into the voice and thoughts of these yearning black men). And embedded in this moment is the cultural discourse about black men and work and its impact on the relationships between black men and black women.[18] The novel sustains attention to Jude's ache, which soon starts to chafe his psyche and ultimately propels his proposal to Nel:

Jude himself longed more than anybody else to be taken. Not just for the good money, more for the work itself. He wanted to swing the pick or kneel down with the string or shovel the gravel. His arms ached for something heavier than trays, for something dirtier than peelings; his feet wanted the heavy work shoes, not the thin-soled black shoes that the hotel required. More than anything he wanted the camaraderie of the road men: the lunch buckets, the hollering, the body movement that in the end produced something real, something he could point to. "I built that road," he could say. (81–82)

And in lieu of a road on which to construct a viable black maleness—since "he stood in lines for six days running and saw the gang boss pick out thin-armed white boys [. . .] and heard over and over, 'Nothing else today. Come back tomorrow'" (82)—Jude chooses marriage and Nel: "He needed some of his appetites filled, some posture of adulthood recognized, but mostly he wanted someone to care about his hurt, to care very deeply. [. . .] He chose the girl who had always been kind, who had never seemed hell-bent to marry, who made the whole venture seem like his idea, his conquest" (82–83).

The equation here is rigged from the start, and Nel figures not as a partner but as a complement or substitution. This unequal communion gains authority from the normative idealization of black marriage, its capacity to recuperate blackness from social and cultural aberration, as Roderick Ferguson has argued.[19] And Nel, who—except for in her long friendship with Sula—has been groomed for domestic normativity, abides as an apt integer in the equation where two become one. Indeed, "Jude could see himself taking shape in her eyes" (83).

This pivotal scene exposes again the fractures of the marriage ideal, especially its racialized imagining of gender. And yet, what makes *Sula* an enduring literary treasure is how its question of marriage revolves not around Jude and his coopting of Nel, or any of the conventional marriages in the story; no, what endures in *Sula* is the investigation of unconventional coupling, the book's study of the ideological limits of and possibilities for relation. Even in this moment between Jude and Nel, the relational dynamics extend to the novel's title character, Sula, and the thrall of her connection with Nel. *Sula* is a quintessential study of the dynamics of black female relation.[20]

For example, though the novel's title is singular, *Sula* teems with couplings, including broken and stressed marriages for nearly all its principal characters—Nel and Jude, Eva and BoyBoy, Hannah and various men, Helene and Wiley Wright. More telling, though, are the extensive nonromantic yet substantial alliances that expose the question of being and relationality: Plum and Eva; Sula and Hannah; the grouping of boys named the Deweys; Eva and Sula; Eva and Hannah; Sula and Ajax; Sula's dalliances with random men, including white ones; Nel and Sula, that iconic girlfriend relationship on which Barbara Smith initiated a call for black lesbian feminist criticism ("Toward"). Even Sula and Shadrack appear as a companionate unit of communal ostracization, described as "two devils" by townfolk when a story circulates that Shadrack tips his hat to a curtseying Sula when they pass on the road. The story is idle gossip, but Shadrack and Sula have a sustained and unusual connection that violates the norms of coupling. As a girl, after the killing of Chicken Little, she enters his shed in a panic, afraid that he might have seen what happened:

> *Ever so gently she pushed the door with the tips of her fingers and heard only the hinges weep. More. And then she was inside. Alone. The neatness, the order startled her, but more surprising was the restfulness. Everything was so tiny, so common, so unthreatening. Perhaps this was not the house of Shad. The terrible Shad who walked about with his penis out, who peed in front of ladies and girl-children, the only black who could curse white people and get away with it, who drank in the road from the mouth of the bottle, who shouted and shook in the streets. This cottage? This sweet old cottage? With its made-up bed? With its rag rug and wooden table? Sula stood in the middle of the little room and in her wonder forgot what she had come for until a sound at the door made her jump. He was there in the doorway looking at her. She had not heard his coming and now he was looking at her. (61–62)*

This moment tenses with fear and yearning, including the unexpected—and inappropriate—erotic description of her entering the room, the gentle push, the finger tips, the single word "more" followed by the phrase "And then she was inside." Morrison's language highlights the threats to female girlhood as well as the impropriety, and still, the scene memorializes Shadrack and Sula in lush encounter, what Barbara Johnson might call the "transforming [of] horror into pleasure, violence into beauty" (171): "More in embarrassment than terror she averted her glance. When she called up enough courage to look back at him, she saw his hand resting upon the door frame. His fingers, barely touching the wood, were arranged in a graceful arc" (Morrison 62).[21] So here is Shadrack, poised and posed, suitor-like, and here is Sula, no longer afraid, walking "past him out of the door, feeling his gaze turning, turning with her" (62). No words pass between them except for the one Shadrack says, "always," which is, among other things, the closing of a love exchange. In the wake of Sula's death nearly twenty years later, Shadrack recognizes a new loneliness that he can't quite countenance. And yet, "More frequently now he looked at and fondled the one piece of evidence that he once had a visitor in his house: a child's purple-and-white belt. The one the little girl left behind when she came to see him" (156). Shadrack recalls how, back then, in that moment, he feared that Sula was frightened by the inevitability of death, and so "he tried to think of something to say to comfort her" (157), the valedictory "always." A love act indeed, and he keeps the belt as an act and symbol of fidelity.

Reading Sula and Shadrack as companions expands on how we think of Sula's subjectivity. That is, though the common wisdom is that "Sula never competed; she simply helped others define themselves" (95), such an assessment obscures the deep investment *Sula*/Sula has in a self-centered relationality. Indeed, the breadth of Sula's intersubjective vitality makes us rethink the conventions of coupling, including notions about object choice and mutuality: Sula may reject marriage as a convention, but her story is a long arc of studying (through) companionship. In this way, *Sula* does what Hortense Spillers astutely described in 1983: it "inscribes a new dimension of being" ("Hateful" 210).[22]

For example, after Sula sleeps with Jude and puts Eva in a nursing home, the townspeople come in harsh for judgment just as the narrative reminds us that Sula "had no intimate knowledge of marriage, having lived in a house with women who thought all men available" (119). This statement opens a steady exploration of Sula's thinking on coupling, particularly her friendship with Nel:

> *She had been looking all along for a friend, and it took her a while to discover that a lover was not a comrade and could never be—for a woman. And that no one would ever be that version of herself which she sought to reach out to and touch with an ungloved hand. There was only her own mood and whim, and if that was all there was, she decided to turn the naked hand toward it, discover it and let others become as intimate with their own selves as she was. (121)*

Strikingly, this passage advocates for self-centeredness in a voice that nearly slips from narrator to character, especially in the way that the first sentence uses the em-dash to delay and highlight the phrase "for a woman." This moment dramatizes the difference between a generic conception of being, where relationality—and mutuality—might be possible, and the restricted subjectivity that is imagined for women. Sula's resolution toward full self-centeredness, then, is shaped by exemption and exception, similar to the childhood realization that aligns her friendship with Nel: "So when they met [. . .] they felt the ease and comfort of old friends. Because each had discovered years before that they were neither white nor male, and that all freedom and triumph was forbidden to them, they had set about creating something else to be" (52). Like brave.

Exemption from being begets an exceptional orientation to being, and this praxis of audacity constitutes how Sula travels through becoming. Indeed, *Sula* is an ars erotica, a tracking of its title character's encounters in relationality through sex. The novel tell us that:

> *Although she did not regard sex as ugly (ugliness was boring also), she liked to think of it as wicked. But as her experiences multiplied, she realized that not only was it not wicked, it was not necessary for her to conjure up the idea of wickedness in order to participate fully. During the lovemaking she found and needed to find the cutting edge. When she left off cooperating with her body and began to assert herself in the act, particles of strength gathered in her like steel shavings drawn to a spacious magnetic center, forming a tight cluster that nothing, it seemed, could break. And there was utmost irony and outrage lying under someone, in a position of surrender, feeling her own abiding strength and limitless power. (123)*

The "matchless harmony" of Sula's embodied experience, this electric habitat of being, constitutes the full possibility of human aliveness. Sula meets herself in the most radical way, couples with herself in a "cluster" of deep relation. Sure, the cluster doesn't hold, but the potency of its happening forms how Sula thinks about herself as a being of relationality—not just her capacity to meet others but the imperative to meet herself.

What follows this determination is Sula's coupling with Ajax, he now thirty-eight and she twenty-nine, a realization of interest piqued nearly twenty years earlier in a moment of salacious and improper flirtation. Ajax and Sula have sex that is so sublime, it initiates in Sula a postcoital desire to rub or scrape off his skin layer by layer so as to study and comprehend materiality. *"If I take a chamois and rub real heard on the bone, right on the ledge of your cheek bone, some of the black will disappear"* (130), the passage begins, extending for nearly a full page of italicized reverie. The scene is legendary in the novel, and it is after this moment that "Sula began to discover what possession was. Not love, perhaps, but possession or at least the desire for it. She was so astounded by *so new and alien a feeling*" (131; my emphasis). Being inquisitive of newness, Sula surrenders fully to the trajectory of feeling, to the possession, which includes making gestures of domesticity that seem contrary to her earlier self-belief: she anticipates and prepares for Ajax's arrival by putting her hair in a ribbon, cleaning the house, setting the table with a rose; she indulges his whininess about life's difficulty by telling him, "Come on. Lean on me" (133).

If we forget that Sula is in-process, then we might read this happening as a lapse or even as a sign of confusing self-betrayal. But Sula is relational, and being with Ajax offers a chance to refine what being is. She is free to risk inquisitiveness about this new feeling, rather than only to conserve or protect herself in keeping with a notion of female frailty. Indeed, since it is true that "[d]uring the lovemaking she found and needed to find the cutting edge" (123), Sula is almost compelled to the risk as an investment in knowing. And if knowing is essential here, then the inquiry of her postcoital fantasy matters more than the specificity of Ajax's presence. In this way, the daydream of dissection and Sula's subsequent display of domesticity are scenes of play, the domain of studying and yielding and feeling; they characterize the capacious totality of her relational being.[25] It might seem odd to call Sula's objectification of Ajax relational, though in doing so I am reminded of two things: one, that what motivates the action here is Sula's surrender to meeting the other—to the risk-full encounter with the other; and two, that relation is not ever perfect mutuality but the capacity of the one to be oriented toward more and more mutuality. Sula does nothing more nor less than approach Ajax as a Thou, and in so doing, she is full of relational capacity.

To be "so astounded by so new and alien a feeling"—this is black female audacity, to be oriented toward the becoming new. And Sula's practice of being extends before and beyond Ajax such that after he disappears, she persists with the studying of difference, including considering the philosophical emptiness that is attachment:

> *Every now and then she looked around for tangible evidence of*
> *his having ever been there. Where were the butterflies? the blue-*
> *berries? the whistling reed? She could find nothing, for he had*
> *left nothing but his stunning absence. An absence so decorative,*
> *so ornate, it was difficult for her to understand how she had ever*
> *endured, without falling dead or being consumed, his magnificent*
> *presence. (134)*

The description lingers on the ornateness of his absence, a lingering that is
wistful, yes, but also clear about the being of encounter. "It's just as well he
left," Sula muses. "Soon I would have torn the flesh from his face just to see
if I was right about the gold and nobody would have understood that kind of
curiosity" (136), to which one wants to add "—in a woman."

This novel is superlative in its characterization of relational
being, and the narrative stretch here concludes with an exemplary expression of audacity: First, Sula falls asleep holding the only material evidence
she has of Ajax, his driver's license that reveals his name to be Albert Jacks
(as in A. Jacks) and therefore not the *objet* at all:

> *Holding the driver's license she crawled into bed and fell into a*
> *sleep full of dreams of cobalt blue.*
>
> > *When she awoke, there was a melody in her head she*
> *could not identify or recall ever hearing before. "Perhaps I made*
> *it up," she thought. Then it came to her—the name of the song*
> *and all its lyrics just as she had heard it many times before. She*
> *sat on the edge of the bed thinking, "There aren't any more new*
> *songs and I have sung all the ones there are. I have sung them*
> *all. I have sung all the songs there are." She lay down again on*
> *the bed and sang a little wandering tune made up of the words*
> I have sung all the songs all the songs I have sung all the songs
> there are *until, touched by her own lullaby, she grew drowsy, and*
> *in the hollow of near-sleep she tasted the acridness of gold, left*
> *the chill of alabaster and smelled the dark, sweet stench of loam.*
> *(137)*

Notice how this conclusion invokes the meditation on Ajax's skin (the references to gold, alabaster, loam) as a signal not of loss or longing, but as the
sublimity of deep feeling and of full aliveness, Sula's "cluster" from earlier.
Indeed, this passage is a characterization of Sula's totality, she who coun-
tenances smallness and obliteration with inventiveness and vigor—with a

self-made song of songs, sung without audience; she whose orientation is of oneness supreme and wide open, full and emptying, a being the world and herself has never seen before.

Like Lorde's speaker in *Cancer*, Sula is of exemption and exception, the relationality to be had in black female self-centeredness. And like Lorde's speaker confronting the possibility of death, Sula offers up a theory of difference from her own deathbed in a definitive confrontation with Nel: "You say I'm a woman and colored. Ain't that the same as being a man?" (142). This statement of difference refuses to have black femaleness stand as the mark of otherness and instead imagines black femaleness as all the difference in the world. A person who is black and female is also a human being and therefore is capable of figuring and being figured through an idea of oneness. Again, it is an understanding of oneness as the difference that doesn't exclude being and that orients toward the relationality of becoming, what Deleuze aptly describes in *Difference and Repetition*: "[I]nstead of something distinguished from something else, imagine something which distinguishes itself—and yet that from which it distinguishes itself does not distinguish itself from it" (28). Or Glissant, who reminds us, "[I]t is possible to be one and multiple at the same time; that you can be yourself and the other; that you can be the same and different" (Diawara 6).[24]

Morrison's Sula is a mighty rendering of black female being through which we can study the whole world of black existence. And yet there is a caution in reading the character (and novel) with this much affection, specifically because of questions about the ethical capacity of a character who is so self-centered. Literary scholar Alex Nissen, for example, argues that Sula "is not fully a moral agent and cannot be a model for emulation" (276), which echoes narrative sentiments about Sula's immaturity. But this conclusion fails to appreciate Sula's philosophical orientation and the ethical capacity of oneness. That is, the full regard Sula tries to have for herself is indeed the full regard she wants to have for other people—to meet other people as if they are of full regard. Sula's orientation depends on this mutuality, on meeting the other as they fully are and can be. (Remember that her meditation on sex claims that she wants to "let others become as intimate with their own selves as she was" [121]). Embedded in relationality is an invitation for open being, and we see this invitation in the way Sula helps others realize potentiality. That she would expect—even demand—fullness in the other makes sense since she is oriented relationally and hungers to be taken fully by the other. This is the ethical compass of Sula's relationality.[25]

Oneness allows one to be more and more human, to seek more and more capacity for good(ness) and right(ness), an ever widening pool of humanness that surpasses narcissism.

Relation is impossible to achieve, even more so for one jostled by social ideas about blackness and femaleness, though relation can be a horizon, an ethos—over and again the attempt to be undone by saying "you," being enough to be able to risk (one's) all.[26] This is Sula's ethos, an I-am-knowing-as-I-am-knowing, where the first clause establishes certainty and the second revels in dissolution, a transcendence that is also an immanence: Not all-knowing as a finality but as a fidelity to what one knows so as to deepen and then surpass that knowing. I am knowing as I am knowing.

One: Beyoncé

The early assessments concluded that *Lemonade* reflected black women's historic marginalization through the betrayal of troubled love. The filmmaker Melina Matsoukas, director of the music video for "Formation," explains that Beyoncé "wanted to show the historical impact of slavery on black love, and what it has done to the black family [. . .] how [black men and women are] almost socialized not to be together" (Okeowo 34). And yet, this characterization understates the philosophical meaningfulness of *Lemonade*'s deployment of black femaleness. More specifically, if *Lemonade* studies the genealogy of betrayal in black marriage, then it achieves its study via the idea of black female audaciousness. That is, rather than a modest exploration of the fraught idiom of a black woman hurt by a black man, *Lemonade* offers an ideological meditation on companionship where what matters is not the coupling per se but the ethical call toward being that coupling inspires. Beyoncé is well known for her commitment to aesthetic excess, but *Lemonade* marshals excess superlatively, in its form and especially in its close focus on a black woman as the axis of relationality. Yes, *Lemonade* is a thesis of the black female (as) one, an audiovisual realization of oneness as an idiom for whatever communion (romantic, social, political) might be possible.[27]

Lemonade's discourse follows the arc of Beyoncé's oeuvre, which worries the trouble that is black (women's) romantic love. Indeed, as she materializes empowerment through songs about the mess of love, Beyoncé participates in a long R&B tradition that perhaps started with blues singers in the post-Emancipation era. Her songs achieve political meaningfulness via what Daphne Brooks terms "black feminist surrogation," "an embodied performance that recycles palpable forms of black female sociopolitical grief and loss as well as spirited dissent and dissonance" (180).[28] And yet, what makes *Lemonade* exceptional are two things: Beyoncé's explicit attention to marriage as a historical conceit, and how this attention correlates to her long-term and—for her—monogamous real-life relationship. *Lemonade* dares to track, explicitly, black female being through heterosexual coupling, that most risky of idioms for black women.

Similar to Morrison's character Sula, Beyoncé's speaker mobilizes the erotic as ontology, and *Lemonade* imagines her being—at once vulnerable and ferocious—as the audacious center of understanding what it is to be human and alive. Certainly, there is not another performer working in contemporary music who exhibits a magnificent and magnanimous sense of self—who deploys magnanimity—as much and as credibly as Beyoncé. But in *Lemonade*, her speaker *luxuriates* in the audacious: she is at once her own particular human self as she is also every black woman.[29] This subjectivity is realized partly by the aesthetic scale of *Lemonade*, but also by its multiple direction of address, how the speaker variably hails black women, herself, her betrayer, black people, and the national imaginary through the varied sonic and visual landscapes as well as through the interspersing of Warshan Shire's poetry.[30] Such capacious address tries to match the discursive breadth of a black woman's domestic subjectivity. Think, for example, about how the singularity that opens "Pray You Catch Me," its chanting in scalar unison with the guitar—and the visual centrality of Beyoncé onstage and then wandering alone through a massive dying cornfield—yields to the figures of black women situated amid a decidedly Southern gothic landscape. *Lemonade* revels in this kind of toggling between the specificity of its speaker and the vastness of human being-ness that is available in her experiences, a thing exemplified best by "Freedom," with its black women covering the ground and the air, and by the tender collage of "All Night."[31]

Though it is not the final track sonically or visually, "All Night" is *Lemonade*'s conclusion: it is where we learn the significance of the work's title; it repeats nearly all of the iconic scenes from the film as a whole and revisits the scalar "huh" that opens "Pray You Catch Me."[32] This final section of *Lemonade* is titled "Redemption," a spiritual term that signals something larger than the reconciliation of coupling, more akin to the scope of the subjunctive from the section titled "Forgiveness": "If we're gonna heal, let it be glorious."

The segment opens with the camera gliding toward a screen door such that the viewer, for a second, is the one who is moving outside, only to have a young black girl (then another and another) bound through the door before us. It is a striking invitation and deferral, as the viewer both becomes and is surpassed by these young ones. This point-of-view subjectivity repeats again; this time, the camera moves toward a split curtain being pulled apart by two black women as the narrator recites the recipe for lemonade. These women who are making entry possible look toward the viewer, as if to say "be ready," and in this visual moment, all of us are walking toward redemption. The deliberateness of point-of-view here, this mixing that allows for a broadening of the film's first person, foreshadows the segment's beautiful collage, which weaves documentary footage of Beyoncé and her family with outtakes of everyday couples in gestures of affection. Here, at the end of things, *Lemonade* exemplifies the collectivity that happens—that can happen—through black femaleness.

Though "All Night" is a love song with lyrics typical of the genre, the audacity arrives in its signal quatrain, spoken first as a preface to the song: "Nothing real can be threatened / True love brought salvation back into me / With every tear came redemption / My torturer became my remedy." Beyoncé sings this transcendent idea deep in her throat as if using the specific gravity of infidelity to articulate a philosophy of being. Fullness this is—not just female endurance of male transgression but a transformation, a reckoning of aliveness. The heft here is supported by the song's interpolation of the horn riff from Outkast's "SpottieOttieDopaliscious," which invokes a sense of marching, dramatic performativity. (The song also ends magnificently on a final punctuated horn note.) But even more vital to an aesthetic of audaciousness is Beyoncé's place in the accompanying images: she largely exists outside the time and narrative frame of the song. Instead, she wanders through a cornfield in a gorgeous Ankara print gown with Victorian-era flourishes. Her hair is pinned up and she hardly ever faces the camera, she this black woman who moves timelessly in a world somewhere else from the song, she who creates and is of all this oneness.

Lemonade reminds us that in the discourse of black coupling, the matter is not marriage but the ontological thinking that ought to be possible through the experience of coupling. And indeed, in this masterwork, we see that a black woman's artistic and representational interrogation of her positionality in a heterosexual marriage can also be a site of her exploration of being. She doesn't have to be consumed by the historicity of the marriage idiom; she can be a subject in regard to and then beyond it. She can be the one of relation.

At its core, *Lemonade* materializes black female oneness.

One

" . . . but some of us are brave." "Brave," they said, brave, that adjective marked by racial and gendered and national specificity, a term that is at once poetic and political, a term describing character and consciousness and will. Brave, as in audacious and ordinary and alive, frail and full of need. Adjective, yes, but also a name; even more radical than that, a statement ontological and imperative: Brave. Undeniably here. Not woman, not black, not of a discourse of authenticity, but something else: human, a maker of things, a god of ideas, a one in and beyond the world, a one in and through black femaleness.

This essay is part of my continued study of what it means to explore black being—being itself—through some of the thinking of black women, particularly examples of black female audacity; it comes from a larger work on black aliveness. I want to thank Nora Daniels for research assistance; Matt Ashby, LaMonda Horton-Stallings, Daphne Lamothe, Mecca Jamilah Sullivan for conversations about being; Denise Davis for astute editing; and Ann duCille for being ever inspiring.

KEVIN QUASHIE is a professor of English at Brown University. He is the author or editor of three books, most recently *The Sovereignty of Quiet: Beyond Resistance in Black Culture* (Rutgers University Press, 2012). He is currently at work on a book on black aliveness.

Notes

1   The anthology's title phrase seems to have originated in the book, though Farah Jasmine Griffin notes how Toni Cade Bambara's introduction to the 1970 collection *The Black Woman* anticipates the title.

2   I am borrowing the phrase "ontology of relations" from the title of Vittorio Morfino's essay, which argues for relationality in Spinoza's work. My thinking about ontology and relation is indebted to three central texts: Martin Buber's *I and Thou*, Emmanuel Levinas's *Totality and Infinity*, and especially Édouard Glissant's *Poetics of Relation*, which posits that there is no difference between the self and the self in relation—as well as a host of works that have sustained my study, including Achtenberg; Cailler; Davidson and Perpich; Drabinski; Hudson; Sas;

and Williams. It is notable, too, that the statement doesn't name white maleness since, in the logic of things, white maleness is of enduring integrity and ubiquity.

3   I was reminded of the Combahee quotation by Alexis Pauline Gumbs, who mobilizes it as her philosophy of everything. My thinking here is motivated by Hortense Spillers's enduring work, "Mama's Baby, Papa's Maybe," which not only offers a philosophical articulation of black femaleness vis-à-vis modernity and coloniality but also resists the impulse to read black female exceptionalism as pathology. For me, Spillers brilliantly uses black femaleness as the subject of abstraction for the sake of trying to understand something about black female being, and blackness as a whole, rather than to reinforce black femaleness

as the essential mark of demeaned otherness. See esp. her description of "being for the captor" as "distance from a subject position" (67). Of all the work "Mama's Baby" does, I find this thread to be most dear.

4　The tendency in philosophy is to think of marriage in regard to morality. See, for example, Elizabeth Brake's discussion in *Minimizing Marriage: Marriage, Morality, and the Law*. I have taken direction from Alain Badiou's *In Praise of Love*, which explores love and coupling through philosophies of relation.

5　The phrasing is from duCille's *Coupling* (4) and riffs on a central idiom from Nina Baym's *Woman's Fiction*. And it is Spillers who noted, definitively, the absence of a concept of black oneness in her essay "'All the Things You Could Be by Now If Sigmund Freud's Wife Was Your Mother': Psychoanalysis and Race," an insight that inspired my exploration of oneness in *The Sovereignty of Quiet* (119–20).

6　This point calls to mind the argument Dwight McBride makes in "Can the Queen Speak?" about Baldwin's assumption of the idiom of the race man that potentially erases or mutes homosexuality.

7　See esp. 74–77 for a rich discussion of Lorde's marriage to Rollins.

8　This tag is included in the essay as it was originally published in *Conditions*, though not when the work is collected as part of *Sister Outsider*.

9　Gill draws on parts of Gumbs's gorgeously poetic dissertation, "We Can Learn to Mother Ourselves: The Queer Survival of Black Feminism 1968–1996," to set up the idea that part of Lorde's project is imagining the self in a practice of becoming. My thinking here learns from Gumbs's dissertation, as well as from the essay it spawned, "m/other ourselves: a Black queer feminist genealogy for radical mothering" in her anthology *Revolutionary Motherhood*, and from Jennifer L. Morgan's exposition on new world slavery's impact on our understandings of black motherhood.

10　Lorde makes this point about self-definition in "Scratching the Surface." Important, too, is the fact that difference is all over Lorde's thinking, as Rudolph P. Byrd notes in his introduction to *I Am Your Sister*: it was the theme of her speech at the 1979 National March on Washington for Lesbian and Gay Rights, as it was central to many of the essays in *Sister Outsider*, including "Scratching the Surface," "Age, Race, Class, and Sex," and "Man Child." Lorde's thinking on difference recalls Spillers from "Mama's Baby": "Every feature of social and human differentiation disappears in public discourses regarding the African-American person, as we encounter, in the juridical codes of slavery, personality reified" (78). For a brief but astute exploration of difference, being, and becoming, see Khalip. Khalip is engaging Lee Edelman, Michel Foucault, Jacques Derrida, and Paul de Man but offers a thoughtful survey of difference as a conceit in contemporary philosophical theory—even as he is less interested in relationality than I am here.

11　My study of Buber is indebted to Maurice Friedman's extensive scholarly work, including *Martin Buber: The Life of Dialogue* and the edited collection *Martin Buber and the Human Sciences*. Since this essay comes from a longer study of relation, I want to note some indebtedness here, including to Glissant and Levinas, whose theorizing informs and, sometimes, is in tension with Buber's. I have been guided especially by Cailler and Sas. Embedded in my thinking is also Luce Irigaray's *To Be Two*, Jean-Luc Nancy's *Being Singular Plural*, and two essays by J. Kameron Carter: "The Inglorious" and "Paratheological Blackness."

12   This claim is related to the argument I made for girlfriend selfhood in *Black Women, Identity, and Cultural Theory: (Un)Becoming the Subject*; see esp. chaps. 1–3.

13   Lorde's grappling with cancer was central in her life and impacts the structure of De Veaux's biography, which is divided into two sections, with cancer marking Lorde's second life. This narrative shape establishes the profundity of *The Cancer Journals* as a text (xi, 269, 271). Notable, too, is the fact that nearly all of the *Sister Outsider* essays and all of *Zami* come in this second life period, after cancer; furthermore, Lorde's ideological investment in being an outsider is linked to cancer (230). Of *The Cancer Journals*, De Veaux writes: "If the publication of *The Black Unicorn* expressed a poetic embracing of African mythologies, for spiritual sustenance, then *The Cancer Journals* signaled Lorde's self-styled transfiguration as Seboulisa incarnate. She becomes a living version of the one-breasted warrior goddess, central to her spiritual links to be a reimagined, mythic Africa. [. . .] [I]t was not simply that Lorde had breast cancer or a mastectomy; it was what she did with those facts" (271). And what she did with those facts was to construct an ontological idiom.

14   The conceptual uses of the black autobiographical are considered in Barbara Christian's "The Race for Theory," Kimberly Nichele Brown's *Writing the Black Revolutionary Diva*, William Andrews's *African-American Autobiography*, and Charles H. Rowell's interview with Farah Jasmine Griffin.

15   Lorde's "Poetry Is Not a Luxury" extends this argument about embodied knowing and imagination; indeed, in my longer study of aliveness, I argue that Lorde offers a philosophical reevaluation of the equation between experience and imagination.

16   I am riffing here on Saidiya Hartman and Frank B. Wilderson's interview, "The Position of the Unthought."

17   The first quotation invokes the title of Nancy's meditation on relation; the second is from Manthia Diawara's "One World in Relation: Édouard Glissant in Conversation with Manthia Diawara" (5). In terms of immanence and transcendence, see Haynes; Smith; Deleuze, *Pure Immanence*; and Rölli. It is also useful to think about Lorde's investment in mythos (especially Afrekete but also her stylization as Zami and her embrace of a Caribbean subjectivity) as a manifestation of a oneness, the transcendent multiplicity of being everything and nothing. See De Veaux 261 and 271.

18   See Jones, as well as Hunter.

19   See also Karen F. Stein's consideration of marriage in the classic essay, "Toni Morrison's *Sula*: A Black Woman's Epic."

20   See the discussion of relationality and the novel in Banyiwa-Horne; McKee; and Nissen.

21   My thinking about Shadrack and Sula's union has been enhanced by a conversation I had with Susanna Apgar years ago. See also Vashti Crutcher Lewis's discussion of the pair in "African Tradition in Toni Morrison's *Sula*."

22 Spillers's essay was really the first to centralize thinking about the ideology of black femaleness in *Sula*. Also see Deborah McDowell's similarly formative argument in "The Self and the Other: Reading Toni Morrison's *Sula* and the Black Female Text" and Diane Gillespie and Missy Dehn Kubitschek's "Who Cares? Women-Centered Psychology in *Sula*," which takes up relational being.

23 I have interpreted this moment as a setback, in *black women, identity, and cultural theory*, so I am offering this reading as another clarification in my sustained study of *Sula*. Indeed, we can read this moment as "the embracing dream [that] provides an image of an expanded self" (Berlant, *Desire/ Love* 6), such that Sula's hallucination creates a romantic scene in which she, Sula, can revel through wanting to feel dependency. (Berlant's insight about the essential fantasy in the love narrative mirrors the case that duCille makes about the marriage plot in *The Coupling Convention*.) These sex reveries are metaphysical and incorporeal as much as they are materially real. I am drawing here on Elizabeth Grosz's arguments in *The Incorporeal*; also see the case Banyiwa-Horne makes for immateriality in the novel.

24 Also see Glissant's claim that the "universal is a sublimation, an abstraction [that relation] doesn't allow" (Diawara 9).

25 The matter of respectability is part of thinking about Sula and ethics; in that regard, see Candace Jenkins's essential *Private Lives, Proper Relations*, Ferguson's *Aberrations in Black*, and Terrion L. Williamson's use of "scandalize" as a way to notice "the black woman who both is and causes a scandal within the field of representation [. . .], the contemplation of a black female subjectivity that attains meaning by way of an *amoral* social order that exists beyond the dichotomous regulatory regimes that structure so much of representational discourse" (19).

26 This is a conclusion that undergirds Glissant's, Levinas's, and Buber's thinking, even as all three of them envision its impossibility differently. See Cailler; Drabinski; and Sas here. Also, it is Buber who makes the most explicit claim for relation as a horizon, writing near the end of the first section of *I and Thou*, "One cannot live in the pure present," and later, "Without It a human being cannot live" (85).

27 As much as the work is personal—and is informed by Beyoncé's marital struggles—*Lemonade* is a performance and an artistic work: the affective and intimate details have been put to creative and discursive use, as Hilton Als reminds us in "Beywatch: Beyoncé's Reformation." Of course, Beyoncé and Jay-Z have long used their iconic coupling to do black cultural work, starting perhaps with "Bonnie and Clyde '03" and continuing right through Jay-Z's *Lemonade* complement, *4:44*. Furthermore, *Lemonade* is not Beyoncé's first foray into explicitly political themes, and indeed there have been many arguments about the meaningfulness of her embrace of or relevance to (black) feminism. See, for example, Brooks; Durham; Weidhase. For a larger scholarly framing, see Durham, Cooper, and Morris; and the essays in Trier-Bieniek's *The Beyoncé Effect*.

28 Brooks's notion of surrogation notices how some black women performers—in this case, Mary J. Blige and Beyoncé—play "with the historically dense liminality of the black female performer singing her way through rock memory and the national imaginary" (188). More specific to *Lemonade*'s use

of black female domesticity is Angela Davis's description of the social and political work of black blues women, how their lyrics and performances are invested with a sophisticated engagement of domestic matters that expose the gendered and racial politics that are often at stake in black women's musical investigations of love. See *Blues Legacies and Black Feminism*, esp. 1–20.

29 Beyoncé's sense of oneness extends to how she deploys motherhood—and pregnancy—especially in the 2017 Grammy Awards performance of "Sandcastles" and "Love Drought." Also see Mecca Jamilah Sullivan's review essay, "Erotic Labor and the Black Ecstatic 'Beyond,'" which discusses this capaciousness (esp. 131–32).

30 In "Beyoncé's *Lemonade*: She Dreams in Both Worlds," Lisa Perrott, Holly Rogers, and Carol Vernallis argue, "*Lemonade*'s unusual form—a long-play music video—gives it the capacity to draw connections between the personal

pain of infidelity and America's terrible history of racism. Twelve video clips are linked by brief passages comprised of poetry, visual tableaux and sound collage. These interludes lean toward avant-garde aesthetics [which offer] the capacity to hold several vantage points in suspension. In *Lemonade*, this capacity allows the work to embody opposites: love and hate, engagement and alienation, forgiveness and revenge."

31 Of all the commentary on *Lemonade*'s expansiveness, see esp. Simmons; and Tinsley.

32 "Formation," which is appended to the film after the closing title, is really a coda. Indeed, I think of "Formation" as functioning similarly to the coda in Morrison's *Beloved*, where the love story ends with Sethe's "me, me," and then the next two pages are a metaphorical replay of the story without the specificity of the characters, a philosophical meditation on human yearning and pain and historical terror.

Works Cited

Achtenberg, Deborah. *Essential Vulnerabilities: Plato and Levinas on Relations to the Other*. Evanston: Northwestern UP, 2014.

Als, Hilton. "Beywatch: Beyoncé's Reformation." *New Yorker* 30 May 2016. https://www.newyorker.com/magazine/2016/05/30/beyonces-lemonade.

Andrews, William L., ed. *African American Autobiography: A Collection of Critical Essays*. New Jersey: Prentice Hall, 1993.

Badiou, Alain, with Nicolas Truong. *In Praise of Love*. Trans. Peter Bush. London: Serpent's Tail, 2012.

Baldwin, James, and Audre Lorde. "Revolutionary Hope: A Conversation between James Baldwin and Audre Lorde." *We Wanted a Revolution: Black Radical Women, 1965–1985: A Source Book*. Ed. Catherine Morris and Rujeko Hockley. Brooklyn: Brooklyn Museum, 2017. 242–51.

Banyiwa-Horne, Naana. "The Scary Face of the Self: An Analysis of the Character of Sula in Toni Morrison's *Sula*." *Sage* 2.1 (1985): 28–31.

Berlant, Lauren. *Desire/Love*. New York: Punctum, 2012.

Beyoncé. *Lemonade*. Parkwood, 2016.

Brake, Elizabeth. *Minimizing Marriage: Marriage, Morality, and the Law*. New York: Oxford UP, 2012.

Brooks, Daphne. "'All That You Can't Leave Behind': Black Female Soul Singing and the Politics of Surrogation in the Age of Catastrophe." *Meridians: Feminism, Race, Transnationalism* 8.1 (2007): 180–204.

Brown, Kimberly Nichele. *Writing the Black Revolutionary Diva: Women's Subjectivity and the Decolonizing Text.* Bloomington: Indiana UP, 2010.

Buber, Martin. *The Eclipse of God: Studies in Relation between Religion and Philosophy.* Princeton: Princeton UP, 2016.

————. *I and Thou.* Trans. Walter Kaufman. New York: Touchstone, 1996.

Byrd, Rudolph P. "Create Your Own Fire: Audre Lorde and the Tradition of Black Radical Thought." Introduction. *I Am Your Sister: Collected and Unpublished Writings of Audre Lorde.* Ed. Rudolph P. Byrd, Johnnetta Betsch Cole, and Beverly Guy-Sheftall. New York: Oxford UP, 2009. 3–36.

Cailler, Bernadette. "*Totality and Infinity,* Alterity, and Relation: From Levinas to Glissant." *Journal of French and Francophone Philosophy–Revue de la philosophie française et de langue française* 19.1 (2011): 135–51.

Carby, Hazel V. *Reconstructing Womanhood: The Emergence of the Afro-American Woman Novelist.* New York: Oxford UP, 1987.

Carter, J. Kameron. "The Inglorious: With and Beyond Giorgio Agamben." *Political Theology* 14.1 (2013): 77–87.

————. "Paratheological Blackness." *South Atlantic Quarterly* 112.4 (2013): 589–611.

Christian, Barbara. "The Race for Theory." *Cultural Critique* 6 (1987): 51–63.

Clifton, Lucille. Untitled ("won't you celebrate with me"). *The Collected Poems of Lucille Clifton, 1965–2010.* Ed. Kevin Young and Michael Glasser. New York: BOA, 2012. 427.

Combahee River Collective. "A Black Feminist Statement." Hull, Smith, and Scott 13–22.

Davidson, Scott, and Diane Perpich. "On a Book in Midlife Crisis." Davidson and Perpich 1–10.

————, eds. *Totality and Infinity at 50.* Pittsburgh: Duquesne UP, 2012.

Davis, Angela. *Blues Legacies and Black Feminism: Gertrude "Ma" Rainey, Bessie Smith, and Billie Holiday.* New York: Pantheon, 1998.

Deleuze, Gilles. *Difference and Repetition.* Trans. Paul Patton. New York: Columbia UP, 1994.

————. *Pure Immanence: Essays on a Life.* Trans. Anne Boyman. New York: Zone, 2005.

De Veaux, Alexis. *Warrior Poet: A Biography of Audre Lorde.* New York: Norton, 2004.

Diawara, Manthia. "One World in Relation: Édouard Glissant in Conversation with Manthia Diawara." *Nka* 28 (2011): 4–19

Drabinski, John. "Future Interval: On Levinas and Glissant." Davidson and Perpich 227–52.

duCille, Ann. *The Coupling Convention: Sex, Text, and Tradition in Black Women's Fiction.* New York: Oxford UP, 1993.

————. "Marriage, Family, and Other 'Peculiar Institutions' in African-American Literary History." *American Literary History* 21.3 (2009): 604–17.

Durham, Aisha. "'Check On It': Beyoncé, Southern Booty, and Black Femininities in Music Video." *Feminist Media Studies* 12.1 (2011): 35–49.

Durham, Aisha, Brittney C. Cooper, and Susana M. Morris. "The Stage Hip-Hop Feminism Built: A New Directions Essay." *Signs* 38.3 (2013): 721–37.

Ferguson, Roderick. *Aberrations in Black: Toward a Queer of Color Critique.* Minneapolis: U Minnesota P, 2003.

Friedman, Maurice, ed. *Martin Buber and the Human Sciences.* Albany: SUNY P, 1996.

————————. *Martin Buber: The Life of Dialogue.* 4th rev. ed. New York: Routledge, 2002.

Gill, Lyndon K. "In the Realm of Our Lorde: Eros and the Poet Philosopher." *Feminist Studies* 40.1 (2014): 169–89.

Gillespie, Diane, and Missy Dehn Kubitschek. "Who Cares? Women-Centered Psychology in *Sula.*" *Black American Literature Forum* 24.1 (1990): 21–48.

Giovanni, Nikki. "Ego Tripping (there may be a reason why)." *The Collected Poetry of Nikki Giovanni, 1968–1998.* New York: William Morrow, 2003. 125–26.

Glissant, Édouard. *Poetics of Relation.* Trans. Betsy Wing. Ann Arbor: U of Michigan P, 1997.

Griffin, Farah Jasmine. "Conflict and Chorus: Reconsidering Toni Cade's *The Black Woman: An Anthology.*" *Is It Nation Time? Contemporary Essays on Black Power and Black Nationalism.* Ed. Eddie S. Glaude Jr. Chicago: U of Chicago P, 2002. 113–29.

————————. "An Interview with Farah Jasmine Griffin." Interview by Charles H. Rowell. *Callaloo* 22.4 (1999): 872–92.

Grosz, Elizabeth. *The Incorporeal: Ontology, Ethics, and the Limits of Materialism.* New York: Columbia UP, 2017.

Gumbs, Alexis Pauline. "m/other ourselves: a Black queer feminist genealogy for radical mothering." *Revolutionary Mothering: Love on the Front Lines.* Ed. Alexis Pauline Gumbs, China Martens, and Mai'a Williams. Toronto: PM Press, 2016. 19–31.

————————. "We Can Learn to Mother Ourselves: The Queer Survival of Black Feminism, 1968–1996." PhD diss. Duke University, 2010.

Hartman, Saidiya V., and Frank B. Wilderson. "The Position of the Unthought." *Qui Parle* 13.2 (2003): 183–201.

Haynes, Patrice. *Immanent Transcendence: Reconfiguring Materialism in Continental Philosophy.* New York: Bloomsbury, 2012.

Hudson, Stephen. "Intersubjectivity of Mutual Recognition and the I-Thou: A Comparative Analysis of Hegel and Buber." *Minerva—An Internet Journal of Philosophy* 14 (2010): 140–55. http://www.minerva.mic.ul.ie/vol14/intersubjectivity.pdf.

Hull, Gloria T., Barbara Smith, and Patricia Bell Scott, eds. *All the Blacks Are Men, All the Women Are White, But Some of Us Are Brave: Black Women's Studies.* New York: Feminist Press, 1982.

Hunter, Tera. *To 'Joy My Freedom: Southern Black Women's Lives and Labor after the Civil War.* Cambridge, MA: Harvard UP, 1997.

Irigaray, Luce. *To Be Two*. Trans. Monique M. Rhodes and Marco F. Cocito-Monoc. New York: Routledge, 2001.

Jenkins, Candace. *Private Lives, Proper Relations: Regulating Black Intimacy*. Minneapolis: U Minnesota P, 2007.

Johnson, Barbara. "'Aesthetic' and 'Rapport' in Toni Morrison's *Sula*." *Textual Practice* 7.2 (1993): 165–72.

Jones, Jacqueline. *Labor of Love, Labor of Sorrow: Black Women, Work, and the Family from Slavery to the Present*. New York: Vintage, 1995.

Jordan, June. "Poem for South African Women." *Directed by Desire: The Collected Poems of June Jordan*. Ed. Jan Heller Levi and Sara Miles. Port Townsend: Copper Canyon, 2007. 278–79.

Khalip, Jacques. "Still Here: The Remains of Difference." *differences* 21.1 (2010): 161–68.

Levinas, Emmanuel. *Totality and Infinity: An Essay on Exteriority*. Trans. Alphonso Lingis. Boston: Kluwer Academic, 1991.

Lewis, Vashti Crutcher. "African Tradition in Toni Morrison's *Sula*." *Phylon* 48.1 (1987): 91–97.

Lorde, Audre. *The Cancer Journals*. Spec. ed. San Francisco: Aunt Lute, 1997.

———. *Sister Outsider: Essays and Speeches*. New York: Crossing, 1984.

McBride, Dwight A. "Can the Queen Speak? Racial Essentialism, Sexuality, and the Problem of Authority." *Callaloo* 21.2 (1998): 363–79.

McDowell, Deborah. "The Self and the Other: Reading Toni Morrison's *Sula* and the Black Female Text." *Critical Essays on Toni Morrison*. Ed. Nellie McKay. Boston: G. K. Hall, 1988. 77–90.

McKee, Patricia. "Spacing and Placing in Toni Morrison's *Sula*." *Modern Fiction Studies* 42.1 (1996): 1–30.

Morfino, Vittoria. "Spinoza: An Ontology of Relation?" *Graduate Faculty Philosophy Journal* 27.1 (2006): 103–27.

Morgan, Jennifer L. *Laboring Women: Reproduction and Gender in New World Slavery*. Philadelphia: U Pennsylvania P, 2004.

Morrison, Toni. *Sula*. New York: Plume, 1987.

Nancy, Jean-Luc. *Being Singular Plural*. Trans. Robert D. Richardson and Anne E. O'Byrne. Stanford: Stanford UP, 2000.

Nissen, Axel. "Form Matters: Toni Morrison's *Sula* and the Ethics of Narrative." *Contemporary Literature* 40.2 (1999): 263–85.

Okeowo, Alexis. "The Provocateur behind Beyoncé, Rihanna, and Issa Rae." *New Yorker* 6 Mar. 2017: 34–39.

Perrott, Lisa, Holly Rogers, and Carol Vernallis. "Beyoncé's *Lemonade*: She Dreams in Both Worlds." *Film International* 2 June 2017. http://filmint.nu/?p=18413.

Quashie, Kevin. *Black Women, Identity, and Cultural Theory: (Un)Becoming the Subject*. New Brunswick: Rutgers UP, 2004.

—————————. *The Sovereignty of Quiet: Beyond Resistance in Black Culture.* New Brunswick: Rutgers UP, 2012.

Rölli, Marc. *Gilles Deleuze's Transcendental Empiricism: From Tradition to Difference.* Trans. and ed. Peter Hertz-Ohmes. Edinburgh: Edinburgh UP, 2016.

Sas, Peter. "A Relation to End All Relations: On Badiou's Scandalous Closeness to Levinas and Buber." *Critique of Pure Interest* (blog) 7 May 2012. http://critique-of-pure-interest.blogspot .com/2012/05/relation-to-end-all-relations-on_6111.html.

shange, ntozake. *for colored girls who have considered suicide / when the rainbow is enuf.* New York: Scribner, 1997.

Simmons, LaKisha Michelle. "Landscapes, Memories, and History in Beyoncé's *Lemonade.*" UNC Press Blog 28 Apr. 2016. https://uncpressblog.com/2016/04/28/lakisha-simmons -beyonces-lemonade/.

Smith, Barbara. "Toward a Black Feminist Criticism." *Radical Teacher* 7 (1978): 20–27.

Smith, Daniel W. "Deleuze and Derrida, Immanence and Transcendence: Two Directions in Recent French Thought." *The Proceedings of the Twenty-First World Congress of Philosophy.* Ed. Paul Patton and John Protevi. London: Continuum, 2003. 123–30.

Spillers, Hortense J. "'All the Things You Could Be by Now If Sigmund Freud's Wife Was Your Mother': Psychoanalysis and Race." *Critical Inquiry* 22.4 (1996): 710–34.

—————————. "A Hateful Passion, A Lost Love." *Toni Morrison: Critical Perspectives Past and Present.* Ed. Henry Louis Gates Jr. and K. A. Appiah. New York: Amistad, 1993. 210–35.

—————————. "Mama's Baby, Papa's Maybe: An American Grammar Book." *Diacritics* 17.2 (1987): 65–81.

Stein, Karen F. "Toni Morrison's *Sula*: A Black Woman's Epic." *Black American Literature Forum* 18.4 (1984): 146–50.

Sullivan, Mecca Jamilah. "Erotic Labor and the Black Ecstatic 'Beyond.'" *American Quarterly* 69.1 (2017): 131–47.

Tate, Claudia. *Domestic Allegories of Political Desire: The Black Heroine's Text at the Turn of the Century.* New York: Oxford UP, 1992.

Tinsley, Omise'eke Natasha. "Beyoncé's *Lemonade* Is Black Woman Magic." *Time* 25 Apr. 2016. http://time.com/4306316/beyonce-lemonade-black-woman-magic/.

Trier-Bieniek, Adrienne. *The Beyoncé Effect: Essays on Sexuality, Race, and Feminism.* Jefferson: MacFarland, 2016.

Weidhase, Nathalie. "'Beyoncé Feminism' and the Contestation of the Black Feminist Body." *Celebrity Studies* 6.1 (2015): 128–31.

Williams, Robert R. *Hegel's Ethics of Recognition.* Berkeley: U California P, 2000.

Williamson, Terrion L. *Scandalize My Name: Black Feminist Practice and the Making of Black Social Life.* New York: Fordham UP, 2017.

Woods, Jamila. "Holy." *Heavn.* Jagjaguwar, 2017.

REBECCA WANZO

The Cosby Lament:
Rape, Marital Alibis, and Black Iconicity

*T*wenty years after Anita Hill came forward to testify that Supreme Court nominee Clarence Thomas had sexually harassed her in the workplace, Thomas's wife Virginia inexplicably called Hill and asked her to apologize. In a voicemail message left on Hill's office phone at Brandeis University, she asked that the professor "consider an apology sometime and some full explanation of why you did what you did with my husband" (Savage). Hill had come forward at deep personal cost and has never recanted the testimony she gave before the all-male Senate Judiciary Committee in 1991,[1] so Thomas's sudden phone call invites us to read the possible multidirectional performativity of it. We could read the call on its face as a sincere appeal to a woman she believed had done her and her husband wrong. Virginia Thomas probably believes that her husband did not harass Hill. She could be performing that spousal faith so that others will believe him, too, and to buttress her own belief as well. Regardless of the reason for the telecommunication (which might not even be apparent to Thomas herself), the episode calls attention to the role wives frequently play in addressing sexual injuries by men.

Volume 29, Number 2   DOI 10.1215/10407391-6999788

© 2018 by Brown University and d i f f e r e n c e s : A Journal of Feminist Cultural Studies

Wives are good victims, shoring up a belief in the husband's goodness, as innocent parties victimized by the accuser. And as a white woman married to a black man, Virginia Thomas was deployed as a white victim in a narrative of rape and blackness but with a profound difference. Thomas (in)famously called his confirmation hearing a high-tech lynching, evoking the idea of black woman Hill as a false accuser, while his wife served as part of his victimization: "I can't tell you what my wife has lived through" ("Nomination" 200). As Ida B. Wells famously revealed in 1892, black men were often accused of raping white women in the early twentieth century when the white community was threatened by black success. In a role reversal, Hill was allegedly attempting to thwart black male success, and white wife Ginni was simultaneously representing support of black manhood *and* victimization by blackness. Conservative Thomas had not proven himself to be a friend of African American civil rights—nor would he, once confirmed on the court—but the accusation nonetheless mobilized many black people to align themselves with Thomas against Hill. He became someone to defend even if he was not loved before, because an attack on black male success was treated as an attack on the race.

In a *New York Times* op-ed, the famed African American sociologist Orlando Patterson publicly accused Hill of ignoring black heteronormative scripts. He was "convinced" that Hill knew that Thomas was not harassing her but simply practicing a "down-home style of courting." For Patterson, Hill was aligning herself with "neo-Puritan feminization with its sacralization of women's bodies" and against black culture. Hill, as an educated, black professional woman, was a foil for black success. Similar accusations were hurled at actress Robin Givens, who married boxing champion Mike Tyson in 1988 and would quickly seek a divorce. Givens accused Tyson of battery but would defend him in a television interview as "gentle" ("Story"). Like many boxing heroes before him, Tyson was a celebrated figure to many in the black community; thus accounts of his abuse were dismissed by those who saw Givens, and later, the black beauty pageant contestant Desiree Washington, whom he was convicted of sexually assaulting, as victimizing *him* (Sharpley-Whiting 48). Bad wives and women "who should know better" are an excuse for maltreatment, while good wives serve as proxies for not only the goodness of the accused celebrity but for the betrayed audience as well.

This essay is an attempt to work through the nature of the cultural injury produced by the African American male celebrity—injuries that are frequently acts of intimate violence—and to hypothesize why the public accusations of such injuries affectively challenge many black subjects. Remedies for these injuries often gesture toward heteronormative or otherwise regulatory racialized sexual scripts. Stories of African American male celebrities accused of sexual harassment and assault are frequently marked by stories of marital alibis. Comedian and "America's favorite Dad" Bill Cosby had *two* wives come to his defense—his real wife, Camille Cosby, and his television wife, Phylicia Rashad—when dozens of women came forward to accuse him of drugging and sexually assaulting them. As Cosby's story continued to unfold in 2016, the actor-director Nate Parker was heralded as making an important intervention into representations of black slavery on film with his Nat Turner biopic, *The Birth of a Nation*, when the reemergence of a rape accusation against him in college shifted the conversation from his filmmaking to his past. Parker would often reference his wife and daughters in defending himself against the rape charge, and some black feminist critics read the rape of Turner's wife in the film biographically and thus symptomatic of how Parker reads women. When the black basketball star Kobe Bryant was accused of sexual assault in a high-profile case in 2003, his wife Vanessa was the public face of support and injury: Bryant made a point of treating her as the victim. And even pop star Michael Jackson, a celebrity not usually associated with heteronormativity, was quickly married after an accusation of child sexual abuse was leveled against him. Part of what we must discard in cases of such injuriousness is giving any succor to the respectability claims proffered by wives, as such arguments are largely shaped by the cognitive refusal to believe in compartmentalized violence: that good and bad can exist simultaneously in one subject.

I put the final touches on this essay in 2017, in the wake of dozens of allegations of sexual harassment and assault against Miramax founder Harvey Weinstein. Post-Weinstein, many women (and some men) have come forward to tell stories of their victimization by powerful men in the entertainment industry. Social media became filled with #metoo (a phrase initiated by a black woman) (Garcia), an acknowledgment that sexual harassment, assault, or abuse is an almost universal experience of women (Almukhtar et al.). As man after man fell from power, a small number of women intimates publically expressed their struggle to negotiate their love for them with accounts of the injuries to other women.[2] This essay dwells in that space of negotiation, but, as is the case with so many experiences in life, it also dwells on a black difference. While many people are mourning the loss and betrayal of entertainers they respected and who gave them joy, black performers encourage defense on a different register.

The marital alibi makes hypervisible the belief that black people will lose too much if we address these injuries. I am interested in exploring how the idea of black male guilt circulates in the media as a black cultural injury and the various ways that heteronormative scripts are mobilized to offer not only innocence but also repair. I am not producing a definitive account of the accused's guilt. Instead, I interrogate the affective and social costs of losing iconic black male love objects, as revealed by an archive of public responses to the injury. Discursive analysis of the triangular relationship between the icon, his art, and the floating signifier of the marital alibi illustrates how victims of sexual violence are displaced in favor of privileging cultural injuries. The marital alibi, as placeholder for our desire or betrayal, is not the Rosetta Stone for these incidents. The complexity of the black love object lost to the audience through his injuriousness can be interpreted in many ways, one of which should be through centering the victims who are obscured in a discursive privileging of romantic love, patriarchy, and racial injury. But as proxies for the familial and the intimate, the marital alibi can help us understand the intimate relationship between black audiences and popular love objects. This essay makes somewhat fanciful use of the wife as analogy and proxy for the fan tied to the injurious love object through memory, affinity, and even economics. Of course, fandom is not like marriage, even though some fandoms turn on romantic fantasy. But if the institution of marriage provides a mechanism for achieving economic security and social and state recognition mobilized through real and idealized notions of affinity, marriage is as good an analogy as any for thinking through the nature of intimate attachments to celebrity. Methodologically bridging the relationship between theories of media effects, a psychoanalytic theory of object relations, and black cultural studies (a tendentious trio, to be sure), this essay explores why popular black love objects matter and why the loss of them is material.

Kill Bill (and Clair, Too)

Fans are often accused of disproportionate attachments to celebrities, a criticism that often becomes most pronounced when fans display grief over their idols' deaths.[3] Such framings of appropriate objects and rituals of grief are but one example of how public and private affective attachments are consistently regulated. Mourning the loss of any person or thing who gives us pleasure is an understandable response. If mourning, as Freud describes it, is "the reaction to the loss of a loved person, or to the loss of some abstraction which has taken the place of one, such as one's country, liberty" or "an ideal," then grief over celebrities who so often represent ideals would seem inevitable and likely (243). Ideals that are understood to contribute to antiracist projects nonetheless perform different work for the fan and can produce racially inflected injuries.

Love objects that many African Americans grew up with, like Michael Jackson and Bill Cosby, become doubled in a subject's consciousness; they are both real people who continue to exist in external reality and idealized fantasies who become incorporated into the fan's sense of self. Melanie Klein argues that adult grief replicates the states of mind in childhood when we learn to negotiate our relationship to good and bad objects and that our parents and family members are not the only people who help us develop a sense of self. Our pleasurable experiences with all loved objects help us develop as subjects. In some ways, twenty-first-century indictments of appropriate attachments and grief are premodern formulations of affective attachments that resist the ever growing presence of mass media in everyday life. As Donald Horton and Richard Wohl recognized in 1956, mass media have produced what they call "para-social interactions" in that these media give the illusion—and, importantly, they do not describe it as a *delusion*—"of a face-to-face relationship with the performer." The parasocial interaction describes the relationship that subjects have with a variety of media stars. They argue that the persona "can claim and achieve an intimacy with what are literally crowds of strangers, and this intimacy, even if it is an imitation and a shadow of what is ordinarily meant by that word, is extremely influential with, and satisfying for, the great number who willingly receive and share it" (216). Although Horton and Wohl were focused on the phenomenon of personae on television and their quotidian impact, multimedia platforms and social media have evolved beyond the pair's supposition that the audience does not truly interact with the performer or the production of the text. Fans can easily find others with shared affinities, with celebrities and many televisions shows increasingly responsive to audience response.

The quotidian nature of popular culture means that popular media and objects that give pleasure are introjected by the subject. Once internalized, these doubles are even more fantastic than they are as personae that subjects consume. Klein suggests that when external situations, objects, and people become doubles of real situations, the inner world is "built up" and then becomes "inaccessible to the child's accurate observation and judgment, and cannot be verified by the means of perception which are available in connection with the tangible and palpable object world" (149). Part of the challenge of the internal good objects in the development of the subject is the tendency to either idealize or devalue. The challenge of integrating the complexity of good and bad into the same subject is part of psychological development. Subjects find an ability to hold onto flawed loved objects.

In the wake of the sexual assault accusations against the comedian and television star Bill Cosby that gained traction after decades, many people argued that we should not hold onto a love object marred by reports that he had drugged and sexually assaulted dozens of women. Cosby's iconicity, like that of many black celebrities, begins with his media scarcity. He became famous in 1963 when he appeared on *The Tonight Show* and rose to success as a comedian before becoming the first African American to star in a network drama, *I Spy*, in 1965. However, it was his creation of *The Cosby Show* (1984–1992), one of the most successful sitcoms of all time, that solidified his iconic status. For many, critics and viewers alike, *The Cosby Show* was groundbreaking for its positioning of the black family as a universal ideal, but others argued that the show was a troubling assimilationist narrative that did not acknowledge racial injury in the post–Civil Rights era (Innis and Feagin 692).

The "positive" representation of blackness aids in constructions of the subject in three ways: as phenotypic and cultural mirror, as ideological refutation, and as statement of desire. In other words, we become attached to those who look like us, defend us against racist representations, and imagine that people of color can inhabit spaces we have never been before. While many scholarly studies of race and media effects focus on injury, a long history of African American writing about popular media also documents the pleasure of black representation that combats the white supremacist gaze. Recognition encourages positive self-development. The image outside of the body is always a distortion of what one understands oneself as being, and popular media encourage both idealized and negative distortions. Idealized representations of Cosby, Sidney Poitier, and other black celebrities who emerged in the classical period of the Civil Rights era trafficked in a problematic politics of respectability that combatted a history of racist representations while often eschewing what some black critics would see as more authentic depictions of the black experience.

Popular love objects thus visually manifest the tension between the different versions of those objects that trouble the self. Love objects affirm and protect us. If, in Kleinian object-relations theory, the child must come to terms with the difference between the real parent who inevitably fails to meet every need and the parent-ideal constructed within the child, a similar process makes us struggle to negotiate the relationship between love objects outside of ourselves and our internalized ideas of the love object. Black love objects carry that doubleness within the world, with the tension between the ideal performance and the performer himself. Bill Cosby, however, perpetuated the idea of himself as a double for the lovable patriarch, Cliff Huxtable, on *The Cosby Show*. Moreover, Cosby invites biographical criticism because his stand-up and sitcom were often described as inspired by situations in his own life. His television wife Clair and his real-life wife Camille had the same maiden name; his fictional family the Huxtables resembled the actual Cosby clan, with four girls and one boy; and his fictive son Theo's dyslexia was inspired by his biological son Ennis's struggle with the disability. Cosby and the popular press invited audiences to see his family as the more affluent, but just as ideal, double of his television show. Cosby became the principal signifier not only of black fathers and husbands but of all patriarchs and marital partners, while *The Cosby Show* became the manifestation of the ideal family, replacing *Leave It to Beaver, Ozzie and Harriet*, and *The Brady Bunch* as referents for national normative values.

Heteronormative black families played no small role in Cosby's iconicity, with his real and fictional wives providing cover and defense in his real and fictive lives. Cosby built a career personifying black respectability politics. In 2004, he delivered his famous "pound cake" speech. Black youth, he opined, were "getting shot in the back of the head over a piece of pound cake" (3). He argued that black youth do not take advantage of their opportunities or live up to their responsibilities, evoking a politics of respectability as a salve to racism that many critics condemned as blaming the victim. The icon angered and disappointed many African Americans with his denigration of black youth, but others embraced his conservative message of personal responsibility. Such rhetoric, however, did not produce an ideological conflict around his most beloved production, *The Cosby Show*. Such conservatism was arguably consistent with the heteronormative ideal modeled on the sitcom.

Cosby presents the paradox of what universality does in the logic of black representational politics. If part of the injuriousness of racist discourse is that African Americans are often not seen as human, as representative of something other than or a part of blackness, then the potential of the black subject as universal is key to addressing white supremacy. But if universality depends on emptying out the specificity of blackness, it is a pyrrhic victory. The blackness of *The Cosby Show* was a much debated idea. Cosby clearly desired to present entertainment appropriate for white identification, and the black upper-middle-class family lives of the Huxtables did not reflect the economic realities and life experiences of the majority of African Americans. Racist and antiracist critics alike suggested the show was about characters who only happened to be black, but the fact of the characters' blackness was essential to identification with these HBCU-educated parents who could, in fact, exist and thrive economically in the post–Civil Rights era. Despite the assimilationist and universalist subject positions the Cosby family occupied, some performance of blackness through speech, aesthetics, music, and other cultural expression was essential to the ideality of the show.

Such culturally specific ideality also encouraged the construction of black intimacy on the sitcom, largely facilitated by Clair Huxtable as a representation of an idealized black lady. I have written elsewhere about Clair Huxtable elevating the standards for all sitcom mothers in the 1990s, with success and style that rarely seemed to require effort. Fatigue or professional challenge was rarely an aspect of her persona, and the black rhetorical specificity of her anger—in an age that encouraged feminist rage on television, as exemplified by Julia Sugarbarker on *Designing Women* (CBS, 1986–1993) and the title character on *Murphy Brown* (CBS, 1988–1998)—made it acceptable, without being explicit, for black women to be feminists (Wanzo 380–81). Clair Huxtable, nearly as much as Cosby's real wife Camille, is a large part of Cosby's marital alibi. She made Cliff's gender politics visible.

For the black feminist theorist Brittany Cooper, Clair also functioned as an alibi for Cosby's sexism. She argues that while the show had an overt rhetoric of antisexism, it is ultimately a sham. She writes:

> *How can a man who is a vicious hater of women get all the rhetoric right offering up an idealistic view of what a "good, feminist family man" might look like? It turns out that dudes, or their carefully crafted representatives, can sound right, and seem right, and still be all the way wrong. It turns out that you can have progressive feminist politics on the outside and still be deeply emotionally damaged and fucked up on the inside.*
>
> *And since Bill Cosby is a rapist, his avatar Cliff Huxtable is a representational terrorist, holding us hostage to a Black Family that never was. But let him die. Stockholm Syndrome be damned.*

Cliff Huxtable never actually "was," but Cooper's commentary suggests that part of our attachment was either a belief that he was or that he could be. But what, exactly, is the thing that never was? Is she referring to a black upper-middle class or to progressive gender politics in a black family or any family? Perhaps she is speaking of the idealism of the sitcom nuclear family, always an impossible standard? Cooper offers up other twenty-first-century models from different genres: melodramas with African American women protagonists who are flawed and, some would argue, antiheroes. "Perhaps," she suggests, "we needed to slay Clair Huxtable" to imagine more complicated political and erotic lives for black women that aren't beholden to impossible standards.

The censure of the ideal sitcom wife is fairly standard in feminist media studies criticism, which over the years has given way to attempts to rehabilitate some of these characters for feminists (Spangler). Clair may not be in need of rehabilitation except for the guilt of her association. While Cooper points to moments in the show indicative of a patriarchal politics in which fathers feel they have a right to protect their daughters' bodies from other men, for the most part the show does possess, as she claims, good gender politics. Thus the stakes of her question are whether (or not) we can still love an admirable (albeit fictive) woman whose very existence is owed to a rapist. Many writers, and of course the actress Phylicia Rashad herself, would contribute to the creation of the character of Clair Huxtable, but *The Cosby Show* exists because Bill Cosby was a star—which leads to the broader questions posed by affective attachments to objects lost through injuriousness. Do we lose everything when our love objects inflict injury? Do we have an ethical responsibility to lose everything? Should we be leery of our attachment to the genius, which overdetermines our relationship to the creations? If we take the death of authorship seriously and think about the ways in which we have a relationship to things outside the conditions of their production, then perhaps it is the space in between us and the love object that we are really trying to preserve, the place where we create and imagine. That play, that revelation, that aesthetic and pleasure, that struggle and redefinition which took place because of our love object may be part of our becoming. This is particularly the case with members of oppressed groups looking for representation—so much so that when we totally discard the lost object, we discard part of ourselves.

If Cosby's television wife was instrumental in shaping the sense of injury to fans, his real-life wife facilitated the silencing and the attempt to shame publically women who accused her husband of assault. Camille Olivia Hanks married William Henry "Bill" Cosby in 1964. The two of them were arguably the most high-profile black couple in Hollywood for decades, held up as an ideal representation of "black love" and prominent black phi-lanthropists. Women have come forward with accounts of being drugged and sexually assaulted by Bill Cosby that date back to the beginning of the couple's marriage (Kim, Littlefield, and Etehad). And while it is unclear when Camille Cosby would first learn of these allegations, we know that she did play a role in some settlements with his accusers. As with Ginni Thomas, we cannot know the inside of Camille Cosby's head. But in understanding the wife as alibi and proxy for public attachment, we can see that this woman's personhood became completely entwined with her husband's. Her fame, wealth, and future hinged on his success. She seems to have sacrificed other women for self-preservation. To a lesser extent, the faithful fan can commit that injury, though with much less material interest at play.

In 2005, a few women reported being drugged and sexually assaulted by Bill Cosby (Meadows). The story, however, did not stick in the public consciousness. Curiously, it took comedian Hannibal Burress's call-ing Cosby a rapist in a 2014 standup routine for the story to gain traction. By 2016, sixty women would come to accuse Cosby of sexual assault (Este-ban and Roig-Franzia). I confess that the story did not stick with me either. Perhaps *The Cosby Show*, as childhood love object, is the reason for such willful forgetting. Eventually, the staggering number of accusers made it impossible for anyone to ignore or forget. The ideal television husband and patriarch's real-life marital alibis, however, never doubted him in public. Camille Cosby continually supported her husband, and Cosby's television wife Phylicia Rashad claimed that the sexual assault charges were a cultural assault: "[T]his is not about the women. This is about something else," she charged. "This is about the obliteration of legacy" (Jue). Rashad's ambiguous "this" pointed to the truth of what much of the black media coverage was about: not his victims, but the loss of an iconographic building block in the black popular imagination.

Ebony magazine emphasized *The Cosby Show*'s foundational sta-tus with a November 2015 cover depicting an earlier portrait of the cast marred by shattered glass. The new cover story explores "the intensely complicated relationship between the fallen icon, his most beloved character and the bro-ken hearts of black America" (Taylor 101). The family issue is part of a long tradition of the representational politics of the Johnson Publishing Company, whose publications have focused on black celebrities and the black middle class. Writer Goldie Taylor opens the cover story with the Moynihan Report, the 1965 assessment of the state of the black family that has haunted public discourse and policy with discussions of a "black matriarchy" and "tangle of black pathology." Like many scholars and commentators, Taylor treats *The Cosby Show* as an answer to the Report that "provided emotional relief from the stereotypes in newspapers" but "inadvertently told America that Moynihan and Reagan were right" (103). Taylor's argument performs a complicated slippage. She maintains that by reinforcing the "widely held virtues of the nuclear family," *The Cosby Show* suggested that "if we could just pull ourselves together and find a good (educated, middle-class) soul mate, everything would be OK." With members of a dominant group, a media depiction of one kind of family would not usually suggest that it is a representation of what all families should be. But in the context of a community often conceived of as monolithic, idealizing the normative family structure can function as an even greater indictment of households that do not fit the formula. At the same time, treating the sexy, intimate, loving relationship between black heterosexual soul mates as injurious to black people—as opposed to one of a set of possible desires—illustrates the inescapability of injury in black representational politics. No family model can be read outside of pathology.

Part of the injury of these accusations against Cosby—particularly given the suggestion that for some of the women, Cliff Huxtable's function as double for Cosby facilitated their trust in him—is the heightened sense that black pleasures are pathological. As Stuart Hall has said of black popular culture, it is not where we discover who we "really are" but "where we discover and play with the identifications of ourselves, where we are imagined, where we are represented, not only to the audiences out there who do not get the message, but to ourselves for the very first time" (32). Cosby as rapist contaminates nostalgia for a text already situated by some as injurious to "real" blackness, and attachment to him as creator of these pleasures becomes an attachment to someone who hurts women. If African Americans wish to hold onto the pleasures they experienced in *The Cosby Show* as a site for recognition and desire because they once incorporated it into stories they told about themselves and the world, then what they see and what they hope for becomes suspect, leaving a hole that cannot be filled by something experienced now. They cannot re-create the stories of becoming through more appropriate attachments; thus what's left is always already pathology.

I Want to Marry Michael: Pop Gods and Monsters

The temporality of our desires is part of what makes it a challenge to work through the injury caused by the lost black love object. Audiences project innocence and guilt over time; if the attachment is formed when the love object was transparently innocent, it can be hard to abandon the ideal image. At the same time, the audience may read back deviance onto earlier images, as some kinds of monstrosity are understood as inherent. But previous innocence also becomes evidence of later innocence. The emergence of injurious deviance invites a rereading and rewriting of not only the loved object's developmental script but also our own.

Few figures illustrate a fan base's commitment to temporal grace like Michael Jackson. In 1994, Jackson paid $25 million to settle a civil suit claiming that he had sexually abused thirteen-year-old Jordan Chandler (Wapshott). Jackson maintained his innocence, claiming that he "reluctantly chose to settle the false claims only to end the terrible publicity and to continue with" his life and career (Vineyard). The son of one of Jackson's maids also said the pop star molested him (Leduff). In 2005, Jackson was indicted on multiple counts for sexually molesting thirteen-year-old Gavin Arvizo, which he again denied. After a lengthy trial in a California superior court, he was acquitted on all fourteen counts. Wade Robson, a boy who was a character witness for Jackson during that trial, said after Jackson's death that the pop star had abused him as well (Dawn). If one were to tell a story about a wealthy man who was accused of sexual assault multiple times, who described emotional and physical intimacy with children not related to him, and who created a home that was a fantasy world for children that attracted them to the space, very few people would be able to avoid presumption of guilt. For those who believe Michael Jackson was "a God who became a mere celebrity," the idea that the pop star could be a pedophile is a sacrilege (Brown). Regardless of one's stance on his guilt, it is reasonable to contemplate what it would mean for someone foundational to the subject formation of so many people to be guilty of such injurious acts.

Part of what it means, for some, is to rethink an attachment to an idol for teens and adolescents who was the object of or soundtrack to romantic desire. People rarely talk about Jackson in relationship to heteronormative scripts, but he did participate in them. In the August 1972 issue of *Teen's Star Magazine*, the soon-to-be-crowned King of Pop, then the young lead singer of the Jackson 5, is asked whether he likes kissing a girl on the first date.

> *I can dig it! I think that if you dig a chick enough to ask her out, you're crazy if you don't want to kiss her. And if she accepted the date, she likes you and probably wants to be kissed! So I couldn't think of any reason why I shouldn't! I think I'd like to wait until*

the end of the date before I kissed her though! I think most girls are afraid you're comin' on too fast if you kiss them right away. But if I could tell that chick was just waitin' to be kissed, I wouldn't mess around wastin' time! I'd take her in my arms, bend her back to rest on the back of her seat, and slowly lean toward her, gazing into her eyes and talking in a slow, smooth voice. Then I'd press my lips against hers, gently at first, then harder and harder until we're both lost in a soul kiss of true love. (Jackson)

Jackson was thirteen or fourteen at the time of this publication, and this representation of him performs the paradoxical mix of juvenescence and the romantic and erotic sophistication of the teen idol. The sexualized child star has a long history in u.s. culture, with children from Shirley Temple through Justin Bieber suggesting their worldliness on stage and in front of the camera (Warwick). "Boy bands," Mark Duffett argues, "emphasize masculinity at various states of maturation for a female target audience who are portrayed as vulnerable to the fantasy of coupling with the performers" (192). Rooting his discussion in the 1990s phenomenon of white boy bands, Duffett maintains that the teen idol and male musical groups have a long history of mobilizing the desire of adolescents. Innumerable women have recounted declaring, "I want to marry Michael," when they were young and foisting the clearly less talented and desirable brothers off to friends. The teen idol encourages fans to see him or her as youthful and capable of adult desires and acts at the same time. Moreover, the invisible object of desire in the song performance can be a mechanism for queer desire as well.

In the spoken word opening to "Who's Lovin' You," a young Michael says he "may be young, but I know what it's all about," and goes on to discuss falling out with a girl in the sandbox before singing a soulful rendition of the song. This was an early example of the romantically sophisticated adolescent that would become a standard trope of the boy band. As arguably the only teen idol male singer who became spectacularly more successful as an adult and whose youthful music is considered part of his genius, Jackson—whose youth and adulthood were always intertwined—would cultivate a childlike persona and continued to present himself as such with his "Neverland" ranch throughout his fifth and final decade of life. This attachment is part of what would place him under suspicion for pedophilia.

Some people in the media argued that one of Jackson's responses to the child sexual molestation accusations was marriage (Cress). A year after he was accused of sexually abusing Jordan Chandler in 1993, he married Lisa Marie Presley, the daughter of the rock-and-roll legend Elvis Presley. If the marriage was, in fact, an effort to frame Jackson as "normal," this performance of heteronormativity was met with derision and laughter. Shortly after the surprise nuptials, Jackson walked with his new wife onstage at the MTV Video Music Awards, saying, "Just think, nobody thought this would last," before giving her an extended kiss ("Video"). An appearance that seemed to serve no purpose other than as an extended performance of heterosexual, adult desire was widely described as an awkward public relations stunt designed to restore his image ("Top Ten"). And, indeed, it seems the naysayers were right: the couple divorced not even two years later. Regardless of how we read the newlyweds' MTV spectacle, the choice to perform public intimacy is indicative of a desire to silence gossip with a public declaration of marital desire and love, just as Nate Parker would do two decades later.

Part of what is fascinating about Jackson's relationship to heteronormative desire is that it has been so linked to his adolescence. As James Kincaid has explained, "[O]ur culture has enthusiastically sexualized the child while just as enthusiastically denying that it was doing any such thing" (13). Tavia Nyong'o argues that looking at Michael Jackson points "toward an incoherence in the ideology of the Child, an inconsistency that popular musical performance is perhaps uniquely equipped to reveal" (42). The temporal dimensions of Jackson's desirability are slippery; some of his most iconic love songs were produced when he was a child, and as an adult his performances simultaneously became more sexual and sexually ambiguous. While he famously grabbed his crotch throughout the 1980s and 1990s, his commitment to plastic surgery made him appear more androgynous, and he was rarely associated with lovers of any gender. In other words, some of his most normative representations of romance were as a child and adolescent.

Nyong'o contends that after Jackson's death in 2009, he noticed a kind of national "nostalgia for the young Michael: the brown-skinned, Afroed, big-nosed Michael of the Jackson 5. [. . .] This nostalgia was particularly pronounced amongst (black bohemian) intellectual types eager to hold on to a Michael that the mass media had passed over," he explains, "a soulful more pop Michael, a Michael who danced and sang as an exemplar of a community rather than as an idiosyncratic and estranged individual, a Michael from the past that the Michael of the present might not even recognize" (44). Nyong'o's observation illustrates how black fandom paradoxically depends upon the representative nature of black icons even as their atypicality is what usually propels them to stardom. Moreover, the "Afroed, big-nosed Michael" is a sign of blackness in the way that the older Jackson—post plastic surgeries, post (white) wives—was not. To love and want to marry a youthful, Motown Michael is also to love a kind of quotidian, recognizable blackness.

When a person of color overcomes poverty or social disadvantage to achieve fame, it is considered a benefit not only to the individual but also to an entire group of people. Nicole Fleetwood's work on racial iconicity highlights this cultural difference in celebrity attachment. The black icon is both "an exceptional and common figure," she writes, and black iconicity represents "the interworkings of misfortune and opportunity, of terror and visibility, of injustice and hopefulness, of death and immortality" (10, 13). By attaining a piece of cultural capital and maintaining a place in a culture that is dominated by whiteness, successful people of color are perceived as opening doors and doing important political work. Thus an investment in and sometimes a defense of a celebrity is often a point of racial pride and progress, and the removal of a celebrity of color from that limited and closely guarded space creates a hypervisibility and sense of shame that disavows the suitability of the oppressed from privilege.

Many fans who are not of color profess "love" for Michael Jackson for reasons that are linked to his skill, the pleasure they attach to the productions he presented to them, and the general sense of possibility offered by all celebrities. But the love from people of African descent can also be about a love of a self that receives public approbation, which is also true for people who do not meet gender norms in our culture. Thus the refrain, "We love you Michael," marked on signs, emerging in conversations, or proclaimed on call-in radio shows when his reputation was threatened, was not only made by an international, hysterical, pubescent, white audience. It was also a pronouncement on the part of black and queer people (not mutually exclusive) that "we" love an icon who looks like, is like, us. Often an assertion that "we" love blackness and queerness and that blackness and queerness can be loved by the world, this public declaration of love announces a psychological, polyamorous union, a public affirmation of affinity and intimacy. Such a relationship comes with a set of expectations on both sides.

But Jackson rarely seemed to harbor any preference for black audiences and did not always make the projection of racial pride onto his body easy. He was ambivalent, at best, or resistant to being a specifically black love object. Lightening his skin, allegedly in response to vitiligo, and undergoing plastic surgeries to obtain features dissimilar to those of many people of African descent, he appears to have been retreating from blackness.

But his physical and behavioral transformations cannot be contained by the classically problematic accusation of "acting white." As David D. Yuan has suggested, "If Jackson had merely wanted to look Caucasian, he could have done so without taking his cosmetic reconstruction nearly as far as he has [. . .]. Jackson has constructed for himself a mask that calls attention to the fact that it is a mask." Yuan argues that this ambiguity demonstrates the star's universality: "[T]he effect of Jackson's alterations is to make him look androgynous rather than feminine, multiracial rather than black or white [. . .]. It is as if Jackson, who has long aimed at entertaining all the world's peoples despite profound differences of language, culture, and race, has tried to make himself look the part of universal entertainer" (379). In this reading, he made himself totally other in order to construct himself as a universal ideal. The example of Jackson demonstrates how the wholly other can be simultaneously strange and comforting. His otherness is similar to that of the colonial object who, as Homi Bhabha argues, generates a "productive ambivalence" and is "at once an object of desire and derision" (67). Such otherness can make him a site of desire.

Jackson made productive ambivalence an art form in the construction of his body and in the stories he used to sell his music visually, stories in which he often configured himself as an alien other. When his character in the *Thriller* video states, "I'm not like other guys," he evokes both heterosexual romance scripts of the exceptional soul mate *and* the generic convention in thrillers and horror narratives that warn the audience of peril. This ambivalence is frequently at play in the cultural scripts that circulate in the media after real killers are revealed: they did, indeed, seem like other guys—or did not. The movement between the invisibility, on the one hand, and the legibility, on the other, of bogeymen in our midst serves a cultural function; it is, in fact, productive. It forces us to recognize that we cannot always "tell" who could commit such injuries. This failure of recognition is often modeled by mothers and wives: "How," people ask, "could they not have known?" But acknowledging the public possibility of such failures of recognition and attachments outside of familial or religious acts of forgiveness might allow us to radically reimagine what it means to love those who are socially constructed as lacking value.

Holding onto Bill Cosby's work posed a problem after the sexual assault accusations because a big part of his performance was selling an idealized representation of black domestic life, a representation he used to prey on women. By contrast, Jackson's increasingly troubled persona, ironically, may have constructed more room to bifurcate his gifts and his injuriousness. The idea of Jackson as pedophile makes Jackson as love object a real person, whose corporeal reality attacks the ideal that fans may have carried with them. But if Jackson is somehow still the little boy who so many dreamed of marrying, the prospect of pathological difference—dangerous otherness—may open the door to incorporating love objects into a sense of self outside a strict binary of good and bad. To imagine the possibility of something good in a love object who has committed a heinous crime like child sexual abuse is typically seen either as making excuses for bad acts or as betraying not only the individual but the culture. Regardless of his guilt or innocence, Jackson and his biography could help us think our way through public conversations about what it means to value someone who may have committed grievous injury, perhaps encouraging a new vocabulary that does not reduce celebrities to gods or monsters.

Did I Mention I Have a Lovely Wife?

Deification is not limited to pop gods. People both within and without the African American community can be quick to identify black messiahs. Such was the case with Nate Parker, who was described as hold-ing "almost messianic promise" (Scott). After the Sundance Film Festival in 2016, the black interweb was buzzing about a new film written, directed, and starring the young African American actor. *The Birth of a Nation*, whose title is an intentional "clapback" to D. W. Griffith's white nationalist landmark in epic filmmaking by the same name, was described as an anti-dote to cinematic and televisual representations of slavery that some critics suggest fetishize black subjection (Wilson and Lewis). Loosely depicting Nat Turner's life and the Southampton slave rebellion of 1831, Parker's film won the grand jury prize at Sundance, and the debut director received the biggest distribution deal in Sundance history (Siegel and Ford). Almost overnight, Parker was heralded as a black auteur and hero for taking time off from his acting career to raise funds for a project that depicted strong black masculinity and resistance to white supremacy in a Black Lives Matter moment.[4] He seemed destined for more success and awards—until reports of a seventeen-year-old rape case involving Parker and his cowriter Jean Celestin resurfaced and his seemingly inevitable trajectory from virtual unknown to cultural icon collapsed (Jones and Bashein).

While students at Penn State in 1999, Parker and Celestin were charged with raping a classmate who had been drinking and who claimed she was too incapacitated to consent. Celestin was convicted of sexual assault and Parker was acquitted on all charges. For those well versed in sexual assault cases on college campuses, the reasons for a not-guilty verdict in Parker's case in 2001 while his codefendant was judged culpable appears illustrative of classic rape scripts. The accuser had performed a consensual sexual act with Parker prior to the evening in question. Given the split verdicts, we can safely conclude that the jury presumed prior consent meant ongoing consent and believed the alleged victim also agreed to have sex with Parker that night. But the jurors also apparently believed that there was some incapacitation, because they convicted Celestin of sexual assault. His conviction was later overturned on the grounds of ineffective counsel, and the prosecution reportedly decided not to retry the case because of how challenging it would be to track down all the witnesses (most of whom had presumably graduated and moved elsewhere) (Stockton). Some of Celestin's supporters who were at Penn State at the time have treated the decision not to retry the case as clear evidence that he was innocent of the charges ("Exclusive").

Many feminists, particularly black feminists, called on people to boycott the film because, as Roxane Gay argued in the *New York Times*, she could "not separate the art and the artist" or her "blackness" and "continuing desire for more representation of the black experience in film" from her "womanhood," "feminism," "own history of sexual violence," and "humanity." The film did not perform well at the box office, and black feminists were accused of being "petty," a claim that spoke to the perpetual argument that antiracist projects and feminism are politically incompatible, resulting, particularly, in the destruction of black manhood (Fee). Such conflicts highlight culturally shaped responses in the African American community around sexual assault. Because of the history of racially motivated accusations of sexual assault against black men and disparate treatment under the law, some African Americans greet claims of white women accusing black men of assault with skepticism, but as Anita Hill, Robin Givens, and Desiree Washington demonstrate, black women who accuse black men of assault are also doubted. Supporters of Parker and Celestin who were at Penn State argue that the two men experienced constant racial harassment on campus from the investigators. However, racist treatment and guilt are not mutually exclusive. If we take as a given that racial discrimination is embedded in the criminal justice system, a black man could be discriminated against and still be culpable. And ironically, the same people distrustful of racial justice from the courts can treat acquittals as evidence of innocence. Nate Parker maintained that he was innocent, and there is unlikely to be a rapprochement between those who read the available evidence and saw an all-too-common account of men sexually assaulting an incapacitated woman on a college campus and those who saw a woman who did not take responsibility for sexual acts to which she consented.

Unlike some African American celebrities who have shored up years of love and attachment and can be appropriately described as icons, Parker was relatively unknown. While lacking the iconic status of Cosby or Jackson, Parker nevertheless used as a major part of his defense the same element that makes African Americans' falls from grace so injurious: their representativeness of something larger than themselves. "The important thing," he argued, "is this isn't about me. The story of Nat Turner as an American, as American people, to know the story about a man who was erased from history, at some point, I think that's where our focus should be" ("'Birth'"). His argument that this moment is "bigger than me" was simultaneously a self-aggrandizing attempt to position himself as the savior of black revolutionary history and a rightful acknowledgment that the reverberations of the controversy rippled beyond him and his film. Because the "rapist" is a prevailing stereotype almost synonymous with black manhood, to see Parker as a rapist is to see him as "always already having been" an example of pathological blackness (Young 122). If Cosby and Jackson represent something larger than life, Parker was representing an everyday black masculinity elevated by his use of a black icon. Parker and Celestin's actions are in no way indicative of who black men are as a group, but some people will read them that way. Racist hermeneutics facilitate what Beth Richie has referred to as the "trap of loyalty" and become the grounds for ignoring misogyny, rape, and intimate violence because to acknowledge such injuries reinforces white supremacist narratives that do not allow black people to be individuals (44). Because sexual violence is both perpetuated by individuals and something that must be seen as structural, any systemic pathology or violence attached to (black) masculinity produces rhetorical challenges inside and outside of the black community. It is thus both inexcusable to ignore sexual violence and a truth to be acknowledged that individual acts by black bad actors become tools for racist attacks on black people as a group. As Nicole Fleetwood explains, the black iconic image carries "a sort of public burden, in their attempts to transform the despised into the idealized" (4).

Respectability discourse has often played a role in African American people's representational defenses. In addition to suggesting that his body stood in for the iconic Nat Turner and that the public strangely would not be able to know about him without his fictionalized account, Parker used his wife and children as instruments in his defense. "I've got five daughters and a lovely wife," he declared. While other signs of empathy—stating that he brought his mother to live with him and that he had little sisters—were attachments produced in his youth, the wife and children marked a change in status (Smith). His present—as a family man with children—is a sign that his past cannot be a mechanism for reading his present. For some, his interracial marriage became part of the controversy; a few people questioned his commitment to the black community because his wife is white. Parker felt called upon to defend the marriage in relation to his role as representative black man: "She's not of African descent but she reads the books that I give her. She knows that she's raising Black kids [. . .]. I say that to say that I know I came under criticism for that and not that I have to speak to it. But I want everyone that can hear my voice to know that I love my wife but I love ya'll, too" (Diaz).

As with Jackson, Parker's declaration is a performance of affinity and illustrative of the various ways cultural love is attached to black popular cultural productions; in the case of "good" popular texts, their existence is often described as evidence of loving black people. Parker as black auteur becomes as much of a text in black consumption practice as his film. Both the film's existence and Parker's success—despite the reality that the creator's survival so often depends on white audiences' consumption—are understood as evidence of black people's value and worth. The creator is thus, by extension, loving black people and deserving of love. Parker finds himself defending interracial intimacy (even though the high profile black feminist commentaries that are allegedly so damaging are entirely unconcerned with who he married or sleeps with), because he understands that he has been building a profile enmeshed with discourses of ideal black masculinity that are shaped by biography and his affective attachments. Parker's avowal of black love directs black people away from reading his exogamy as a rejection of black women, pushing against essentialist readings of black masculinity.

Parker's statement is also illustrative of the heightened demand for reciprocity between popular love objects and their consumers in African American communities. The pro forma "I love you" from celebrities to fans can sometimes function on a different register with subjected groups that receive little public approbation. Love objects are obviously not always romantic or sexual, but the indeterminacy of Parker's love somewhat haunts his declaration. Jennifer Nash has given a compelling account of how black feminist theorists have framed love as a political act—as self-care and utopian political world-building. They imagine a "collectivity marked by communal affect held together by public feeling rather than imagined—and enforced—sameness" (19). Parker is by no means practicing a black feminist politics, but his case illustrates how black communal affect can be as much about preservation of the normative as it can be transgressive. Love for the race can be an act of resistance by loving what is so often reviled, but it can also be a conservative project shaped by nostalgia and community regulation. Parker's extension of love was undoubtedly an effort to receive and sustain it in response to the accusation that he committed a misogynist act, but love—romantic, erotic, marital, political—is often the accused's defense against allegations of intimate violence. At the same time, black love and the political expectation of it can be a complex defense mechanism against iconicity's failure.

In Nat Turner, Parker arguably chose a tendentious black cultural love object to serve as the subject of his directorial debut. Long valued among black people as a cultural hero for leading the largest slave rebellion in history, Turner nonetheless holds a contentious place in an American history that values white nationalist violence but disparages black violence as an inappropriate form of protest. Turner's religious zealotry may have posed some challenges for Parker, who crafted a motion picture modeled on traditional Hollywood filmmaking structures and thus makes Turner into a black cultural hero for the twenty-first century. His Turner is inspired by God and preaches to his followers, but his character's motivations do not seem tied, as the historical record suggests, to the belief that he is a prophet. Turner's wife, Cherry, is not mentioned in Thomas R. Gray's 1831 as-told-to interview, *The Confessions of Nat Turner* (not to be confused with William Styron's 1967 novel), but the relationship between the rebel and his wife nonetheless takes center stage in Parker's story of Turner's life. And while nothing in the archive suggests that such an assault occurred, the gang rape of Turner's wife serves as a narrative trigger for the uprising in the film.

Cherry's victimization, Salamishah Tillet argues, "is cast as secondary to Turner's heroism." Her voice is "sidelined to the plot of Turner's realization of his own manhood in the horror of slavery." In the logic of American violence, the rape of his lovely wife is a marital alibi for Turner's violence. While sexual assault was a constant in many slave women's lives, the insertion of a brutal gang rape, which the archive does not suggest occurred, works to make Parker's narrative choices seem patriarchal. That is to say, the fictionalized rape of Turner's wife allowed Parker to treat an assertion of black masculinity and the protection of black women as one of the galvanizing impulses for the rebellion. Such a narrative move makes the new film a true double for the original *Birth of a Nation* cinematic adaptation of Thomas Dixon's 1905 novel, *The Clansman: A Historical Romance of the Ku Klux Klan*, in which the Klan avenges the honor and death of white ingénue Flora, who in an infamous scene chooses suicide to escape being raped by the grotesque, freed slave Gus. The doubling is a plot device that invites audiences to read Parker's biopic in relationship to the earlier film. If Cosby appears to have used heteronormativity in his work as a defense mechanism for predation, and Jackson's work, as well as his use of marriage, felt very separate from the injuries he was accused of committing, Parker's *linkage* of rape and marriage in his work has been read by some as a means of shoring up belief in both Turner's normativity and his own.

Apology Rings and Displacing Restorative Justice

Unlike some of the entertainers I have discussed, one group of black male celebrities often admired in the u.s. for their exceptional gifts but who simultaneously seem almost to carry the *expectation* of criminality are African American athletes. These athletes are often categorized as good or bad, with players like Michael Jordan representing the ideal "race-less" icon. By contrast, other players who commit crimes can function as alleged evidence for racists who believe in the inherent criminality of black people, whose actions are not seen to be shaped by economic circumstances (Leonard). In the late 1990s, Kobe Bryant, a point guard with the Los Angeles Lakers, was heralded as the next Michael Jordan as much for his spotless image as for his skills on the court. After spending much of his childhood in Europe, Bryant became a star high school athlete and made headlines for forgoing college basketball and becoming the youngest player in the history of the NBA when he joined the Lakers in 1996 (Thomsen).

Sports commentators watched Bryant mature on the court, joining Shaquille O'Neal in leading the Lakers to the championship in 2000. Commentators suggested that Bryant had lived up to the hype and had taken a course others should follow. The catalyst for becoming a better player and teammate after a slower start, Bryant stated, was his 2001 marriage to Vanessa Laine: "Being married forces you to be a better communicator" (Ballard). Bryant was touted by one commentator as better than the reigning golden-guy player in the NBA, Jordan: "Here's a young man who speaks fluent Italian, is married and has a child, and never shows up in the back of a squad car" (Reilly).

A few months after these words of praise appeared in *Sports Illustrated*, Bryant was accused of sexually assaulting a nineteen-year-old hotel employee in Eagle, Colorado (McCallum and Dohrmann). He initially denied the accusation and claimed the sex was consensual, making the true victim of the incident his wife, Vanessa. After he was formally charged with sexual assault, she accompanied him to a press conference, where the two were the picture of a loving couple, steadfastly clasping each other's hands throughout the media event. Bryant went on to deliver a tortuous statement, his mouth often contorting as he appeared to struggle to find the right words. Declaring that he was innocent at least four times during the speech, he also proclaimed that he was "furious" and "disgusted" with himself "for making a mistake of adultery." He seemed to fight back tears as he praised his spouse: "I love my wife with all my heart. She's the backbone. You're a blessing," he managed to choke out, at points turning slightly to address his wife directly. "You're the beats to my heart and the air I breathe. And you're the strongest person I know. And I'm so sorry for having to put you through this and to put our family through this."

This scene shows perhaps the most insidious side of the way the marital alibi works: in making Vanessa the victim, Bryant turned the woman who accused him into the actual offender, as the wounded wife looked on stoically. Their handholding carried a certain symbolic significance. Three days after prosecutors announced he would be charged with sexual assault, Bryant bought his "rock" a rock—an "apology ring"—with an eight-carat purple diamond reportedly valued at four million dollars.

The heteronormative logic of husbands buying themselves out of minor and major domestic injuries is nothing new, and neither is the displacement such actions often perform. The apology ring was a hypervisible displacement of the alleged injury from the accuser. The multimillion-dollar purple diamond was a mechanism for preserving the tarnished love object and also redirected the look. Redirecting the gaze to another injury takes attention away from the crime and can reframe interpretation of the incident itself. Jewelry is a traditional signifier of the transgressive husband, if not the criminal one. In the Kobe Bryant case, the ring affirmed the idea that the real injury was adultery and not a crime. The extravagant excess of the gift was also marked for the highly visible performance of black capital that could make things better. In Bryant's case, it was individual redress. In Cosby's case, some—including his television wife and defender—maintained that the sexual violence accusations were an attempt to keep the actor-comedian from lucrative entertainment contracts. While Bryant claimed in his press conference that what was at stake had "nothing to do with endorsements" and was about family, the idea that there can be financial costs not only to an individual but also to the black community, which holds comparatively little wealth, redirects a claim about intimate violence into one of economic threat.

People often target celebrities for money, but in the case of African Americans, the threat to the affluent can be a threat to black capital, to one of the few black sources of charity for black causes, and one of the few models of significant black wealth. Protecting black love objects, then, can be treated as protecting black capital, which reinscribes old scripts that treat sexual violence as an issue of property by making the stakes economic. Such readings are also inflected by a history of white citizens lynching black men in the name of white female protection, when the actual "crimes" for which they were punished were financial success and social progress. African Americans are so haunted by the specter of false accusations that redirecting the gaze from the accusation is often treated as an ethical and political imperative informed by history's lessons. The struggle to reconcile the possibility of the black icon's guilt with the inevitable racist treatment and costs of the guilt becomes an unnecessary oppositional binary. Black individuals don't get to be individuals; their transgressions—whether social or criminal—don't get to be singular.

But unusually for such cases, Vanessa Bryant was not the only one who received an apology. After the prosecutors dropped the criminal case, because the victim did not wish to proceed, and the accuser agreed not to use his words against him in her civil lawsuit, Bryant made a fairly unprecedented apology for a celebrity accused of felony sexual assault. "Although I truly believed this encounter between us was consensual," he said, "I recognize now that she did not and does not view this incident the same way I did. After months of reviewing discovery, listening to her attorney, and even her testimony in person, I now understand how she feels that she did not consent to this encounter" ("Kobe"). The distance between acknowledging the woman in question "did not feel" she consented and acknowledging that she did not consent and that he failed to recognize that fact may be as close to an admission of guilt for sexual assault we are likely to hear from a celebrity. Part of what makes Bryant's apology generative for exploring public responses to sexual violence is that it highlights the inevitable inadequacy of mea culpas given the actual injury and her subsequent injuries via public vilification. For many feminists concerned with prison abolition, the prison-industrial complex is not a remedy for sexual violence, but it is also hard to see this recognition of his injury to her—a requirement of restorative justice projects—as truly restorative.

Bryant and the challenge of a restorative response to sexual violence on the part of the offender is an intriguing shadow to the Nate Parker story. At the same time that Parker was doing a publicity tour in an effort to turn the story away from sexual assault, Bryant was playing his final season. One criticism frequently leveled at Parker is that he has failed to apologize for the assault. But given that he has maintained his innocence, the expectation that he would publicly acknowledge guilt is a somewhat puzzling one. It is unlikely that any statement he could make would be truly restorative. The young woman who brought charges against him committed suicide, and her family blamed Parker, Celestin, and the university for contributing to her depression and death. The temporality of violence in defining the subject is at issue here: once one has been a batterer, a rapist, or a murderer, is one always a batterer, a rapist, or murderer (Polone)? Part of the challenge of redefining the self in relationship to what one has done is that the status is determined not only by the offender's consciousness but also by his victim. And in the case of someone like Parker, whose cultural work and importance may depend on his representational value, restoring him would require work on the part of the audience. The audience would have to commit to forgiving, forgetting, or reconciling the act with the subject.

Attachment to love objects often leads to reification. People become ideals and the ideals become real. The affective similarities between the evolution of the love object for the fan and for the spouse are part of what make the marital alibi a generative figure for examination. The love object is idealized, tied to its other through marriage, but it inevitably disappoints when the ideal gives way to a real person. We make choices to become attached to celebrities, but we often do so without being conscious of our connectedness. Black fans, however, are frequently *called* to these attachments. Loving a successful black person is a point of racial pride. Doing the work of being realistic about our love objects is something spouses are compelled to do, but fans are not. In both cases it can be hard—even injurious—to let go of the ideal because our love objects not only reflect on us but in some way become us.

But perhaps through their objecthood, we may get back to their personhood—and our own. We have to find a way to live with those who we should not forgive. More people are connected through attachments to iconographic love objects than through other everyday interactions. When we grieve the death—literal or figurative—of a celebrity who was truly meaningful to multitudes, recognition of the similar ways we are pleasured can become a moment of communion despite the common belief in the popular as a mode of alienation. Similarly, the loss of a black love object through injurious acts could become a moment of communion. Rather than bemoan the cultural attachment to celebrities and the loss of them, we can continue to work toward an ethical relationship to representational injury. We can find new modes of black intimacy in what the failure of recognition in injurious acts can model, the struggle to reconcile love and rage, and the commitment to believing that our earlier attachments need not be reread as always already pathological.

In the midst of what Bill Cosby killed, in my disappointment in his marital alibis, my concern over the young who are inevitably cast as liars in accounts of Michael Jackson's relationships with children, and my rage over the dismissal of women who are allegedly a threat to black futurity, I know the only way to negotiate the injury privately and publicly is to embrace the possibility of reconciling good and bad objects. I have just as much responsibility to the person I was who found meaning in what I loved as I do to the person who finds power in the responsibility to condemn violence wrought by our most loved icons.

REBECCA WANZO is an associate professor of women, gender, and sexuality studies at Washington University in St. Louis. She is the author of *The Suffering Will Not Be Televised: African American Women and Sentimental Political Storytelling* (State University of New York Press, 2009).

Notes

1 For a complete account of the hearings, see Miller and Totenberg.

2 Comedian Sarah Silverman asked this question publically after many women said that popular comedian Louis C. K. had masturbated in front of them without their consent. Samantha Guthrie, cohost of the *Today Show*, was in tears on the day it was revealed that cohost Matt Lauer had been let go from the show because of sexual harassment allegations.

3 For discussions of fan attachment to celebrities after death, see Radford and Bloch.

4 See, for example, a review that appeared after the Sundance screening:

Cinema does not exist in a vacuum, any more than any other medium does, and there's something undeniably powerful about seeing this story, from this perspective, at this point in time. When one slave laments, "They killed people everywhere for no reason at all but being black," it's impossible not to hear echoes of all those recent police shootings and the Black Lives Matter movement. When Nat is beaten or insulted or bossed around by white overseers and masters, there's an extratextual fuck you in the knowledge that in real life, Parker himself was the one calling the shots on set. (Han)

Works Cited   Alexander, Leslie. "'The Birth of a Nation' Is an Epic Fail." *The Nation* 6 Oct. 2016. https://www.thenation.com/article/the-birth-of-a-nation-is-an-epic-fail/.

Almukhtar, Sarah, Michael Gold, and Larry Buchanan. "After Weinstein: 42 Men Accused of Sexual Misconduct and Their Fall from Power." *New York Times* 13 Dec. 2017. https://www.nytimes.com/interactive/2017/11/10/us/men-accused-sexual-misconduct-weinstein.html.

Ballard, Chris. "Roll of a Lifetime." *Sports Illustrated* 3 March 2003. https://www.si.com/vault/2003/03/03/338925/roll-of-a-lifetime-pouring-in-points-by-the-score-and-leading-the-lakers-back-into-contention-kobe-bryant-is-following-a-master-plan-he-devised-as-a-teen.

Bhabha, Homi. *The Location of Culture.* London: Routledge, 1994.

"'Birth of a Nation' Star Nate Parker Speaks Out." ABC *News* 3 Oct. 2010. http://abcnews.go.com/GMA/video/birth-nation-star-nate-parker-speaks-42521617.

Brown, Helen. "Michael Jackson and Motown: The Boy behind the Marketing." *Telegraph* 26 Jun. 2009. http://www.telegraph.co.uk/culture/music/michael-jackson/5651468/Michael-Jackson-and-Motown-the-man-behind-the-marketing.html.

Cooper, Brittany. "Clair Huxtable Is Dead: On Slaying the Cosbys and Making Space for Liv, Analise, and Mary Jane." *Crunk Feminist Collective* 23 Oct. 2014. http://www.crunkfeministcollective.com/2014/10/23/clair-huxtable-is-dead-on-slaying-the-cosbys-and-making-space-for-liv-analise-and-mary-jane/.

Cosby, Bill. "Dr. Bill Cosby Speaks at the 50th Anniversary Commemoration of *Brown v. Topeka Board of Education* Supreme Court Decision, May 22, 2004." *Black Scholar* 34.4 (2004): 2–5.

Cress, Coug. "All Shook Up: Jackson-Presley Marriage Is Confirmed, but Match Gives Rise to More Questions." *Atlanta Journal Constitution* 2 Aug. 1994: C1.

Dawn, Randee. "Wade Robson: 'Pedophile' Michael Jackson Abused Me for 7 Years." *Today* 16 May 2013. https://www.today.com/popculture/wade-robson-pedophile-michael-jackson-abused-me-7-years-1C9948163.

Diaz, Evelyn. "Watch Nate Parker Defend His White Wife: 'She's Raising Black Kids.'" BET 6 Sept. 2016. http://www.bet.com/celebrities/news/2016/09/06/nate-parker-white-wife.html.

Duffett, Mark. "Multiple Damnations: Deconstructing the Critical Response to Boy Band Phenomena." *Popular Music History* 7.2 (2012): 185–87.

Esteban, Chiqui, and Manuel Roig-Franzia. "Bill Cosby's Accusers Now Number 60: Here's Who They Are." *Washington Post* 3 Aug. 2016 https://www.washingtonpost.com/graphics/lifestyle/cosby-women-accusers/.

"Exclusive: Nate Parker's Former Classmates, Penn State Alumni Speak Out in Support." *Root* 25 Aug. 2016. http://www.theroot.com/exclusive-nate-parkers-former-classmates-penn-state-a-1790856519.

Fee. "Birth of a Nation's Box Office Flop and the Unrepentant Pettiness of Black Feminists." *Medium* 2 Oct. 2016. https://medium.com/@inthe9thhouse/birth-of-a-nations-box-office-flop-and-the-unrepentant-pettiness-of-black-feminists-9f3f598819aa.

Fleetwood, Nicole R. *On Racial Icons: Blackness and the Public Imagination.* New Brunswick: Rutgers UP, 2015.

Freud, Sigmund. "Mourning and Melancholia." 1917 (1915). *The Standard Edition of the Complete Psychological Works of Sigmund Freud*. Trans. and ed. James Strachey. Vol. 14. London: Hogarth, 1957. 237–58. 24 vols. 1953–74.

Garcia, Sandra E. "The Woman Who Created #Metoo Long before the Hashtags." *New York Times* 20 Oct. 2017. https://www.nytimes.com/2017/10/20/us/me-too-movement-tarana-burke.html.

Gates, Henry Louis, Jr. "TV's Black World Turns—but Stays Unreal." *New York Times* 12 Nov. 1989. http://www.nytimes.com/1989/11/12/arts/tv-s-black-world-turns-but-stays-unreal.html.

Gay, Roxane. "Nate Parker and the Limits of Empathy." *New York Times* 19 Aug. 2016. https://www.nytimes.com/2016/08/21/opinion/sunday/nate-parker-and-the-limits-of-empathy.html.

Hall, Stewart. "What Is This 'Black' in Black Popular Culture?" *Black Popular Culture*. Ed. Gina Dent. Seattle: Bay Press, 1992. 21–33.

Han, Angie. "Nate Parker's 'The Birth of a Nation' Is Powerful, Necessary Storytelling." *Slashfilm* 27 Jan. 2016. http://www.slashfilm.com/the-birth-of-a-nation-review/.

Horton, Donald, and Richard Wohl. "Mass Communication and Parasocial Interaction: Observations on Intimacy at a Distance." *Psychiatry* 19 (1956): 215–29.

Inniss, Leslie B., and Joe R. Feagin. "The Cosby Show: The View from the Black Middle Class." *Journal of Black Studies* 25.6 (1995): 692–711.

Jackson, Michael. "Teen Star Magazine Interview, 1972." *Jackson 5 abc.com*. http://www.jackson5abc.com/dossiers/presse/1972-TeenStarMag.php.

Jones, Nate, and Rachel Bashein. "A Timeline of the Nate Parker Rape Scandal, and the Damage Control That Has Followed." *Vulture* 3 Oct. 2016. http://www.vulture.com/2016/08/timeline-of-the-nate-parker-rape-scandal.html.

Jue, Teresa. "Phylicia Rashad Claims She Was Misquoted When Defending Bill Cosby." *Entertainment Weekly* 8 Jan. 2015. http://ew.com/article/2015/01/08/phylicia-rashad-misquote-cosby/.

Kim, Kyle, Christina Littlefield, and Melissa Etehad. "Bill Cosby: A 50–year Chronicle of Accusation and Accomplishments." *Los Angeles Times* 17 June 2017. http://www.latimes.com/entertainment/la-et-bill-cosby-timeline-htmlstory.html.

Kincaid, James. *Erotic Innocence: The Culture of Child Molesting*. Durham: Duke UP, 1998.

Kittelson, Mary Lynn. *The Soul of Popular Culture: Looking at Contemporary Heroes, Myths, and Monsters*. Chicago: Open Court, 1998.

Klein, Melanie. "Mourning and Its Relationship to Manic-Depressive States." *Selected Melanie Klein*. Ed. Juliet Mitchell. New York: Simon and Schuster, 1987. 146–76.

"Kobe Bryant's Apology." *ESPN* 2 Sept. 2004. http://www.espn.com/nba/news/story?id=1872928.

Leduff, Charlie. "Son of Former Maid Testifies That Jackson Molested Him." *New York Times* 5 Apr. 2005, http://www.nytimes.com/2005/04/05/us/son-of-former-maid-testifies-that-jackson-molested-him.html.

Leonard, David J. *After Artest: The NBA and the Assault on Blackness*. Albany: SUNY P, 2012.

McCallum, Jack, and George Dohrmann. "The Dark Side of a Star." *Sports Illustrated* 99.3 (2003): 42–45.

Meadows, Bob. "Cosby and His Accusers." *People* 28 Feb. 2005: 109–10.

Miller, Anita, and Nina Totenberg. *The Complete Transcripts of the Clarence Thomas–Anita Hill Hearings, October 11, 12, 13 1991.* Chicago: Academy Chicago, 2005.

Miller, Julie. "'Birth of a Nation' Supporters Suggest Rape Scandal Is Part of a Smear Campaign." *Vanity Fair* 24 Aug. 2016. https://www.vanityfair.com/hollywood/2016/08/nate-parker -rape-smear-campaign.

Nash, Jennifer. "Practicing Love: Black Feminism, Love-Politics, and Post-Intersectionality." *Meridians* 11.2 (2011): 1–24.

"Nomination of Judge Clarence Thomas to Be Associate Justice of The Supreme Court of The United States: Hearings before the Committee on the Judiciary United States Senate. Part 4 of 4 Parts." 11–13 Oct. 1991. https://www.congress.gov/supreme-court/GPO-CHRG-THOMAS-4.pdf.

Nyong'o, Tavia. "Have You Seen His Childhood? Song, Screen, and the Queer Culture of the Child in Michael Jackson's Music." *Journal of Popular Music Studies* 23.1 (2011): 40–57.

Patterson, Orlando. "Race, Gender, and Liberal Fallacies." *New York Times* 20 Oct. 1991. E15.

Polone, Gavin. "Remember When Kobe Bryant Was Charged with Rape? I Didn't Forget and Neither Should You." *Hollywood Reporter* 20 Apr. 2016. http://www.hollywoodreporter.com /news/kobe-bryants-rape-charge-i-885653.

Radford, Scott K., and Peter H. Bloch. "Grief, Commiseration, and Consumption following the Death of a Celebrity." *Journal of Consumer Culture* 12.2 (2012): 137–55.

Reilly, Rick. "Like Mike, or Even Better." *Sports Illustrated* 98.9 (2003). https://www.si.com /vault/2003/03/03/8098947/like-mike-or-even-better.

Savage, Charlie. "Clarence Thomas's Wife Asks Anita Hill for Apology." *New York Times* 19 Oct. 2010. https://www.nytimes.com/2010/10/20/us/politics/20thomas.html.

Scott, A. O. "In Nate Parker's *The Birth of a Nation*, Must-See and Won't-See Collide." *New York Times* 6 Oct. 2016. https://www.nytimes.com/2016/10/07/movies/the-birth-of-a-nation -review-nate-parker.html.

Sharpley-Whiting, T. Denan. "When a Black Woman Cries Rape: Discourses of Unrapeability, Intraracial Sexual Violence, and the *State of Indiana v. Michael Gerard Tyson.*" *Spoils of War: Women of Color, Cultures, and Revolution.* Ed. T. Denan Sharpley-Whiting and Renee T. White. Lanham: Rowan and Littlefield, 1997. 47–58.

Siegel, Tatiana, and Rebecca Ford. "Sundance: 'Birth of a Nation' Sets Record with 17.5M Deal to Fox Searchlight." *Hollywood Reporter* 26 Jan. 2016. http://www.hollywoodreporter.com /news/sundance-birth-a-nation-sets-857365.

Smith, Nigel M. "The Birth of a Nation Director Nate Parker Talks about Being Accused of Rape." *Guardian* 12 Aug. 2016. https://www.theguardian.com/film/2016/aug/12/nate-parker -birth-of-a-nation-film-college-rape-trial.

Spangler, Lynn C. *Television Women from Lucy to Friends: Fifty Years of Sitcoms and Feminism.* Westport: Praeger, 2003.

Stockton, Halle. "Ex-Wrestler Gets New Trial in Assault Case." *Daily Collegian* 1 Nov. 2005. http://www.collegian.psu.edu/archives/article_321ef6da-9f6c-511e-82b5c8c506f7820d.html.

"Story: Mike Tyson." ABC *20/20.* 30 Sept. 1988. Transcript print date 2 Jan. 2018. 1–27. Transcription Company.

Taylor, Goldie. "Cliff-Hanger: Can 'The Cosby Show' Survive? Should It?" *Ebony* Nov. 2015. 101–5, 120.

Thomsen, Ian. "Show Time!" *Sports Illustrated* 88.17. (27 Apr. 1998): 40+.

Tillet, Salamishah. "How 'The Birth of a Nation' Silences Black Women." *New York Times* 12 Oct. 2016. https://www.nytimes.com/2016/10/16/movies/how-the-birth-of-a-nation-silences -black-women.html.

"Top Ten Michael Jackson Moments: An Unexpected Union." *Time.* http://content.time.com /time/specials/packages/article/0,28804,1907249_1907255_1907251,00.html (accessed 5 Mar. 2018).

"Video Music Awards." MTV 8 Sept. 1994.

Vineyard, Jennifer. "Jackson Says $25M Settlement Is Not an Admission of Guilt." MTV*News* 17 Jun. 2004. http://www.mtv.com/news/1488501/jackson-says-25m-settlement-is-not-an -admission-of-guilt/.

Wanzo, Rebecca. "Can the Black Woman Shout? A Meditation on Real and Utopian Depictions of African American Women on Television." *African Americans on Television: Race-ing for Ratings.* Ed. David J. Leonard and Lisa Guerrero. Santa Barbara: Greenwood, 2013. 373–89.

Wapshott, Nicholas. "Jackson Paid Boy's Family $25m Hush Money." *Times* (London) 17 Jun. 2004: 15.

Warwick, Jacqueline. "'You Can't Win, Child, but You Can't Get Out of the Game': Michael Jackson's Transition from Child Star to Superstar." *Popular Music and Society* 35.2 (2012): 241–59.

Wilson, Riley, and Shantrelle P. Lewis. "'The Birth of a Nation': The Biggest Clapback in Hollywood History or Yet Another Slave Movie?" *Colorlines* 2 Feb. 2016. https://www.colorlines .com/articles/birth-nation-biggest-clapback-hollywood-history-or-yet-another-slave-movie.

Young, Iris Marion. *Justice and the Politics of Difference.* Princeton: Princeton UP, 2011.

Yuan, David D. "The Celebrity Freak: Michael Jackson's 'Grotesque Glory.'" *Freakery: Cultural Spectacles of the Extraordinary Body.* Ed. Rosemarie Garland Thomson. New York: New York UP, 1996. 368–84.

Something Old, Something New: Black Women, Interracial Dating, and the Black Marriage Crisis

*I*t is a beautiful wedding, set in an outdoor garden. The black bride, gorgeous in her white dress, is about to be married to her ideal black man. But just before they kiss, a siren goes off, chaos ensues, and the bride wakes up to her morning alarm. That dream sequence opens the 2006 romantic comedy *Something New*, which tells the story of Kenya McQueen, a beautiful, well-educated, and highly successful black professional searching for love. She and her equally well-educated, similarly successful black female friends are all single. On Valentine's Day, they go out with each other instead of with dates and lament that well-educated professional women like them are even less likely than other black women ever to find partners. "Where" asks one of the women, "are the brothas?" Involved with white women, the film suggests, as it pans to a black man and white woman sharing a romantic dinner.

  Something New reflects the political and cultural zeitgeist of its day, as black women in the 2000s were warned that they might never tie the knot because of a shortage of suitable black men. In 1960, 61 percent of blacks over the age of eighteen were married; by 2010, only 31 percent of blacks

Volume 29, Number 2 DOI 10.1215/10407391-6999802
© 2018 by Brown University and d i f f e r e n c e s : A Journal of Feminist Cultural Studies

were. In comparison, 55 percent of whites over eighteen were married in 2010 (Cohn et al. 8). Researchers linked the decline in black marriage rates to a shortage of marriageable black men. Because of their poor economic prospects, high incarceration rates, and lower life expectancy, by 2014 there were only 51 employed black men for every 100 black women between the ages of twenty-five to thirty-four (Wang and Parker 34). There were, in short, few attractive black male partners for black women who, in larger percentages than whites, feel a husband needs to be economically stable and a good provider (Mouzon). No surprise, then, that the working title for *Something New* was the significantly less catchy "42.4," which referred to the supposed percentage of black women who were single.

Even though college-educated black women are actually *more* likely to marry than their less educated sisters, *Something New* embraces the very common framing of the marital crisis as especially acute for middle-class black women and as due, in part, to black women's insistence on holding out for an ideal black man.[1] The film thus reflects the discourse in both public media and popular culture that portrays the decline in black marriage rates as "a middle-class issue, and, more specifically, a problem for Black women" (Hightower). Ralph Richard Banks's controversial 2011 book, *Is Marriage for White People?*, epitomizes this common narrative: within just a few pages, Banks shifts from the general question of his title to focus exclusively on the plight of middle-class women. Banks acknowledges that the marriage crisis is more acute for lower-income black women, and yet he still portrays college-educated black women as especially disadvantaged—because fewer black men than women attend college, because well-educated black men are more than twice as likely as black women to marry outside the race,[2] and because the shortage of successful black men means that they have little incentive to settle down or to be monogamous.

Something New and *Is Marriage for White People?* share not only a common framing of the problem—that successful black women cannot find suitable mates because the too few educated black men available are either "players" or prefer white women—but also a potential solution that, according to the film, is in fact something *new*: that educated black women address their marital woes by seeking partners outside the race. In the film, Kenya finds love with the white landscape architect she has hired to design her yard. To reach her happy ending, she has to overcome her own fears about whether a white man can truly understand her, as well as the opposition of friends and family. The film ends with a real wedding, not a dream one, this time between Kenya and her ideal white man. Banks's book also urges successful black women to date and marry outside the race and does the film one better by arguing that if more black women marry out, it will lead black men to reconsider their unwillingness to settle down and marry.

But the film and Banks's book are not alone in offering this supposedly "new" solution to black women's dating woes. In fact, this same idea has become the cornerstone of an entire genre of advice literature since the mid-2000s, with a number of real-life "Kenyas"—black middle-class women who themselves have found happiness with white men—making the case for intermarriage in ezines, blogs, articles, and books. These outspoken advocates of intermarriage, all of whom are or have been interracially married themselves, include Christelyn Karazin, a black writer and the coauthor of *Swirling*, who created the blog *Beyond Black & White* to provide advice for interracially dating black women after finding no supportive information when she began dating her white husband in 1999; Eve Sharon Moore, the founder of the *Black Female Interracial Marriage* blog and author of four self-published books aimed at black women; Karyn Langhorne Folan, a former law professor turned author who was driven to write a book exhorting black women to "look for love beyond racial boundaries" (11) after seeing the controversy generated by her 2008 *Washington Post* opinion piece "What Mildred [Loving] Knew"; and Halima Anderson,[3] a black Brit, who began the blogspot *dateawhiteguy.com* in 2007 and has published books available in the U.S. for both black women considering interracial dating and white men interested in relationships with black woman.

This essay explores this self-help literature and what it reveals about both the state of black marriage and the views of black women who see themselves as the primary victims of declining marriage rates. The perceived need for books and blogs urging black women to overcome their reservations about interracial dating might seem to embrace the idea that black women are in fact to blame for their single state because they have failed to get on board as the rest of American society has become more tolerant and accepting of interracial relationships. But the promotional literature urging black women to date interracially offers less a narrative of blame than of empowerment. Black women, it suggests, have the power and agency to change their situation. In arguments that illuminate contemporary perspectives on long-standing debates among blacks about when and how to put down the burdens of history, about racial identity and authenticity, and about the loyalty an individual owes to the community, these advocates of intermarriage urge black women to see themselves as powerful and to embrace something new: their desirability in American society and their ability to chart their own personal happiness.

Yet at the same time, the literature traffics in ideas that are quite old. Suffused with a nostalgic desire for a world where men are providers, women can be the weaker sex, and traditional marriage serves as a path to both personal and group advancement, the advocacy literature unwittingly reinforces cultural narratives that have stigmatized the black community—and especially poor black women—for their low marriage rates. And while offering a positive and powerful vision of a world where black women have the freedom and power to chart their own futures free from the burdens of history and racism—that is, in focusing on black women's agency—these writers fail to grapple with the ways in which black women in fact remain disadvantaged on the marital market. As a result, a literature grounded in the rhetoric of freedom and empowerment may actually disempower black women seeking ways to challenge sexual and systemic racism effectively.

The Marriage Crisis as Intermarriage

To understand how a literature based in empowerment becomes disempowering requires, first, a brief historical investigation of how it is that anyone might even plausibly suggest that interracial marriage might be a suitable solution to a "marital crisis" in the black community. Until recently, it would have been ludicrous to link black women's single state to their supposed reluctance to intermarry or to black men's willingness to do so. When the u.s. census first started tracking interracial marriages in 1960, there were only 51,000 black-white couples in the entire country (and almost no interracial marriages of any other kind involving black partners). More-over, those 51,000 marriages involved a roughly equal number of black men and black women. Indeed, in 1960, there were slightly more black women with white husbands than there were black husbands with white wives. *Loving v. Virginia*, the 1967 Supreme Court case that overturned all state bans on interracial marriage, involved a black woman married to a white man.

But things have changed since the 1960s, as both the number of blacks who marry across color lines has climbed and a significant gender gap has emerged between those who intermarry. By 1970, there were nearly twice as many black men married to white women as there were black women married to white men (41,000 to 24,000). In the 1980s and 1990s, that gap continued to widen, and by 2000, there were 2.8 intermarried black men for every intermarried black woman. While the gender gap has closed somewhat since 2000, it still remains significant. In 2010, the u.s. census reported a total of 690,000 interracial marriages involving a black spouse; 495,000 marriages between black men and nonblack women and 195,000 marriages between black women and nonblack men, for a ratio of 2.45 intermarried black men for every intermarried black woman.[4] Data from 2015 show that 24 percent of black male newlyweds married a partner of a different race, while only 12 percent of black female newlyweds did (Livingston and Brown). Overall, as a result of these gendered patterns, there are approximately 300,000 more married black men than there are married black women in the United States today.

As I explored in greater detail in my 2003 book on black-white marriages in the postwar era, neither structural nor demographic factors offer an easy explanation for why the number of black men who marry white women has soared since 1970 while the number of black women married to white men has risen so much more slowly. Black women are as, or even more, likely than black men to meet potential white mates in spaces like colleges and professional workplaces. Moreover, as there are more black women than available black men because of higher life expectancy and lower incarceration rates, they should be more rather than less likely to intermarry (Romano 231–32).

Many black women in the decades after the Civil Rights movement attributed the gender gap in intermarriage to the continuing influence of racism on black men. They claimed that black men had been told for so long that white women were "forbidden fruit" that they had come to equate marrying a white woman with personal freedom. Black men, they charged, had internalized white standards of beauty and saw marriage to a white woman as a way to advance their own status in the world and leave behind some of the stigma associated with blackness. In a 1980 survey of twelve hundred African Americans, 12 percent of the women said they thought black men preferred white women to black women; only 4 percent of men made the same claim (Romano 234).

Black women in the 1970s and 1980s, especially those in the middle class, frequently described black men's interracial relationships as a threat to them personally and to the larger black community. They filled the pages of *Ebony* magazine with letters that accused white women of stealing their men and charged black men with abandoning them. Countless articles and popular cultural representations featured black women expressing their dismay and disgust at black men's dating habits, as in the famous scene in Spike Lee's 1991 film *Jungle Fever*, where a group of black women sit around complaining about no-good black men. The actresses quickly went off-script, according to Lee, instead "just vomiting that stuff up" based on their personal experiences (qtd. in Romano 259).

Black women who were critical of black men dating and marrying outside the race pointed out that they did not have the same option to do likewise. They had little confidence that white men would find them attractive or suitable marital partners. Black women had never been "forbidden fruit" for white men. And neither were white men symbols of freedom for black women; they were more likely to be reminders of historical sexual exploitation. Unlike in the case of black men and white women, there were no existing cultural stereotypes that might make black women and white men particularly attractive to one another. Moreover, many black women claimed to have little interest in interracial dating. They were committed to the project of building strong black families as a way to advance the goals of the black community. As one black woman wrote in 1970, for the community to prosper, black people needed to love themselves "so much that we would want to see the blood of our heritage running in and through the veins of our children" (qtd. in Romano 243). Marrying interracially, in this view, reflected a lack of dedication to the future of the race.

Perhaps because of their perceived disadvantage in the world of interracial dating or perhaps because their loyalty to the community led them to favor marriages to black men, black women—according to some quantitative studies from the early 1990s—both disapproved of intermarriage more than their male counterparts and were somewhat more hesitant to date outside the race themselves (Romano 259). Whether black women are in fact more opposed to interracial dating and marriage than other groups is difficult to gauge, but black men's higher outmarriage rates nevertheless remain a common theme in discussions of the contemporary black "marital crisis" (Djamba and Kimuna).[5] Blogs and magazines like *Essence* are replete with articles by black women lamenting their black male peers' rejection. Some contributors even vow to change the script for future generations by consciously raising their sons to "bring me home a black girl" (Edwards 176). The solution for black women, these works suggest, is to persuade black men to value black women and the black community.

The View from the Advocates

This is not how the women who have built careers around encouraging black women to date outside the race see it. Rather than trying to convince black men that they need to "bring home a black girl," the advocates at the heart of this essay instead seek to persuade black women that they don't need to bring home a black boy. This small but active group of writers urges black women to let go of their dream of the perfect black man and to search instead for their ideal mate from the whole "global village" of men. In making their case, they explicitly address both of the core critiques of interracial marriage that black women expressed in earlier decades: that marrying out represents a betrayal of the race and the community and that it is not an option for black women in the same way that it is for black men. In contrast, these advocates insist that black women today are limited only by their own attitudes, not by sexual or structural racism. And they reassure readers that women, unlike men, can pursue individualistic goals and still serve the race. Their blogs, articles, and books all insist that black women who are willing to dislodge their "mental chains" and tear down the self-constructed "invisible roadblocks" that lead them to be perpetually and involuntarily single (Anderson, Interview; Karazin and Littlejohn 14) can find happiness with nonblack men and that they can do so while still remaining committed to the common good of the race.

While promoting a positive vision of black women's ability to craft their own lives, this literature thus portrays an idealized world, one where black women no longer need to imagine themselves as limited by racism and its legacies; where they—unlike most men—can date interracially and still maintain a strong black identity; and where they can pursue individualistic goals and still promote the health of the community. It offers, in short, something of a fairy tale, and like all fairy tales, it ultimately has a dark side. But before we can unpack the dark side, we first need to understand the story.

The first element of the fairy tale is the advocacy literature's insistence that history no longer limits black women's choices in the way many seem to believe it does. Black women, advocates assert, have new forms of power that they have not yet fully acknowledged, including the power to reject and rewrite a script that portrays them as the inevitable victims of white men and of sexual racism. Given the long history of being vulnerable to white male sexual assault, black women in the past had reasonably sought "freedom *from* White men," rather than "the freedom to choose

White men as lovers and friends" (Patricia Hill Collins qtd. in Folan 17). But for advocates of interracial dating, women today who continue to reject white men because of the legacy of slavery are no longer exercising meaningful agency; they are instead misguidedly holding onto a misplaced anger that obscures how much the status of black women has changed in American society. Advocates urge their readers to let go of their blanket anger at all white men because of the acts of their ancestors. "Anger is for losers," "LET IT GO," and "pour away the hate!," they pointedly tell their readers (Moore, *Black* 69; Anderson, "Give"). Focusing on the wrongs white men have done to them historically not only forces "every white man we meet into a narrow box" but also denies how much times have changed since the days of slavery. It is "not realistic to simply draw a straight-line comparing white behavior then and now" or to assume that white men today are "equally invested in maintaining" racist structures, the advocacy literature argues (Folan 20; Sal-Anderson, loc 8742; Moore, *Black* 70). By holding onto anger or letting others use the history of slavery to discourage them from interracially dating, black women are sacrificing their own happiness on the basis of an outdated state of hostility toward white men. "You are not," Anderson preaches, "bound or obliged to continue ancient feuds and to sacrifice your life for them" ("Give"). Black women, advocates insist, limit themselves by living in the past rather than embracing the realities of the contemporary world.

In another call to let go of the burden of history, these writers urge black women to liberate their minds from the false assumption that sexual racism and the derogatory sexual stereotypes that developed during slavery still disadvantage them on the dating market. Too many women, advocates insist, continue to think that white men see them as hypersexual Jezebels, sexually deviant Venus Hottentots, shrewish Sapphires, or asexual Mammies, and thus they doubt that any white man can truly find them desirable. But this "most common form of defeatism" is simply wrong, advocates charge, and "only true if you think it's true" (Sal-Anderson, loc 15009; Folan qtd. in Misick). Black women themselves can change the script: "If you believe you are beautiful to a wide cross section of men, chances are good that a wide cross section of men will find you appealing" (Folan 107). If you focus on the "literally millions of men all over the planet who desire you," these writers assure black women, and give white men "the green light" to approach, you will find eager white men waiting (Karazin and Littlejohn 62; Moore, *Black* 130).

If black women are single, advocates insist, it isn't because white men don't want them. It is because black women either push them away—"turning off hordes" of potential suitors because of their "less-than-receptive attitude" (Moore, *Black* 130, 128)—or because they judge white men according to unfair sexual stereotypes of their own. Too many black women, advocates charge, assume the worst of any white man who expresses interest in them: that he only wants sex, that he has some kind of "master complex," that he hopes to live out some fetishistic fantasy about the exotic other. They project their own hang-ups onto white men (85). Worse, some black women themselves believe the sexual myths that black men are more generously endowed and better in bed than their white or Asian counterparts, myths that developed out of Reconstruction-era white racism. Black Americans have twisted an idea that "sprang from a history in white racism [. . .] into a source of pride," Folan warns. Any woman aware of that fact needs to take a "fresh look" at her dating options (231)—sentiments echoed by Karazin and Littlejohn, who add that, given their own long fight against negative sexual stereotypes, black women should know better than to project similar "plantation baggage" onto others (167). For these writers, black women remain single not because they are stigmatized by sexual racism, but because they themselves practice it.

Underlying these arguments is a deep and profound belief that black women are powerful in ways that clinging to the past obscures. Portraying all white men as powerful abusers or assuming that black women are not desirable to men outside their race casts black women as victims when, in fact, black women in contemporary America have, as Folan describes it, "chipped huge holes in the system of white male authority" (18). Black women's identities have not yet caught up to the immense changes in their status that have taken place in the last fifty years, Folan insists. But it is time to stop seeing the struggle "in terms of blacks against whites" (Folan 32, 34). History need not burden black women unless they let it.

Neither, according to these advocates, should they be yoked to outdated notions about their own black female racial identity. Again reflecting their belief in black women's power to craft an identity for themselves unlimited by the past, writers like Folan, Moore, and Anderson unapologetically deny the charge that the African American community should be able to define what blackness means. Black women, they assert, often eschew interracial dating because they have been conditioned to believe that dating or marrying outside the race makes one "less black," a charge that they argue is directed at women more than men. Instead, these authors preach their own form of what the black cultural critic Touré has called "post-blackness," which he describes as the end of "a narrow understanding of what Blackness means" (xv). Like Touré, they critique the idea of "authentic blackness" or that anyone who breaks certain codes of behavior—dating interracially, wearing preppy clothes, listening to rock music—is somehow less black. For interracial dating advocates, the idea that black women lack racial consciousness because they have white partners "illustrates just how much work we still have to do to define—or redefine—black identity." Such thinking is a form of "blackthink" that "steals our choices," Folan argues, while Karazin and Littlejohn describe rules and sanctions that aim to discourage black women from interracially dating as violating the "very definition of freedom" (Folan 161, 170; Karazin and Littlejohn 35). Black women who allow themselves to be dissuaded from interracial dating because they fear being labeled sellouts are buying into an outmoded and harmful form of black identity, advocates warn.

In rejecting essentializing tests of black authenticity, this literature takes pains to reassure black women that they can marry outside the race and still maintain a strong sense of their black identity. "You can still advocate for change and love your blackness if you have a non-black spouse," Karazin insists (qtd. in Frederick), pointing particularly to examples of Jewish women who marry people of different religions and still raise their children as Jews. In fact, she and other advocates argue, black women in interracial relationships often feel *more* black and "more connected to their African American-ness" because they live with someone of another race (Karazin and Littlejohn 32). As Anderson puts it, those most likely to date outside the race will be black women whose sense of racial identity is "not so flimsy as to cause them to run a mile from other races for fear that their convictions will be shaken" (Sal-Anderson, loc 13720). Interracially married women can both follow their hearts and maintain a positive black racial identity.

Following this similar, somewhat contradictory, logic—that black women should not be beholden to limited forms of black identity but that intermarriage doesn't mean a rejection of blackness in any case—advocates also argue that while black women should not deny their personal happiness for the sake of the "black community," marrying outside the race does not necessarily harm the common good. Advocates making this case unapologetically embrace a double standard, characterizing black men who date outside the race as "self-haters" who explicitly reject black women and place their individual welfare above any sense of a common good. But black women, the argument goes, cross the color line not because they hate themselves or spurn black men, but because their own men have rejected them (Moore, *Black* 169). By opening themselves to interracial dating, they actually help their community rather than harm it.

Given their emphasis on individualism, it is no surprise that these advocates argue against women sacrificing their own personal happiness for the sake of some misguided sense of loyalty to the black community—misguided because black men have already jumped ship. Black men have made clear their lack of commitment to the larger common good; for proof, claim the advocates, one need only look at the huge number of single-parent homes headed by women. "If black nationhood was a priority for black men," Anderson pointedly asks, "do you think 70 percent of black children would be born outside wedlock with the attendant poverty and lack of safety these children are more likely to experience?" ("Do"). Black men are "self-server[s]," driven by the desire for individual economic gain and not the "higher principle of 'community outlook'" ("My"), yet black women are unfairly expected to be the backbone of the black community, the people who have held and continue to hold everything together while sacrificing for the sake of the larger good (Karazin and Littlejohn 55). Indeed, advocates characterize black women as so conditioned to put community ahead of self that they end up sacrificing their own health and happiness in a life of "servitude without reward" (Anderson, "Interracial Dating 101: Further Notes").

It is time for black women to rethink their priorities these writers argue. They need no longer be the "mules of the race" who are "*never* to know even a slip of happiness," Karazin insists ("Verdict"), but they have to be willing to recognize that black men have absolutely no interest "in building a black nation hand in hand with black women" (Anderson, "Some"). So black women do not, advocates explain, have to abandon their own commitments to the community, but they do need to understand how dating outside the race may offer the best way to pursue them. "You can uplift your race and follow your bliss," *Swirling* suggests (Karazin and Littlejohn 57). There is no reason why an interracially married black woman can't "participate in the same activities, have the same friends, work to uplift her community, if she chooses in any number of the same ways that she would if her man were black," Moore charges. "Each woman lifting herself will lift the entire community" (*Black* 33–34, 22). Intermarriage here offers a path that allows black women to support *more* effectively the needs of the black community than if they remained tied to black men.

Black men who urge black women to seek their happiness within the race not surprisingly challenge these claims. Steve Harvey, a black comedian and popular talk and game show host who has a side career offering relationship advice to black women (writing books with titles like *Act Like a Lady, Think Like a Man* and *Straight Talk, No Chaser: How to Find and Keep a Man*) categorically denies the claims put forward in the advocacy literature. "Black men adore, honor and absolutely love sisters," Harvey insists in his advice column in *Essence*. It is a myth that "brothers prefer everyone but" black women, Harvey contends, a falsehood women embrace as an excuse for their dating woes (94). The black filmmaker Tyler Perry likewise suggests in many of his movies that the problem lies not with black men but with professional black women and their snobbish refusal to give decent working-class brothers a chance. If college-educated women would only get past their superficial need to have a man who makes as much money as they do, this argument goes, they would find no shortage of black men who want them.[6]

Mansplaining arguments to the contrary, many black women—not just interracial dating enthusiasts—share the belief that black men's interracial dating habits reveal their negative views of black women. The sociologist Erica Chito Childs found in a 2004 study that college-age black women viewed black men's choice of white women as a personal rejection of them. "For single young women," she argues, "a Black man's choice to be with a white woman is seen as a specific betrayal of Black women because the decision to date interracially does not mean just choosing white women but also rejecting black women" ("Looking" 551). These young women, according to Childs, believed that black men preferred white women because they had internalized white standards of beauty and because they perceived white women to be more submissive (558). Similarly, the African American scholar Tiya Miles admits being demoralized and feeling personally rejected when her male relatives bring home white dates. As she acknowledged in a recent blog, their willingness to date white women affirms "a social hierarchy based on race in which whiteness is prized."

But since the advocacy literature denies that society more generally devalues black women's worth and beauty, it has nowhere to place the blame except on supposedly ungrateful and selfish black men. Thus, advocates of intermarriage express far more anger toward their brothers than women like Miles. Miles expresses dismay and regret rather than red-hot fury about her male relatives who bring home white women; she wishes them "luck and joy in their relationships," even if she is disappointed by their choices. Similarly, the women Childs interviewed were angry not with individual black men or with interracial couples, but with a "society that devalued their worth as women" (Childs, "Looking" 551). Yet the advocacy literature blames black men for not putting "their stamp of approval on black female beauty and desirability," for participating in a "massive campaign" to denigrate black women as unappealing and hard to live with in order to cover up for their own failures and inadequacies (Moore, *Black* 74), and for having such a "deep resentment and dislike" of women of their own race that they have become black women's "chief antagonists" (Anderson, Interview). In this fairy tale, black men are definitely the ogres.

And that means, of course, that the white knights must be white (literally) or at least nonblack men. Perhaps the most traditional aspect of the story the advocates promote is their insistence that black women who cross the color line will find men who will treat them like princesses, or even better, like *black* princesses. White men, they insist, will enable black women to embrace their own unique beauty more fully. By looking outside the race, they will finally learn what it is like to be treated well, to be protected and provided for, and to be comfortable in their own skin. Even as the advocacy literature urges black women to free themselves to try something new, it reassures them that what they are really pursuing is something quite old: traditional gender roles, the right to be protected, and a secure marriage with a good provider.

In direct response to the voices in the African American community—Steve Harvey and Tyler Perry foremost among them—urging successful black women to embrace relationships with less-educated black men, these advocates tell their readers unequivocally that there is no reason to settle for a less successful man. "It's okay to want someone on the same income and education level as you," Karazin reassures her readers. It "doesn't make you a gold-digger" and it doesn't mean that you are somehow weak. There is absolutely nothing wrong "with choosing a mate who is financially capable of supporting you at least temporarily while you bear his children within wedlock," she insists (Karazin and Littlejohn 59, 55). We need to stop apologizing for expecting a man to "bring to the table fidelity, education, and if not financial security, some ambition or plans for his future," Folan argues (46). Black women deserve men who know they are supposed to be the breadwinners.

They also deserve to be the weaker partners for once. Having learned "almost before birth" that it is their responsibility to hold everything together at work and at home, it is time for them to let go of the myth of the black superwoman, advocates charge (Karazin and Littlejohn 51). Black women's own strength has become unhealthy, leading them to buy into "superpatriarchy" in their search for men who are even stronger than they are. Women too often choose swagger, toughness, and a cool pose over qualities that are more meaningful, like stability, decency, and kindness, advocates warn their sisters. But if black women can "surrender their infatuation with bad-boy traits," they will find that white men offer a version of masculinity—a kinder, more gentle version—that will allow them to embrace more traditional feminine gender roles (Folan 93). And shouldn't men "be the backbone," one woman writes on Moore's blog. The failure of black men to step up "has stripped some of our women of their femininity, dignity, and hope that we could depend on a man to be a man," she laments (Meli qtd. in Moore, *Black* 108). Black women need to find men who "behave like real *men,*" Moore concurs, if they ever hope to live like "real" women (*Black* 174).

For these advocates, contemporary gender dynamics between blacks are so out of alignment that they violate some kind of "natural" order. Thus, one interracially married woman who wrote into Karazin's blog describes protection as an innate male trait that black men fail to fulfill. "Men from different cultures by nature protect women," and while her Asian-Indian husband is no tough guy, she knows he would defend and shield her unquestioningly if she were threatened. It's liberating, she insists, "to not have to be strong," but fears that most of her peers will never know what that feels like (zoriansmom). Moore sees a different violation of the natural order in black women's desperate efforts to compete for scarce black men. "The overwhelming majority of males in the animal kingdom compete for female attention—not the other way around. Why work against nature" when you could let a rainbow global village of men compete for you, Moore asks (*Black* 117–18).

Those willing to take the plunge will reap a reward, the advocacy literature reassures readers, for they will discover that other men know how to treat a black woman far better than black men do. "White men tend to be more polite and chivalrous," a post on one website claims. "They open the car door, pull out the chair, pay for dinner, or just make a special call to say 'I had a good time last night.'" And concern about offending a woman of another race makes nonblack men especially sensitive to black women's feelings ("Why"). Folan describes the behavior of her future husband in glowing terms. On their first date, he picked her up, paid for dinner, and didn't expect anything in return from her. "He was an absolute gentleman" (8). Anderson, meanwhile, answers her own question about whether a white man makes a better partner than a black one by noting that black women "who are taken for granted and expected to do a lot of heavy lifting within their communities [. . .] might suddenly find it a refreshing experience to be with a man who has no such expectations of them" ("Interracial Dating 101: Further").

It would also enable them to embrace their own beauty more fully. In what is perhaps the most romanticized of this fairy tale's idealistic claims, advocates argue that white men are less burdened with historical baggage and stereotypes about race and beauty than black men are. White men care less about skin tone and thus have no qualms about how dark a woman is, Folan claims (113), while Moore insists that they appreciate "a *much* wider range of black female beauty than the majority of black men I've encountered, heard about, or read about" (*Black* 134). Banks tells the story of a woman whose white husband encouraged her to go natural with her hair rather than continuing the difficult and sometimes painful practice of relaxing it, something no black man she dated ever endorsed. Her husband's ignorance about race may have irritated her, Banks argues, "but it also liberated her" (176). The film *Something New* offers the exact same storyline: the black heroine's white boyfriend encourages her to go natural, but when she later starts dating a black man, he asks her to use a relaxer. White men, these advocates suggest, are more comfortable with black women's natural beauty, and as a result, can enable a sister to "get more in touch with loving herself as a black woman" (Childs, *Fade* 86). The bottom line, then, is that women in interracial relationships can be not only more feminine but more beautifully black than those in intraracial liaisons.

As I suggested above, while these authors portray themselves as offering something radically new, their perspective on traditional gender roles and binaries reflects much older value systems. Some of the literature goes so far as to describe heterosexuality as part of the "natural order," completely failing to acknowledge queer couples or the existence or experience of black lesbians. Moore supports her claim that black women dating nonblack men is absolutely normal by arguing for the primacy of biological gender categories over racial ones: "We were biologically females and males *before* we were ever politically defined as 'black' and 'white.'" And since "[m]ales and females are just wired to be attracted to each other," she claims, heterosexual interracial relationships are completely natural, an argument that implies that same-sex relationships are not (*Black* 31).

In its most ambitious claim, the advocacy literature suggests that if black women were more open to dating nonblack men they would not only find fulfilling marriages for themselves, but they could also help restore traditional values and gender roles among blacks. Banks believes that women dating outside the race will help bring equilibrium back to a community reeling from the effects of a gender gap that has left black men with "disproportionate power to establish relationships that are intimate but not committed, that entail sex but not marriage, and that offer benefits without responsibilities" (62). In a chapter tellingly titled "Saving Black Marriage," Banks makes the case that by intermarrying, black women will reduce the gender imbalance, shift the unequal power dynamics in the community, and bring black men back into the fold. "For black women," he insists, "interracial marriage doesn't abandon the race, it serves the race" (181). In her response to Banks, Karazin muses on whether his analysis might be right. If more black women intermarried, she wonders, "could we finally see a return of 'the black family' where the wife isn't a mule and the husband provides and protects his wife and children like Professor Banks does?" ("Could"). Promoting something new—intermarriage—here appears as the best way to save something old: a strong black community rooted in traditional gender roles.

A Dangerous Fairy Tale?

The idea that black women can close the marriage gap by opening their minds and hearts to the possibility of interracial dating is seductive and even romantic. Black women, this narrative insists, have the ability to shape their own destinies and to find love and fulfillment with a caring and respectful partner. "[B]lack women," Anderson puts it bluntly, "can make things happen" (Sal-Anderson loc 1992). They have the power to forge their own destinies if only they would use it. For Folan, the key question for those women who are hesitant to date interracially is whether "we see ourselves as black people in need of power or do we feel powerful." Those who allow fear to dictate their life choices are throwing away "power that you have earned and that you deserve" (159). Black women, these advocates insist, have the capacity to craft their own fairy tales.

This kind of fairy tale is today splashed on the pages of *People* magazine, as the media touts the marriage of England's Prince Harry to the biracial Californian Megan Markle. Apparently, the white male royal not only treats Markle like a princess, but he will make his "black" woman "Her Royal Highness" in what *People* and the rest of the popular press—along with Twitter and the blogosphere—dub "*her* real-life fairy tale." In another media-made example, the romance narrative of black women finding true love with white men became the basis for a whole season of ABC's reality dating show, *The Bachelorette*, which made history in 2017 when it featured its first black female star, Rachel Lindsay, choosing a husband from male contestants eager to compete for her hand. The season ended with Lindsay deciding between two finalists, neither of whom was black. Love, she later said, is color blind; she had no qualms about dating or marrying outside her race despite the fact that she knew she "would feel pressure from certain audiences that would say you 'had to pick a black man.'" Some people might not be happy with my decision, Lindsay reflected after she chose and became engaged to one of the two men, "but I needed to be selfish in this journey and find the one who was perfect for me" (qtd. in Dugan and Stone). With a ring on her finger, Lindsay seems to be living proof that black women can compete on the dating and marriage market, especially if they are willing to expand their romantic horizons.

But how much reality does this reality television show and its narrative of black women's power to craft their own destinies on the dating market offer? *The Bachelorette*, like its parent show *The Bachelor*—where a single man chooses from a bevy of beautiful women—has always presented its viewers a fairy tale, where two people find true love as they have romantic dates in exotic places around the world. The 2017 season represented a twist on the pattern by staging a colorblind, racial fairy tale as well, one in which, despite a few episodes that dealt with racial controversy caused by one white contestant, the people involved rarely talked about race, and Rachel and her suitors presented themselves as colorblind.

While not complete fantasy—all of us have some ability to shape the direction of our own lives based on our individual choices—this solution to the marital crisis that focuses on black women's agency and power is rooted as much in romantic thinking as in reality. It is a compelling and attractive story precisely because it suggests that individuals have the capacity and power to craft the lives they choose, that they are not in any way limited by the legacies of history or the manifestations of racism today. But like all fairy tales, the narrative promoted by these advocates of interracial dating has a dark side. By emphasizing black women's individual agency to find a husband, it downplays or obscures the deeper issues of systemic racism that do far more to explain declining marriages for black women and blacks overall than a supposed unwillingness to date across the color line. This interracial romance paints a picture of a world that simply does not exist, one where men are colorblind and the marriage market is free from bias and racism, thus offering one more arena where black women's lived experience is delegitimized. And like most fairy tales, it is rooted in and promotes traditional norms, in this case by reinforcing the centrality of the institution of marriage to racial progress and full citizenship for black people.

The Individualist Fantasy

There is without question a gender gap in the black community. There really are fewer marriageable black men than there are black women looking for partners. A recent Brookings Institute study found that while white women have "no shortage of options," among blacks, "concerns about a shortage of marriageable men are much more consistent with the evidence" (Sawhill and Venator 5). But in focusing on the disparate rate of intermarriage as a key factor in that shortage, the advocacy literature offers an individualistic solution to a problem that is far better understood as a reflection of structural racism. Black women's low marriage rates reflect the impact of broader social trends and a more pessimistic reality than most advocates of intermarriage are willing to admit. The decline in marriage rates correlates closely with the escalation of the War on Drugs in the 1980s. For most of the period from 1890 to 1980, roughly 10 percent of black men over thirty-five had never married, but that number began to climb precipitately in 1980 with policies that led to new forms of mass incarceration. By 1990, 15 percent of black men over thirty-five had never married. In 2010, that figure stood at around 25 percent ("Marriage").

Recent sociological work theorizes that a good part of blacks' lower marital rates, even among the black middle class, stems from their relatively disadvantaged economic status in American society. A 2015 study found that marriage is less of a social imperative and economic necessity for women than it once was, which has had the ironic effect of making wedlock something that people want to enter into only once they have achieved some kind of economic stability and security (Raley et al.). Marriage rates for people of every race have fallen fastest and furthest among those with the least education and the most precarious economic position. While middle-class blacks are more likely to marry than poorer blacks, they likely marry less than whites of the same social class due to economic factors and fewer familial resources. The contemporary racial gap in marriage rates, then, is largely due to "differences in employment, earnings, and wealth," the study concludes (Raley et al.).

Moreover, even if interracial dating offers options that can help some individual women navigate these broader structural issues, the advocacy literature fails to acknowledge that its solution is not equally accessible to all black women. By focusing almost exclusively on the middle class, the advocacy literature fails to consider how broadening one's dating horizons might be unrealistic for a poor black women living in highly segregated urban areas. A 2006 study found, for example, that "lower-class blacks are largely excluded from the interracial marriage market," while black men and women who have attended some college are 35 percent more likely than those with just a high school degree to be intermarried (Gullickson 686). The solution of intermarriage thus has the potential to deepen the already cavernous class divide in the black community.

Imani Perry, the Hughes-Rogers Professor of African American Studies at Princeton University, pointedly notes this disconnect between the actual problem and the solution proposed by intermarriage advocates in her review of *Is Marriage for White People?* While the book "identifies a devastating social reality for black men as the foremost explanation for low African-American marriage rates," Perry writes, it offers a solution that "treats the problem as an individual one rather than as societal or structural." Where, she wonders, are the solutions focused on the discrimination black men face in workplaces, schools, and the criminal justice system? The advocacy literature, in short, does not address the underlying economic and institutional structures that contribute to a decline in marriage rates in the first place; indeed, it cannot do so because that would require coming to grips with the fact that black women do face more barriers on the dating and marriage market than women of other races.

The Colorblind Fantasy

To put it bluntly, the so-called marriage market is not as fair and free of racial bias as promoters of interracial dating claim. While the advocates insist that it is a lie that no "non-black man will ever want you" (Karazin and Littlejohn 52), there is at least some ugly truth to black women's fears that men outside their race might not consider them attractive dating and marriage partners. Indeed, multiple studies find that nonblack men are reluctant to date black women. Over 90 percent of the men in a 2009 study of fifteen hundred white Internet dating profiles refused to consider dating black women. Indeed, white men are 2.5 times more likely than white women to exclude blacks completely from their dating preferences (Feliciano et al.). And it isn't just white men. A report by the online dating site OkCupid finds that 82 percent of all nonblack men (which includes Asians, whites, and Latinos) show some bias against black women, who not only receive the fewest messages of all OkCupid users (Rudder) but also are often ignored when they contact nonblack men. As the authors of a study of the online behaviors of almost a million Internet daters conclude, "Black daters, particularly black women, are largely confined to a segregated dating market" (Lin and Lundquist 204, 209).[7]

These patterns likely reflect deeply rooted perceptions of beauty and negative stereotypes about black women, despite claims by advocates that nonblack men better appreciate black female beauty than black men do. On dating sites, white men, Asian men, and Latino men rate black women as 18 percent, 16 percent, and 22 percent less attractive than average, respectively (Rudder).[8] A study of 134 white men—nearly half of whom are middle class and 70 percent of whom have some kind of college education—found that "deep frames" of long-standing sexual and racial stereotypes shape their views of black women. Men interviewed for the study described black women as domineering and unattractive and black culture as inferior and pathological. Asian and Latino men hold similarly negative views, which, the study's author hypothesizes, may explain the very low rates of interracial marriage between black women and nonwhite men overall (Slatton 9).

Authors like Banks and Moore have tried to discount the importance of these findings. As Banks explains, while studies find that men who express racial preferences in their partners disfavor black women, not all men in the studies express racial preferences. What really matters, he argues, is the absolute numbers, not the percentages. Since black women are only 13 percent of the u.s. population, even if two-thirds of white men refuse to date them, there will still be plenty of men to go around (Banks 127–28). Moore sidesteps the issue by explaining to critics that her "philosophy" is that black women are "as desirable as any woman from any group to a progressive, non-racist, open-minded man" while failing to ask just how many men like that are in fact out there in the world (*Black* 188). She and other advocates aren't claiming that there is some kind of "mainstream white male stampede for black women," Anderson insists, but she still asserts that the odds of a black women finding a white man are good and perhaps even better than of finding a black man ("I Think"). Advocates, in other words, routinely downplay the extent to which negative stereotypes continue to disadvantage black women on the dating and marriage market.

The argument that the biggest barrier to black women finding love across the color line is their own resistance to interracial dating, then, contradicts the stark evidence of the continued power and presence of sexualized racism. It peddles fantasy rather than grappling with a painful reality, much as *The Bachelorette* did during its 2017 season. But that one season of the show should not obscure what a longer history of that franchise reveals: that whites do not consider blacks equally attractive romantic partners. Indeed, for most of its thirty-three seasons, both *The Bachelor* and *The Bachelorette* have been stunningly white. No African American before Rachel Lindsay had ever been the star of the show, and very few of the black contestants in any given season have even made it past week five. Nearly 60 percent of black contestants on both programs have been voted off within the first two episodes, when the average contestant lasts ten weeks (Fitzpatrick).

The claim that black women only have to open themselves to interracial dating in order to find happiness has the potential to reinforce the belief that black women's low marriage rates reflect their individual failings rather than larger cultural or structural issues—a story that at least some young black women still internalize. As one black female blogger explained in 2015, she and her friends end up blaming themselves when white guys walk away once things get serious. We imagined that we weren't pretty enough or accomplished enough, she admitted, "because we did not want to grapple with the morose reality that we could be denied the most fundamental of human experiences—love—because of the color of our skin." Her antidotal, self-affirming refrain, "It's not your fault. It's never been your fault," suggests the ways in which this colorblind fantasy can negatively affect individual women (Bennett). As Childs concludes, "Black women alone do not have the power to change the current situation." The problem they encounter in searching for partners is "racism and sexism, where Black women are devalued based on their race and gender" ("Looking" 559). Meaningful change, Childs argues, can only come by addressing these long-standing racial and gender inequalities. Focusing on the supposed unwillingness of black women to date across the color line or suggesting that the dating market is, in fact, colorblind, denies and delegitimizes many black women's own lived experience.

The Marriage Fantasy

If the advocacy literature peddles something of a fairy tale by promoting an individualistic solution to a problem with deep structural roots—and then minimizing the barriers that stand in the way of even that individualistic solution—it is a fairy tale with deep roots, one that reinforces what might be considered a somewhat mythic narrative that marriage is the best path forward for blacks seeking full citizenship and racial justice.

In "Marriage as Black Citizenship," the legal scholar R. A. Lenhardt makes a compelling argument that the narrative about black marriage enhancing the quest for full citizenship is in fact wrong and even damaging. Instead, Lenhardt explores how the regulation of marriage has been used as a tool of racial subordination, a way to impose standards whites consider respectable on people they consider inferior and to stigmatize nonwhite groups that in any way deviate from these gender and sexual norms. Marriage regulations have also, Lenhardt argues, facilitated the hyperregulation of black families and served to stigmatize blackness, whether through bans on interracial marriage that communicated that blacks were inferior or in interaction with other forms of regulation, like the welfare system. Yet there has been little interrogation of this deeply held idea that marriage is a path to citizenship or racial advancement, and in the contemporary u.s., Lenhardt insists, even as some forms of nonmarital relationships are being normalized for nonblacks, African Americans are stigmatized as deviant and lacking in ambition for having lower marital rates than other groups.

The advocacy literature that promotes dating and marriage accepts and reinforces this narrative that marriage is the best path forward for the black community. All the advocates convey this message in their unacknowledged emphasis on how finding a marital partner is the right way for black women to achieve happiness, economic security, and stability. Moore goes furthest among them in emphasizing the vital importance of marriage as an institution in society. "Family starts with marriage and family is the basic building block of any community or nation." It is impossible to improve the black community until blacks begin choosing mates properly and marrying in large numbers, she insists, calling a marriage contract a "highly valuable piece of paper" that is especially important for economic advancement. People who are better off economically got there and "remain there for generations largely *because* they marry," according to Moore ("Marriage"). Banks, too, touts the benefits and importance of marriage in *Is Marriage for White People?* While wedlock is no longer a legal or economic necessity, it is still "a marker of status and achievement," he asserts (21). The decline in marriage among the black middle class restricts its "growth and security" and undermines the future, since many middle-class women will remain childless. Both Moore and Banks present marriage as key to the continued vitality of the black bourgeoisie (10).

But arguments that promote marriage as a path to economic advancement for the black community are both unrealistic and stigmatizing to blacks who do not marry. As Lehnhardt explains, such arguments "vastly overstate the economic benefits of marriage to African Americans in particular" and especially to low-income black families (1355). Indeed, poor families often face a marriage penalty, losing low-income tax credits or welfare benefits if they marry. Moreover, by promoting interracial marriage as the solution to black women's problems, advocates further reinforce the idea that marriage should be the yardstick for judging the health and success of black people. But "so long as marriage continues to be the metric against which all black loving relationships, married or unmarried, are evaluated, African Americans, at least given current statistics, will continue to fall short," Lenhardt asserts (1361). Arguments about racial progress linked to marriage offer a neoliberal vision of social inequalities best addressed through private individual actions. No wonder that the conservative pundit Andrew Sullivan recently praised evidence of an increase in black women's intermarriage rates as "terrific news," a sign that black women are finally "making it" and breaking out of the culture of welfare dependency. Like other conservatives who tout interracial relationships as a way to address racial inequalities, Sullivan prefers love to be the answer, not legislation or government programs (Romano 287).

In this genre of advocacy literature, solving the marriage crisis for middle-class black women is easy. Black women have "more choices than they realize," Folan insists (12). The only thing holding them back is their own reluctance to embrace interracial dating. This is without question a positive vision and a compelling narrative, one that suggests that black women have power and agency, that they live in a time where they can build their own futures unburdened by the constraints of history and racism, and that they can marry outside the race without sacrificing their own black identity or their commitment to the black community. Perhaps it is ironic to suggest that black women can most effectively embrace their black identity, their power, and their beauty by moving outside the black community and dating men from across the racial spectrum. But there is no irony for these advocates, who portray black women who are open to interracial dating as successfully laying down the burden of America's racial history, overcoming internalized negative stereotypes, and standing up to insist on being treated with respect. It should not be surprising that they believe such women can maintain, and even strengthen, their own black identity and the black community while marrying outside the race.

But while the prescriptive advice these black women advocates offer differs dramatically from that of folks like Steve Harvey, who advise black women to be more demure, to allow their men to lead, and to stop being so outspoken, both positions share the underlying conviction that the key barrier black women face stems from their behavior and attitudes. The advocacy literature puts the onus on individual black women to solve problems that are systemic and institutional. It offers the fantasy that race is no longer determinative in the marriage market despite the evidence that black women—whatever their attitudes toward intermarriage—face extra challenges in finding partners. And it further reinforces a cultural narrative that deep and enduring racial disparities and inequalities can best be addressed by promoting black marriage. Advocating intermarriage may offer black women something new, but it also plays into old patterns that have long contributed to the stigmatization of black women and the black community.

RENEE ROMANO is the Robert S. Danforth Professor of History and Professor of Comparative American Studies and Africana Studies at Oberlin College. She is the author or coeditor of five books, including *Race Mixing: Black-White Marriage in Postwar America* (Harvard University Press, 2003). Her most recent book is the coedited collection, *Historians on Hamilton: How a Blockbuster Musical Is Restaging America's Past* (Rutgers University Press, 2018).

Notes

1   In fact, 70 percent of black female college graduates are married by age forty, as compared to only 60 percent of black female high school graduates. See Nittle.

2   Thirty percent of college-educated black men marry someone of another race, compared to only 13 percent of similarly situated black women. See "How Higher Education Impacts the Likelihood of Interracial Marriage."

3   Anderson publishes as both Halima Anderson and Halima Sal-Anderson. For the purposes of this paper, she will be referred to in the text and in parenthetical references to her blog as Anderson, while citations to her book, which she published as Sal-Anderson, will use that name.

4   In 2010, there were 2.3 black men married to white women for every black woman married to a white man. The disparity in numbers was greater for other kinds of interracial marriages.

For example, of the 48,000 black-Asian marriages, only 9,000 involved a black woman.

5   Djamba and Kimuna's 2014 study found no statistically significant difference between the percentage of black women and black men who said they would strongly approve of a relative marrying outside the race (54.3 percent of women and 52.8 percent for men).

6   Banks offers a more extensive analysis of this issue and of Perry in *Is Marriage for White People?* (87–93).

7   This pattern held true regardless of their educational qualifications, physical characteristics, or the demographic of the black women. And white men with college degrees were no more likely to respond to black women; indeed, the study found that white men and women with college degrees contacted and responded to whites without college degrees more than to similarly educated blacks.

8   Black men rated black women as 3   they gave to white women, sug-
     percent less attractive than aver-   gesting the "average" includes
     age, which was the same rating   other racial makeups.

Works Cited   Akil, Jamila. "Don't Date Massa!! A Note on Slavery and Swirling." *Beyond Black & White* (blog). 22 Apr. 2012. http://www.beyondblackwhite.com/dont-date-massa-a-note-on-slavery -and-swirling/.

Anderson, Halima. "Do Black Women Actually Know What It Takes to Build the 'Strong Black Community' They Keep Talking About?" *Dateawhiteguy* (blog). 1 Jan. 2009. http:// dateawhiteguy.blogspot.com/2009/01/do-black-women-actually-know-what-it.html.

————. "Give It Up or Embrace the Fruits Thereof." *Dateawhiteguy* (blog). 27 July 2009. http://dateawhiteguy.blogspot.com/2009/07/give-it-up-or-embrace-fruits-thereof.html.

————. "Interracial Blogger's Key Assumptions (Part 1)." *Dateawhiteguy* (blog). 8 Jan. 2009. http://dateawhiteguy.blogspot.com/2009/01/interracial-bloggers-key-assumptions.html.

————. "Interracial Dating 101: The Basics." *Dateawhiteguy* (blog). 13 May 2008. http:// dateawhiteguy.blogspot.com/2008/05/interracial-dating-101-basics.html.

————. "Interracial Dating 101: Beginning of Your Strategy." *Dateawhiteguy* (blog). 11 July 2008. http://dateawhiteguy.blogspot.com/2008/07/interracial-dating-101-begining-of -your.html.

————. "Interracial Dating 101: Further Notes." *Dateawhiteguy* (blog). 5 June 2008. http://dateawhiteguy.blogspot.com/2008/06/interracial-dating-101-further-notes.html.

————. Interview with Glee. *"Supposing I Wanted to Date a White Guy." Offbeat Marriage: Sharing the Gift of Extra-Challenging Unions.* http://offbeatmarriage.com/black -women-dating-crisis/ (accessed 3 Mar. 2018).

————. "'I Think You Glorify White Men and Make Them Out as Saviors.'" *Dateawhite- guy* (blog). 3 June 2009. http://dateawhiteguy.blogspot.com/2009/06/i-think-you-glorify-white -men-and-make.html.

————. "My Thoughts on a Range of Things." *Dateawhiteguy* (blog). 10 Sept. 2009. http://dateawhiteguy.blogspot.com/2009/09/my-thoughts-on-range-of-things.html.

————. "A Response That Deserves a Comment." *Dateawhiteguy* (blog). 14 July 2009. http://dateawhiteguy.blogspot.com/2009/07/reponse-that-deserves-comment.html.

————. "Round Up for the Year 2009!" *Dateawhiteguy* (blog). 31 Dec. 2009. http:// dateawhiteguy.blogspot.com/2009/12/round-up-for-year-2009.html.

————. "Some 1st Week July Thoughts about Black Unity." *Dateawhiteguy* (blog). 3 July 2009. http://dateawhiteguy.blogspot.com/2009/07/some-1st-week-july-thoughts.html.

Banks, Ralph Richard. *Is Marriage for White People? How the African American Marriage Decline Affects Everyone.* New York: Dutton Adult, 2011.

Bennett, Amanda. "(Black) Girl, Unnoticed." *Huffpost Black Voices* (blog). 10 Nov. 2015. http:// www.huffingtonpost.com/amanda-bennett/black-girl-unnoticed_b_8499200.html.

Childs, Eria Chito. *Fade to Black and White: Interracial Images in Popular Culture.* Lanham: Rowman and Littlefield, 2009.

————————. "Looking Behind the Stereotypes of the 'Angry Black Woman': An Exploration of Black Women's Responses to Interracial Relationships." *Gender and Society* 19.4 (2004): 544–61.

Cohn, D'Vera, et al. "Barely Half of u.s. Adults Are Married—A Record Low." *Pew Research Center's Social and Demographic Trends.* Washington, DC. 14 Dec. 2011. http://assets.pewresearch.org/wp-content/uploads/sites/3/2011/12/Marriage-Decline.pdf.

Djamba, Yanyi K., and Sitawa R. Kimuna. "Are Americans Really in Favor of Interracial Marriage? A Closer Look at When They Are Asked about Black-White Marriage for Their Relatives." *Journal of Black Studies* 45.6 (2014): 528–44.

Dugan, Christina, and Natalie Stone. "Rachel Lindsay and Bryan Abasolo on Their Interracial Relationships: 'Love Is Blind—We're Just a Man and Woman in Love.'" *People tvwatch.* 8 Aug. 2017. http://people.com/tv/bachelorette-rachel-lindsay-bryan-abasolo-talk-interracial-relationship/.

Edwards, Audrey. "Bring Me Home a Black Girl." *Essence* Nov. 2002. 176–79.

Feliciano, Cynthia, et al. "Gendered Racial Exclusion among White Internet Daters." *Social Science Research* 38 (2009): 39–54.

Fitzpatrick, Molly. "A History of Black Contestants on 'The Bachelor' and 'The Bachelorette.'" *Splinter* 2 Feb. 2016. www.splinternews.com.

Fletcher, Brody. "12 Most Common Stereotypes about Black Women and White Men Relationships." *I Support and Love Interracial Relationships Facebook Page.* 6 Jan. 2011. https://www.facebook.com/notes/i-support-and-love-interracial-relationships/12-most-common-stereotypes-about-black-women-and-white-men-relationships-written/178480052184323/.

Folan, Karyn Langhorne. *Don't Bring Home a White Boy: And Other Notions That Keep Black Women from Dating Out.* New York: Gallery, 2010.

————————. "What Mildred Knew." *Washington Post* 12 June 2008. http://www.washingtonpost.com/wp-dyn/content/article/2008/06/11/AR2008061103171.html.

Frederick, Candice. "Black Women and Interracial Dating: A Q and A with Relationship Expert Christelyn Karazin." *Black Girl Nerds* (blog). 16 Apr. 2015. https://blackgirlnerds.com/black-women-interracial-dating-qa-relationship-expert-christelyn-karazin/.

Gullickson, Aaron. "Education and Black-White Interracial Marriage." *Demography* 43.4 (2006): 673–89.

Harvey, Steve. "Setting the Record Straight." *Essence* Aug. 2010. 94.

Herman, Melissa R., and Mary E. Campbell. "I Wouldn't, But You Can: Attitudes toward Interracial Relationships." *Social Science Research* 41 (2012): 343–58.

Hightower, Joy. "Where Are the Brothas? How the Continued Erasure of Black Men's Voices on the Marriage Question Perpetuates the Black Male Deficit." *Harvard Kennedy School Journal of African American Public Policy: A Student Publication* (blog). 25 Apr. 2016. http://hjaap.org/where-are-the-brothas/.

"How Higher Education Impacts the Likelihood of Interracial Marriage." *Journal of Blacks in Higher Education* 30 May 2017. https://www.jbhe.com/2017/05/how-higher-education-impacts-the-likelihood-of-interracial-marriage/.

Karazin, Christelyn. "Could What Ralph Richard Banks Said in His Book Be True Regarding How Swirling Might Help Black Women Marry Black Men?" *Beyond Black & White* (blog). 22 Oct. 2014. http://www.beyondblackwhite.com/ralph-richard-banks-said-book-true-regarding -swirling-might-help-black-women-marry-black-men/.

——————. "The Verdict Is In: All Black Women MUST Consider Swirling." *Beyond Black & White* (blog). 23 Sept. 2013. http://www.beyondblackwhite.com/verdict-black-women-must -consider-swirling/.

Karazin, Christelyn D., and Janice Rhoshalle Littlejohn. *Swirling: How to Date, Mate, and Relate: Mixing Race, Culture, and Creed.* New York: Atria, 2012.

Lenhardt, R. A. "Marriage as Black Citizenship." *Hastings Law Journal* 66 (2015): 1317–64.

Lin, Ken-Hou, and Jennifer Lundquist. "Mate Selection in Cyberspace: The Intersection of Race, Gender, and Education." *American Journal of Sociology* 119.1 (July 2013): 183–215.

Livingston, Gretchen, and Anna Brown. "Intermarriage in the U.S. 50 Years after *Loving v. Virginia.*" Pew Research Center. May 2017. http://www.pewsocialtrends.org/2017/05/18 /intermarriage-in-the-u-s-50-years-after-loving-v-virginia/.

"Marriage in Black America." *Black Demographics.* 2014. http://blackdemographics.com /households/marriage-in-black-america/ (accessed 2 Mar. 2018).

Miles, Tiya. "Black Women, Interracial Dating, and Marriage: What's Love Got to Do with It?" *HuffPost* (blog). 5 Nov. 2013. http://www.huffingtonpost.com/tiya-miles/interracial-dating -and-marriage_b_4213066.html.

Misick, Bobbi. Interview with Karyn Folan. "'Dating Out': Single Black Females and Inter-racial Dating." *Essence* 6 Mar. 2010. https://www.essence.com/2010/03/09/single-black-female -interracial-dating.

Moore, Eve Sharon. *Black Women: Interracial and Intercultural Marriage, Book 1—First and Foremost.* 2nd ed. Lancaster: Shareve Communications, 2012.

——————. "Marriage for Wealth-Building, Stability, Raising Children: SOME of the Many BENEFITS of Marriage." *Black Female Interracial Marriage* (blog). 1 June 2017. http://www .blackfemaleinterracialmarriage.com/?p=1124.

Mouzon, Dawne M. "Why Has Marriage Declined among Black Americans?" *Scholar Strategy Network.* Oct. 2013. http://www.scholarsstrategynetwork.org/brief/why-has-marriage -declined-among-black-americans.

Nittle, Nadra Kareem. "The Top Four Myths about Black Marriage." *ThoughtCo* (blog). 11 Sept. 2017. https://www.thoughtco.com/the-top-myths-about-black-marriage-2834526.

Perry, Imani. "Blacks, Whites, and the Wedding Gap." *New York Times* 16 Sept. 2011. http:// www.nytimes.com/2011/09/18/books/review/is-marriage-for-white-people-by-ralph-richard -banks-book-review.html.

Raley, R. Kelley, Megan M. Sweeney, and Danielle Wondra. "The Growing Racial and Ethnic Divide in U.S. Marriage Patterns." *Future Child* 25.2 (2015): 89–109.

Romano, Renee. *Race Mixing: Black-White Marriage in Postwar America.* Cambridge, MA: Harvard UP, 2003.

Rudder, Christian. "Race and Attraction, 2009–2014." *Okcupid* (blog). 9 Sept. 2014. https://theblog.okcupid.com/race-and-attraction-2009-2014-107dcbb4f060.

Sal-Anderson, Halima. *"Supposing I Wanted to Date a White Guy . . . ?" Everything You Need to Know about Interracial Relationships.* Something2Say: 2005. E-book.

Sawhill, Isabel, and Joanna Venator. "Is There a Shortage of Marriageable Men?" *Center on Children and Families at Brookings.* ccf Brief #56. Sept. 2015. https://www.brookings.edu/wp-content/uploads/2016/06/56-Shortage-of-Marriageable-Men.pdf.

Slatton, Brittany C. *Mythologizing Black Women: Unveiling White Men's Racist and Sexist Deep Frame.* Boulder: Paradigm, 2014.

Something New. Dir. Sanaa Hamri. Gramercy Pictures, 2006.

Sullivan, Andrew. "Black Women Make a Date with History." *Sunday Times* 21 July 2002. London.

Touré. *Who's Afraid of Post-Blackness: What It Means to Be Black Now.* New York: Atria, 2011.

Wang, Wendy, and Kim Parker. "Record Share of Americans Have Never Married: As Values, Economics, and Gender Patterns Change." *Pew Research Center Social and Demographic Trends.* Washington, DC. 24 Sept. 2014. http://www.pewsocialtrends.org/2014/09/24/record-share-of-americans-have-never-married/.

"Why Some Black Women Only Date White Men?" *InterracialMatch* (blog). 15 Feb. 2016. https://www.interracialmatch.com/interracial_dating_blog/why-some-black-women-only-date-white-men-140.

zoriansmom. Comment on Christleyn Karazin, "My Story: Jumping the Broom with a 'White' Boy." *Beyond Black & White* (blog). 6 June 2010. http://www.beyondblackwhite.com/my-story-jumping-the-broom-with-a-white-boy/.

ONEKA LABENNETT

"Beyoncé and Her Husband":
Representing Infidelity and Kinship in a Black Marriage

Beyoncé and Her Husband

*T*his article explores infidelity and kinship within represen-tations of the marriage of two superstar African American performers, Beyoncé Giselle Knowles-Carter, popularly known as Beyoncé, and her hus-band, Shawn Carter, whose stage name is Jay-Z. It takes Beyoncé's Peabody Award–winning twelve-track visual album *Lemonade* as its starting point, reading this work as a genre-defying autoethnographic text and situating the project's representation of infidelity alongside Jay-Z's subsequent response record, *4:44.* Both albums and the couple's marital and familial ties are also read alongside popular commentary, including Black Twitter discourses, online gossip and rumors, entertainment news, and cultural critiques.

I argue that *Lemonade* is an exercise in autoethnographic kinship formation, one that employs representations of Beyoncé and her family—defined both in the conventional sense of the nuclear family and biological kin and constructed more broadly to include a sisterhood of fictive kin—to reimagine how black marriage, sexuality, and kinship are popularly under-stood. *Lemonade* and key related performances challenge our conceptions of public and private, celebrity and intimacy, at the same time that they

Volume 29, Number 2   DOI 10.1215/10407391-6999816

© 2018 by Brown University and d i f f e r e n c e s : A Journal of Feminist Cultural Studies

clarify and confront the ways in which the black family has been confined to and captured within a "glass closet" that exposes and impinges on black interiority. In the process, Beyoncé reveals the persistence of damaging stereotypes of race, gender, and "black marriage," even as her attempts at queer solidarities fall short of fully including gender-nonconforming agents in her autoethnographic kinship formation. By parsing the reliance on queer voices in *Lemonade* and *4:44* alongside the erasure of gender-nonconforming bodies in the former, I interrogate how both artists reconceptualize family.

Arguably the "First Family" of the hip-hop generation, Beyoncé and Jay-Z's familial ties emerge in political discourse and online gossip as, on the one hand, an enviable ideal and, on the other, as exemplar of the co-constitutive production of blackness and queerness. Black Twitter[1] is a fruitful starting point for parsing how these spouses are regarded in the public sphere. "Beyoncé and her husband," a recurring quip on Twitter, evinces the unconventional role reversal employed to characterize this celebrity marriage. Fans have used this descriptor to identify Beyoncé as the *real* heavyweight in the duo and to throw shade at Jay-Z for his suspected infidelity, as in this example: "Congratulations to Beyoncé and her husband / Or her husband who's name I forget / The one she made Lemonade about / His name is beyonces husband" (sleep bitch). The terminology, when strategically deployed by Beyoncé's diehard social media fans, popularly known as the BeyHive, shuts down slanderous rumors about the pair, as was the case when a Twitter user wondered if "Jay Z and his wife's" public image masked the possibility that they were abusive parents "behind closed doors." Before being deleted from Twitter, in an exchange that exposes the multiple ways in which the marriage has been queered, this tweet received a harsh rebuke, stating that it was "Beyoncé and her husband" and admonishing the author for making "false accusations." Here, Beyoncé and Jay-Z's union is queered in the sense of contesting heteronormativity in its positioning of Beyoncé's name first and in the sense of being "aberrant" in the (unsubstantiated) accusation of child abuse. Yet, as I will demonstrate in this essay, the couple's performances have also articulated queer sexualities. Queer of color critique has highlighted how black families have long been deemed dysfunctional based on their deviations from heteronormative and patriarchal nuclear family norms (Ferguson). The digital debates around "Beyoncé and her husband" point to the complex ways in which this marital union is represented and understood as both prototypical and queer, a contradiction that this essay interprets to suggest that these two artists reimagine how black sexuality, marriage, kinship, and infidelity are popularly constructed.[2] I respond to attempts to frame the pair's marriage as deviant, in part by deconstruct-ing Beyoncé's autoethnographic kinship formation and by unpacking key moments in the representation of their union.

The critical moments that inform *Lemonade* and *4:44* include the "Single Ladies" song and video, Beyoncé and Jay-Z's public announcements of a miscarriage or miscarriages, the couple's On the Run tour on the heels of Beyoncé's solo act, The Mrs. Carter Show World Tour, and the infamous elevator fight between Jay-Z and Solange Knowles, Beyoncé's sister. These performances position the couple as collaborators and co-conspirators who employ love and matrimony, kinship and fidelity as generative artistic forces and as vehicles to reflect on the pressures of black marriage in the spotlight. They also underscore my argument, first, that the pair is simultaneously rendered as both prototypical and queer and, second, that Beyoncé's oeuvre—anchored by her command, "Okay, ladies, now let's get in formation!"—can be read as a making, or poiesis, that locates black women's sexual liberation in an autoethnographic kinship formation rather than squarely within the confines of the conjugal bond.

Autoethnographic Kinship Formation

Before turning to a gloss of each of these critical examples, a word about what I am calling Beyoncé's "autoethnographic kinship for-mation." Although subject to various interpretations and definitions, I am employing the term *autoethnography* to refer to a "genre that places the self and the researcher and/or narrator within a social context" and a work "that provoke[s] questions about the nature of ethnographic knowledge by troubling the persistent dichotomies of insider versus outsider, distance and familiarity, objective observer versus participant, and individual versus culture" (Reed-Danahay). In theorizing *Lemonade* as an exercise in auto-ethnographic kinship formation, I am retooling a hallmark of anthropo-logical theory—the notion that kinship structures are crucial blueprints for understanding social organization as a whole—while positioning Beyoncé's configuration of "family" as a race/gender project that both adheres to and destabilizes traditional kin structures.[3] By concentrating on how Beyoncé reconceptualizes kin, and arguing that hers is an autoethnographic kinship formation that defines family beyond the construct of the heteronormative nuclear unit, I am exposing how entrenched race/gender ideologies that pathologize the black family persist in the here and now.[4] Autoethnographic kinship formation is also especially applicable due to *Lemonade*'s blurring of genres. Like the pioneering autoethnographic work of Zora Neale Hurston, including her "autobiography" *Dust Tracks on a Road*,[5] *Lemonade* blends ethnographic, novelistic, and autobiographical genres. I therefore apply the term in order to push back against interpretations of *Lemonade* as a squarely autobiographical work.

From Single Lady to Mrs. Carter: Kinship, Feminism, and Marriage before Lemonade

Beyoncé's oeuvre might best be understood in two connected stages: "before *Lemonade*" and "after *Lemonade*." Before *Lemonade*, observers like Aisha Durham honed in on how the socio-politics of the black family played out in Beyoncé's performances. These themes would reemerge in *Lemonade*'s treatment of infidelity and marriage. For Durham, Beyoncé's widely parodied "Single Ladies (Put a Ring on It)" video illustrated that it is the performer's "ability to play the freak and the lady that garners mainstream celebrity while maintaining respectability in the black public sphere" (82). Durham aptly notes that "real single ladies" are interpreted as "potential threats to a perceived fragile black manhood and a broken black family" (82). Deeply generative, Durham's analysis sets the stage for a reading of the diva's work that engages more closely with her autoethnographic elements.[6] It is useful to juxtapose Sasha Fierce's famous refrain in "Single Ladies"—"If you liked it, then you shoulda put a ring on it," an admonition to a suitor reluctant to marry—with Beyoncé's rejection of marriage in *Lemonade* when, in "Don't Hurt Yourself," she flings her ring at the camera and shouts, "If you try this shit again, you gon' lose your wife!" These "ring moments" not only illustrate Beyoncé's/Sasha Fierce's lady/freak trajectory—she moves from straddling the lady and the freak to disavowing both—but also accentuate her evolution as a feminist and signal the centrality of conjugality and fidelity as constant themes in her work.[7] The multiple YouTube parodies that "Single Ladies" spawned articulate how social media open up a critical space in which questions of gender and queer sexualities come into dialogue with Beyoncé's repertoire.

The video for "Single Ladies," which, like much of Beyoncé's work, draws heavily on queer black performance styles, took on a controversial afterlife on YouTube when previous unknowns like Shane Mercado re-created its dance routine in his bedroom and attracted millions of views. Mercado became popularly known as "the queen dancing to 'Single Ladies.'" Durham emphasizes that "both Shane and Beyoncé remind us about the particular bodies that are able to transgress boundaries of gender," pointing out that it is Beyoncé's alter ego, Sasha Fierce, who is "the bad girl [. . .] who has to do Beyoncé's dirty work" (81). This observation, of course, highlights the contradictions of respectability and sexual liberation that the performer has navigated. Beyoncé's at times contested claims to feminism have been wrapped up in how she uses her own body to enact sexual liberation. These claims have also, as I will demonstrate, been inextricably linked to her employment of queer sexuality and gender-nonconforming artists.

Mrs. Carter and On the Run

While Beyoncé legally hyphenated her name after her marriage to Jay-Z in 2008, the title of her 2013–14 Mrs. Carter Show World Tour collapsed the divide between her stage persona and her identity as a married woman, suggesting a transformation from Single Lady/Sasha Fierce into a more "respectable married lady."[8] In so doing, she proudly broadcast her marital status and left cultural critics scratching their heads as they tried to reconcile the performer's previous anthems, such as the Destiny's Child megahit "Independent Women (Part 1)" and "Single Ladies" with what Aisha Harris described as a "step back in the ongoing debate of 'Beyoncé-as-feminist.'"[9] Referencing another of Beyoncé's feminist anthems, "Run the World (Girls)," Harris summarizes the confusion the tour title sparked with the headline, "Who Run the World? Husbands?"

After Beyoncé completed the Mrs. Carter World Tour, the couple launched On the Run, a joint tour. The Bonnie and Clyde theme around which they organized On the Run undercut the respectability suggested in the Mrs. Carter nomenclature and tour aesthetic.[10] The song "Part 2 (On the Run)" channels the couple's real-life reputation as having united a notorious womanizer, bad boy, and former drug dealer and a respectable good girl. Jay-Z's rap verses support this reading with lines such as: "She fell in love with the bad boy, the bad guy / What you doing with them rap guys, them rap guys / They ain't see potential in me girl, but you see it / If it's me and you against the world, then so be it." When the duo performed the song in Paris on the tour's last night, Jay-Z pushed back against any doubts that his lyrics mirrored their actual relationship by offering the following announcement as Beyoncé sang the song's opening lines: "Paris, celebrate this love with us tonight. This is our last night of the On the Run Tour! This place is real special to us. We got engaged here. Our baby, Blue, was conceived here!" At one point during the performance, the couple sways together in a close embrace and Jay-Z once again underscores the authenticity of their tour personae, yelling "This is real!" as Beyoncé smiles knowingly at him. Suffice it to say that, considered in the context of the rumors of marital problems that emerged simultaneous to the tour, Jay-Z's insistence on the reality of the performance can be read as an example of protesting too much.

On the Run further established Jay-Z and Beyoncé, who had already collaborated on a number of projects, as co-conspirators for whom love and marriage are both a generative artistic force and a vehicle for reflecting on the pressures and complexities of being a "power couple." Online rumors of marital strife dogged the twosome throughout On the Run, however, with, for example, a gossip site quoting one of Beyoncé's dancers as describing the couple's onstage chemistry as a kind of mixtape: "It shows the love, it shows the affection," she said. "The love, the *hate*, the relationship, real things that go on in [. . .] relationships" (Rogers). The same article notes that rumors abounded during this time of Jay-Z cheating with the fashion designer Rachel Roy—the ex-wife of his former business partner—and the Barbadian singer and internationally recognized phenom Rihanna among the list of alleged mistresses.[11] Around this time, too, the widely publicized video of a violent confrontation between Beyoncé's sister, Solange, and Jay-Z in an elevator fueled speculations of his infidelity, a video to which I will return shortly.

Considering the proliferation of rumors about marital strife and infidelity, it is perhaps not surprising that Beyoncé rarely grants interviews. Although she has been reluctant to publicly share personal matters, concomitant to the announcement of the Mrs. Carter World Tour, Beyoncé was arguably more candid than she had been to date—revealing previously closely held details around issues of family and childbirth. In her 2013 documentary *Life Is but a Dream*, she discloses both that she is pregnant and that she'd previously had a miscarriage—an intimate and tragic loss she also addresses in what she has called the saddest song she has ever written, meaningfully titled "Heartbeat." As she subsequently explained to Oprah Winfrey in a televised *Next Chapter* interview that aired on February 16, 2013, she shared her experience because, she says, "I felt that there are so many couples that go through that and it was a big part of my story." Oprah's response is telling and suggestive. She provocatively frames a question about whether Beyoncé lived in fear of another miscarriage during her pregnancy with daughter, Blue Ivy: "And when you were dancing on stage and doing all the [Winfrey gesturing by thrusting her head from side to side, before the camera cuts to footage of the performer onstage] were you afraid?" Juxtaposing Knowles's admission of a miscarriage with video footage of her high-energy performances (first writhing on her stomach, knees spread and head thrusting vigorously back and forth toward the floor, and then in a wide stance, suggestively licking her thumb before gyrating wildly), Winfrey lets the end of her loaded question hang in the air expectantly. Posed in conjunction with the videotape, the question intimates that Sasha Fierce's bad girl body rolls were not conducive to carrying a child to term—a suggestion that by extension blames Beyoncé's career for her miscarriage. Beyoncé responds saying, "I was afraid, but my doctor told me that I was completely healthy and don't be crazy and paranoid and to live my life." Here, the married lady and "good mother," Beyoncé, has to rationalize the role the freak/Sasha Fierce might have played in jeopardizing the performer's chances at motherhood.

Significantly, during the interview, both Knowles and Winfrey pivot from the singer's reference to *couples who go through that*" to Beyoncé's individual maternal role, thereby reinforcing the presumption that it is the woman who ultimately holds responsibility for pregnancy and childbirth. This last insight would find complexity, however, when, on *4:44*, Jay-Z seems to take responsibility, rapping, "I apologize for all the stillborns / Cuz I wasn't present / Your body wouldn't accept it."[12] Oprah's interpretative lens and her role as interlocutor for the American public frame the entire exchange. And Winfrey's loaded question situates Beyoncé's miscarriage—despite the singer's insistence that her doctor gave her approval to perform—as a cautionary tale against how this particular working mother's career nearly cost her motherhood. The tale's closure in the form of Jay-Z's admission of culpability places further blame on this black family, whose failure to adhere both to the social conventions of patriarchy (by allowing Beyoncé's sexually liberated work beyond the home) and to the rules of monogamous marriage (in the form of Jay-Z's adultery) endangered the pair's chances at parenthood.

Drunk in Love

The couple's "First Family" status has often been recognized in relation to their friendship with former president Barack Obama and first lady Michelle Obama, an association not lost on the 2016 Republican presidential candidate Mike Huckabee, who denounced the Obamas' parenting and Beyoncé and Jay-Z's marriage in one fell swoop, echoing historical practices that from slavery have defined African Americans as unfit parents and delegitimized their marital ties. Huckabee's complaint was that the Obamas, who are routinely celebrated as model parents, allow their daughters to listen to Beyoncé's music and that their close relationship with the singer and her husband expose the former president and first lady as making poor parental choices. Huckabee honed in on the couple's steamy rendition of the song, "Drunk in Love."

On the heels of the Mrs. Carter World Tour, Beyoncé and Jay-Z performed "Drunk in Love," one of the hits from the album on which the tour was based, at the Grammy Awards in January 2014. Huckabee damned the performance with racially coded praise: "[Beyoncé] is a terrific dancer—without the explicit moves best left for the privacy of her bedroom," he opined, adding derisively, "Jay-Z is a very shrewd businessman, but I wonder: Does it occur to him that he is arguably crossing the line from husband to pimp by exploiting his wife as a sex object?" (qtd. in Howard). Huckabee's criticism not only evokes historical images of black women as sexually aberrant; it also (unsuccessfully) translates the couple's union into the oppressive structures of American patriarchy that posit husbands as responsible for their wives and position black women as property.

The duet also raised eyebrows in more liberal circles. Beyoncé's feminist status came under question because she sang along with her husband as he rapped, "I'm Ike Turner [. . .] baby, no I don't play / Now eat the cake, Anna Mae." The line clearly references a depiction of Ike and Tina Turner's marriage in the 1993 biopic *What's Love Got to Do with It*, which portrays Ike's brutal domestic violence against his wife. Along with the troubling "eat the cake" reference, the song also includes a line in which Jay-Z boasts, "Catch a charge I might / beat the box up like Mike" (a reference to rough sex and to convicted rapist and boxer Mike Tyson). I have suggested elsewhere that these references, and Beyoncé's act of singing along with the "eat the cake" line, complicate her identification as a feminist ("Black"). It is significant that both references evoke celebrity black marriage gone awry. The unions of iconic R&B duo Ike and Tina Turner and the boxing legend Mike Tyson and actress Robin Givens were notoriously tainted by the husbands' domestic violence, with both marriages ending with revelations of deeply disturbing abuse, high profile legal disputes, and divorce.

The "Drunk in Love" performance straddles the uncomfortable line between black marriages marked by domestic violence and a rare and poignant display of love between two black, married consenting adults—as Brittney Cooper interpreted the song's video in her defense of Beyoncé's feminist status ("Beyoncé"). The audience reaction immediately after the performance exposes a public appetite that paradoxically frames the pair as simultaneously aberrant and ordinary. As Beyoncé and Jay-Z end their duet and exit in a tight embrace, the camera shifts to show, in close succession, musical celebrities—including white soul singer Robin Thicke and his then-wife, the African American actress Paula Patton, the then married country music singers Blake Shelton and Miranda Lambert, and the pop star Taylor Swift—all leaping to their feet and applauding enthusiastically with awestruck expressions. All of these onlooking stars have had their own high profile divorces or breakups. It is unclear if their amazed expressions are due to the artistry they just witnessed, to what they take to be a touching enactment of marital love, to knowledge of their own troubled partnerships, or all of the above.[13] The threat to "family values," which Huckabee evoked in his critique of Beyoncé and Jay-Z, was later shown to be present even in the marriage of Shelton and Lambert, once country music's "golden couple" (Bromley; Yahr). Therefore, the juxtaposition of these spectators/peers with the "Drunk in Love" performance shatters the glass house of wrongheaded critiques of the performance like Huckabee's, which focus not on the arguably troubling references to the domestic violence, but rather on notions of the twosome as sexually deviant.

Private Matters in Public: The Elevator as Glass Closet

In his groundbreaking book, *Nobody Is Supposed to Know: Black Sexuality on the Down Low*, C. Riley Snorton reformulates Eve Sedgwick's seminal queer studies analytic of the glass closet in order to attend anew to the co-constitutive production of blackness and queerness. Focusing on popular materials including film, television, and gossip blogs, Snorton argues that the down low, although "commonly understood to describe a group of black men's sexual practices, might actually characterize the condition for black sexual representation" (3–4). For Snorton, "Black sexuality then is figured within a 'glass closet,' a space [. . .] marked by hypervisibility and confinement, spectacle and speculation" (4). While his chapter "Rumor Has It" centers on "the seeming inevitability of 'queer' rumors about black celebrities" (127), and although Jay-Z has long been the subject of such rumors,[14] Snorton's insights on the obsession with black sexual identities vis-à-vis rumor has bearing not only on popular understandings of Jay-Z's masculinity but also on how his union with Beyoncé is read and how we might interpret his infamous confrontation with his sister-in-law in an elevator on the night of the 2014 Met Gala.

When it comes to blackness, Snorton argues, the closet does not represent cover in the folds of darkness. "Comparative interpretations of the closet rely on a set of logics that place darkness and enlightenment and concealment and freedom in opposition to one another," he writes. "These logics are put in crisis in the case of blackness, where darkness does not reflect a place from which to escape but a condition of existence. In other words, there can be no elsewhere when darkness is everywhere. In the context of blackness," he concludes, "the closet is not a space of concealment but a site for observation and display" (18). Read through Snorton's analytic, Beyoncé and Jay-Z's staged renditions of their marriage negotiate the seemingly opposing logics of confinement and display. This configuring of the glass closet serves my reading of the leaked video depicting the infamous elevator brawl. The event took place after Beyoncé, Jay-Z, and Solange Knowles had attended the Met Gala ball and then an after party at the Standard Hotel in New York City on May 5, 2014. The three entered an elevator along with a bodyguard. Captured in black and white footage from a bird's-eye surveillance camera, the soundless video reveals a stunning altercation in which Solange lunges at Jay-Z repeatedly, pelting his head with an accessory and kicking him before being pulled away by the bodyguard, only to lunge at him again and again. The entire scene is rendered under the ghostly glow of an overhead light, with the mirrored elevator panels reflecting the group's bodies: Jay-Z clad in a white tuxedo jacket and black bow tie, the bodyguard in a suit, and the two sisters in elegant couture evening dresses. Jay-Z responds by fending off Solange's blows and at one point grabbing her foot, mid-kick. Beyoncé, who has remained relatively still throughout, gradually moves from her position, hands clasped in front of her, close to and almost behind Jay-Z, to stand between the fighting in-laws and direct words at her sister, who continues yelling at Jay, even as the large frame of the bodyguard engulfs and restrains the considerably smaller but visibly irate younger Knowles daughter. Throughout the scene, the bodyguard and Jay-Z struggle to control Solange's rage, which is only curbed when, upon finally exiting the elevator, Beyoncé positions herself between Jay-Z and Solange.

The footage—three minutes and thirty-two seconds in duration—was sold to the gossip outlet tmz by a hotel employee, eliciting a firestorm of attention from u.s. and international celebrity news outlets. Coverage included the surveillance footage but also photographs and additional video of the quartet immediately after they exited and regained their composure, Solange with a sullen expression, Jay-Z touching his chin and looking stunned, and Beyoncé wearing a thin, pat smile. TMZ reported that if you watch the video closely, you can see the bodyguard hit the emergency stop switch, on the twelfth floor, "presumably to keep the fight private" ("Jay-Z").

In the hours after the elevator footage was released, reports abounded attempting to explain what triggered Solange's attack. Questions about Solange's mental state and about whether she was drunk, along with rumors about Jay-Z's alleged infidelity, dominated the coverage. Tabloid-style blogs summarized the "top theories" explaining Solange's behavior, which ranged from speculation that she is "a nasty drunk," to conjecture that she lashed out because of Jay's supposedly well-established history of infidelity (Morrissey). On May 15, 2017, three days after the video was released, Beyoncé, Jay-Z, and Solange issued their own statement to the Associate Press that read:

> As a result of the public release of the elevator security footage from Monday May 5th, there has been a great deal of speculation about what triggered the unfortunate incident. But the most important thing is that our family has worked through it. Jay and Solange each assume their share of responsibility for what has occurred. They both acknowledge their role in this private matter that has played out in the public. They both apologized to each other and we have moved forward as a united family. The reports of Solange being intoxicated or displaying erratic behavior throughout the evening are simply false. At the end of the day families have problems and we're no different. We love each other and above all we are family. We've put this behind us and hope everyone else will do the same. (qtd. in Nolan)

Those bent on getting to the bottom of whether Jay-Z's cheating triggered the incident might note that the official statement denounced only the rumors concerning Solange's alleged intoxication and "erratic behavior," neglecting to address Jay's alleged infidelity.[15]

The video footage, the reporting on the incident, and the Knowles-Carter family statement can be read as a striking manifestation of Snorton's concept of the glass closet. What the family had imagined as a site of concealment and privacy was revealed as a locus of observation and display. It is not only black masculinity that is the subject of rumor and speculation but this black family as a whole that is queered in the process. The Solange/Jay-Z/Beyoncé elevator as glass closet is precisely a place where the alleged queerness of black family life can be neither confined nor concealed. The grainy footage has been played and replayed ad infinitum, becoming hypervisible, a spectacle, and the subject of intense speculation. The mirrored paneling on the elevator walls served to reflect, distort, and multiply the contained black bodies, amplifying Solange's rage.

All three members of this high-profile black family emerged from the glass closet of the elevator with their claims to respectability and "normalcy" questioned: Why did Solange behave so violently? What did Jay-Z do to trigger her attack? Why did the diva leave it to her sister to reprimand her husband?[16] Invoking the word *family* or *families* four times in its nine sentences, the Knowles-Carter document is sensitive to the ways in which speculation about the incident painted the involved parties as a dysfunctional kin unit; their response endeavors to reframe the event as "no different" because "families have problems." The disconnect between the no longer behind the scenes real-life footage and the camera-friendly exterior the group feigned upon emerging from the elevator cast further doubt on a family that was already the subject of intense scrutiny, giving rise to additional suspicions that the public had finally seen the kin group as it really is: a unit plagued by violent discord.[17] In spite of the trio's attempts at "moving forward," the elevator scandal would continue to be a subject of speculation and rumor for two years.[18] Reactions to the scandal queer the Knowles-Carter family, recasting their interactions as dysfunctional and marred by violence.

The critical moments I've discussed were brought into stark relief after Beyoncé and Jay-Z released *Lemonade* and *4:44*, respectively. I turn now to how collaborative performances framed around kinship and infidelity come to a head in the two albums. I focus on the following principal issues in *Lemonade*: how Beyoncé employs family in conveying themes of marriage and fidelity and how Jay-Z figures into the album. Reading *4:44* as a response to *Lemonade*, I concentrate on Jay-Z's specific admissions and references to infidelity and marriage and how he, too, employs family in that representation. In reading both texts, I consider the place of black queer culture, asking what labor queerness does.

Lemonade

Lemonade was a smash hit that absorbed popular discourse and solidified, if there were still any doubts, Beyoncé's reputation as *the* most popular contemporary performer. There are, of course, a number of perspectives and entry points from which we might analyze this album: it can be read as a visually stunning homage to Julie Dash's masterpiece, *Daughters of the Dust*; it centers black women's social relationships and makes a statement of solidarity with the Mothers of the Movement;[19] it presents a seamless but complex incorporation of cross-genre musical forms (hip hop, R&B, country, rock, reggae) and African diasporic literary, musical, and religious traditions;[20] and on and on.

Heralded as antiracist political commentary and as a "revolutionary work of black feminism" (Bale), *Lemonade* not only garnered massive sales and industry accolades for Beyoncé, it put to bed any lingering questions about her feminist status. While the public discourse surrounding *Lemonade* is perhaps as varied as the genres the visual album incorporates, much of the popular focus on this impactful work centers on how Beyoncé portrays her marital union with Jay-Z, on her treatment of infidelity, and on the journey to forgiving an adulterous husband. This foregrounding of betrayal or infidelity is in keeping with Beyoncé's first words on *Lemonade*: "You can taste the dishonesty / it's all over your breath as you pass it off so cavalier." From here, the artist frames her work within eleven chapters or stages (which appear as titles on the screen at the start of each segment) that chronicle the evolution of her reactions to marital betrayal: Intuition; Denial; Anger; Apathy; Emptiness; Accountability; Reformation; Forgiveness; Resurrection; Hope; and Redemption. The chapter titles function as stages of revelation and recovery, allowing the viewer to accompany the performer as she grapples with each step in her journey toward repairing her marriage.

In the weeks and months after Beyoncé's surprise April 2016 debut of *Lemonade* on Tidal[21] and its subsequent release on HBO, public commentators focused on the degree to which the visual album was autobiographical. Did Jay-Z really cheat on Beyoncé? Who was the woman Beyoncé refers to as "Becky with the good hair"? What was the state of the couple's marriage at that moment? These questions and public reaction to them illustrated much about how black marriage is viewed in contemporary society. When Beyoncé's legions of black women and LGBTQ fans mobilized on social media in the wake of *Lemonade* and subsequently *4:44*'s release, they responded critically to entrenched notions about the dysfunctionality of black marriage and zeroed in on the ways in which Beyoncé's reputation for overshadowing her husband lays bare long-held stereotypes of black women as emasculating black men. Their responses suggested that *Lemonade* engages wide-ranging questions about how we understand black women, black feminism, and black family life.

In a screening of the visual album accompanied by a panel discussion, I argued that rather than reading *Lemonade* as autobiographic, we might instead read it as an autoethnographic text ("Beyoncé's"). Autoethnographic elements appear in the richly layered visual and lyrical references to African American life in the u.s. South, in the weaving of personal experiences alongside cultural mores that resonate with African American traditions, and with diasporic life ways skillfully depicted not only in Dash's *Daughters of the Dust* but also in Hurston's anthropological, folkloric, and autoethnographic writings. If we read *Lemonade* as an autoethnographic text, we become less preoccupied with getting at the "truth" of the Carter-Knowles marriage and more concerned with how Beyoncé *represents* that marriage and with what popular interpretations of the text have to say about black marriage writ large. While some commentators interpreted Jay-Z's admission of adultery on *4:44* as affirming Beyoncé's story,[22] I am more interested in what these two texts reveal about the construction of black family ties, including queer kinship structures and (un)conventional spousal roles.

A Family Affair

Lemonade incorporates home-video-style actual footage of family events and celebrations, such as Beyoncé and Jay-Z's wedding and his grandmother's ninetieth birthday party. The visual album thus encourages a reading of the text as autobiographical by presenting Beyoncé along with her real-life husband and their first child, Blue Ivy; her father, Mathew Knowles; her mother, Tina Knowles, and second husband, the actor Richard Lawson; and Jay-Z's grandmother, Hattie White, the source of the album's title. (Hattie is featured toward the close of the album, after Beyoncé narrates a lemonade recipe passed down from "grandmother," at a celebration of her ninetieth birthday, saying, "I was served lemons but I made lemonade.") This intertextual inclusion of actual kin and family events positions *Lemonade* as an authentic depiction.[23] However, the film also employs Beyoncé, Jay-Z, and Blue Ivy acting in and/or reenacting scenes that serve the exposition of its eleven chapters/stages. The three blur boundaries between reality and fiction by playing themselves and staged roles. In his role as actor, Jay-Z plays both the repentant adulterer and the loving father and husband. Blue Ivy is both a little girl from the past in pristine antebellum Southern dress and daddy's little girl in the present.

The intertextual weaving of multiple performance devices, including family video footage and acting/reacting, position kin as proto-types—in the sense of ideal examples and as mythic characters of another era (especially in the cases of Blue Ivy and Beyoncé, who appear in elaborate Southern antebellum-era scenes shot at Louisiana's Madewood and Destrehan plantations)—and as foils (especially in the cases of Mathew Knowles and Jay-Z, who stand in contrast to the women in the film in their embodiment of betrayal). In this way, Beyoncé's kin are both idealized and realistic, both embodiments of a reconceived haunting past (recast with a commune of black women replacing any signs of slavery), and resolutely of the here and now. They are at once perfect and deeply flawed.

These flaws surface in the country music–inflected song "Daddy Lessons," which tells the story of a father warning his daughter to arm herself against "trouble" in the form of "men like me." With the refrain, "Oh, my daddy said shoot," and a call to bear arms, the song can be read as a "how-to" on survival for a girl-child besieged by men who, like daddy himself, are trouble. Here, themes of intergenerational betrayal echo the reported family history of infidelity in Beyoncé's real life. Following reports in 2009 that her parents, Tina and Mathew Knowles, were divorcing after twenty-nine years of marriage, gossip outlets published rumors that Mathew had been unfaithful to his wife and had fathered a child with another woman. In the album's opening song, Beyoncé emphasizes intergenerational betrayal when she narrates the following lines, inflected with Warsan Shire's poetry: "Where do you go when you go quiet? / You remind me of my father, a magician / Able to exist in two places at once / In the tradition of men in my blood you come home at 3 am and lie to me / the past and the future merge to meet us here / What luck / What a fucking curse."[24] Infidelity becomes a curse that has plagued the Knowles family for generations. This positioning of Beyoncé's father as an adulterer like her husband and the portrayal of infidelity as a generational malady resurface throughout the text. The featured family members call attention to the broader gender message: Beyoncé and her female kin are depicted as survivors who "spun gold out of this hard life" and "conjured beauty from the things left behind / found healing where it did not live / discovered the antidote in your own kitchen." Infidelity is the disease to which these powerful and resourceful matriarchs find the antidote.

Interestingly enough, both husband and father are subsequently depicted as loving family men, a message emphasized particularly in old home videos of Beyoncé and her dad and in scenes showing Blue Ivy playing with Jay-Z. In "All Night," a song about love conquering all, we see Beyoncé's mother dancing in a close embrace with her second husband. The wives ultimately find solace and the husbands are forgiven and redeemed—or replaced. A series of family scenes underlines the redemption: shots of Jay-Z and Beyoncé kidding around in a photo booth; the couple's wedding video footage, in which the bride places a piece of cake in the groom's mouth and he beckons for a kiss; an intimate moment with Beyoncé in bed, dressed only in bra and panties, her hand cupping a very pregnant belly; a shot of the nuclear family at what looks to be Blue Ivy's first birthday party; and lastly, a scene in which Jay-Z and Blue horse around on the field of the Mercedes-Benz Superdome, their private playground for the filming.

Although laden with overlaps with personal life and replete with shots of the conventional nuclear family, *Lemonade* also represents family in an ethnographically broader sense, reenvisioning kin as inclusively defined. Beyoncé, her female kin (Blue Ivy, her mother, Hattie), and her extended fictive kin of "sisters"—who include notable black women like tennis champion Serena Williams, the actresses Zendaya, Amandla Stenberg, and Quvenzhané Wallis, and the Mothers of the Movement—appear, first, to suggest that their sisterhood transcends romantic love and, second, to empathize with black women's suffering at the loss of their sons to racist and/or police violence. This is an autoethnographic kinship formation that employs black women kinfolk to serve as a moral compass, a political point of mobilization, and an "antidote" to what ails black families.[25] The "Redemption" sequence celebrates diverse couples in documentary-style footage. "All Night" stirringly portrays same-sex and interracial couples in street scenes of everyday life that complement the images of Beyoncé's biological/marital family. In the quotidian street scenes, however, nontraditional couples only share arm's-length visual space with Beyoncé and Jay-Z; neither artist appears within the documentary-style scenes alongside the queer couples.

This portrayal of queer couples, both inclusive in its celebration of their love and distancing in that they are not quite on the same plane as Beyoncé's biological/marital family, gestures toward contradictions in her use of queer culture and limitations in the inclusiveness of her autoethnographic kinship formation. The duo's privilege, both in terms of class—revealed, for example, in having the Mercedes-Benz Superdome all to themselves—and in terms of the entitlements that accompany heterosexual unions, undermines their solidarity claims with queer couples.

The privileges attached to heterosexuality reveal themselves again when we consider Beyoncé's controversial use of queer artists. The hit song "Formation" features samples of gender-nonconforming New Orleans artists Messy Mya and Big Freedia. Beyoncé's sample of Messy Mya, a comedian, rapper, and popular social media personality, reflects her contradictory and complex efforts to pay homage to queer artistry. Now famously immortalized on "Formation," Messy Mya was fatally shot in 2010 at the age of twenty-two, becoming "a symbol of [New Orleans's] murder epidemic" (Andrews). Mya's death should also be understood in the context of the alarmingly high numbers of LGBTQ people who are murdered at the national level. Mya's estate reportedly sued Beyoncé for over $20 billion in royalties and other damages, alleging that the singer utilized the sample without permission (Vargas). Known as the Queen of Bounce, Big Freedia had already enjoyed widespread recognition before collaborating with Beyoncé, including starring in a television reality series. In "Formation," we hear Freedia's booming voice delivering the oft-quoted lines, "I did not come to play with you hos! I came to slay, bitch!" Big Freedia's phrase, "I came to slay," and the term "slaying," which are drawn from queer black culture, have become a catchall of sorts for describing the genre/gender-slaying artistry for which Beyoncé is widely celebrated. In other words, Big Freedia's words have become synonymous with Beyoncé. While Messy Mya's untimely death foreclosed the artist's ability to speak about being sampled on Beyoncé's track, Big Freedia has spoken publicly and positively about being featured. That these two artists, whose Creole-accented voices were recognizable in local New Orleans music scenes and to legions of YouTube viewers, were catapulted to a global audience was read as both a show of solidarity and, with the lawsuit filed by Messy Mya's estate, as exploitative.

Significantly, as Jennifer DeClue points out, Big Freedia is sonically present but visually absent in the video for "Formation."[26] I follow DeClue in arguing that this visual absence speaks to how "the history of transwomen in feminist circles or within gay and lesbian communities has been fraught with exclusion and contested admission."[27] For DeClue, it is Big Freedia's "gender queerness, with all the resistance to fixity and perpetual liminality that it produces" that influences Beyoncé's choice to "foreclose on the visual representation of Big Freedia." DeClue insightfully links this erasure to the social violence evidenced in the widespread murders of trans people, arguing, "[T]he violence of erasure, the refusal of visibility, the pain of a contingent inclusion in black feminist world making is actively being produced [in 'Formation]." Messy Mya and Big Freedia's samples, the visuals in "All Night," and the album as a whole position Beyoncé's auto-ethnographic kinship formation as dependent on queer sexuality. Yet, her visual erasure of Big Freedia connotes that while queer voices and queer culture enliven *Lemonade*, Beyoncé has been unable to reconcile gender-nonconforming bodies either within the visualization of her feminist text or within her autoethnographic kinship formation.[28] This absence exposes the limitations of her conceptualization of kin as not confined to blood or marital relations, but rather, as organized around black feminist alliances. By excluding gender-nonconforming bodies, *Lemonade* not only erases the visual presence of artists like Big Freedia and Messy Mya; it also marginalizes queer agents who have been key to the intersectional theory and praxis of black feminism.

While Big Freedia is not granted screen time, *Lemonade*'s gaze privileges symbols of heterosexual marriage such as the bride and groom, the wedding cake, and, notably, the ring. As previously noted, Beyoncé's deployment of a second critical "ring moment" has her angrily removing a gold band from her left hand and tossing it as a "final warning" to her husband. And in the song "Sorry," she offers the spoken lines: "Looking at my watch, he shoulda been home by now / Today I regret the night I put that ring on." The ring emerges, then, as a crucial symbol both of the Knowles-Carter union and of Beyoncé's option to sever it. Also in "Sorry," Beyoncé refers to separating from her husband, adding, "Me and my baby we gon be alright / We gon' live a good life." "Sorry's" tossing aside of the ring, alongside allusions to striking out on her own with her infant daughter position Beyoncé as a woman who was ready to walk away. In the section titled, "Reformation," however, the ring toss is literally reversed: the shot is rewound so that Beyoncé now appears to be catching the ring rather than removing it and throwing it away.[29]

Beyoncé's back-and-forth tossing and reclaiming of the ring demonstrates ambivalence about her marriage and emphasizes tensions between adhering to the nuclear family and replacing it with an autoethnographic kinship formation. Soon after she reclaims the ring, Jay-Z enters as the repentant husband in the song "Sandcastles," whose title alone equates the relationship with ephemerality. We are made to understand that Beyoncé had left him but ultimately forgave him, breaking "the curse" of infidelity and making lemonade out of the lemons she was served. The contrite face her husband wears would find further exposition in his album, *4:44*. Before turning to that text, however, it is important to underscore that by incorporating her female fictive kin and the Mothers of the Movement in "Redemption," the sequence immediately following "Forgiveness," Beyoncé signals that although she may have been speaking of finding a "remedy" in reconciliation with her husband, the embodiment of that remedy rests also in a communal settlement of mourners, farmers, and artists who are women and in a synchronized army of women dancers moving as one in "Formation." Both the stage production in "Freedom" and the unified dancers in "Formation" delineate an autoethnographic kinship formation that is imagined not within the confines of the marital bond, but rather in a sisterhood of black women.

4:44: "I Apologize"

By the time Jay-Z dropped *4:44*, *Lemonade*'s position as a tour de force that powerfully centered black women's experiences even in the context of heterosexual relationships had been well established. *4:44* emerges, then, as a response to a marital battle that Beyoncé had arguably won by outing her husband's bad behavior. Although his producer insisted that Jay-Z's album, released on June 30, 2017 (one year and two months after *Lemonade*), was not a "response album" (Coscarelli, "Man"), cultural critics and fans largely saw it as such.[30] For my purposes, *4:44* is rightfully read as a rap battle response album in the convention of the genre,[31] but with a significant departure: Jay-Z may be singular in rap history as the male emcee who has *admitted defeat* in a response record, and to a woman at that. Beyoncé slays and Jay repents. The opening track, "Kill Jay Z," acknowledges his own murder/suicide and shifts between speaking about himself in the second and third person. He recalls the elevator scandal admitting, "You egged Solange on / Knowin' all along all you had to say was you were wrong." Here, the rapper also confirms that because of his infidelity, he almost lost his wife: "You almost went Eric Benét / Let the baddest girl in the world get away / I don't know what else to say / Nigga, never go Eric Benét!" The reference to Halle Berry's ex-husband, whose notorious cheating and sex addiction led to the couple's divorce, not only positions Jay-Z as an adulterer but also situates him as unworthy of his gorgeous wife. While Berry's celebrity status only increased after the split, the far less successful Benét is popularly regarded as "a punchline for ruining his relationship with one of the most beautiful women in the world" (Yuscavage).

In five key tracks on his album, "Kill Jay Z," "Smile," "4:44," "Family Feud," and "Legacy," Jay-Z revisits the themes of kinship, marriage, betrayal, and infidelity so brilliantly delineated in *Lemonade*. However, where *Lemonade*'s autoethnographic kinship formation connects personal loss with an attempt to unify a broader sisterhood of black women and queer allies, *4:44* remains introspective in its conceptualization of accountability and couches its more expansive familial and sociopolitical lessons around the transfer of patriarchal wealth and the racialized politics of class mobility and financial security. Personal culpability and self-deprecation abound in *4:44*, but these mea culpa decrees are rationalized in allusions to the rapper's own absentee father. In "Kill Jay Z," he raps, "You'll never be enough [. . .] / Fuck Jay-Z [. . .] you gotta do better, boy, you owe it to Blue / You had no father, you had the armor." In the title song, the emcee also corroborates Beyoncé's portrayal of intergenerational male betrayal with lines such as "Like the men before me, I cut off my nose to spite my face."

    4:44 is a concession to guilt: the title track offers an unfiltered apology, "Look, I apologize, often womanize / Took for my child to be born, to see through a woman's eyes / Took for these natural twins to believe in miracles / Took me too long for this song, I don't deserve you / I harassed you out in Paris." Jay-Z presents himself as a man who came dangerously close to having lost his wife and his children in the name of pursuing other women. The searing depiction not only unmasks his near destruction of the family bond but effectively queers the pair's idealized "First Couple" reputation by confirming rumors of infidelity, marital discord, and (perhaps) multiple miscarriages, offering a glass closet spotlight under which they might have been destined, as he raps on *4:44*'s eponymous track, to "cry and die alone in these mansions."

The Glass Closet Revisited

    4:44 engages queerness in multiple ways, not only in the sense that it renders Jay-Z's marriage as "deviant" but also by featuring a personal narrative from the rapper's lesbian mother. The confessional framework extends beyond Jay-Z's individual struggles with preserving a monogamous marriage to include his mother Gloria Carter's voice on the song "Smile." Following in the footsteps of *Lemonade*, another Carter matriarch contributes to the artistic production, bringing the couple's rendition of powerful women who "spun gold out of this hard life" full circle. However, Jay-Z's collaboration with Gloria serves the dual purpose of bringing both mother and son out of the glass closet. One might argue that, in fact, it is the son rather than the mother who figuratively comes out in the song. When I discussed the lyrics with an emcee who has been active in hip-hop music and culture for over two decades, she proclaimed, "But we already knew his mother was gay!" Although rumors of his mother's sexual identity had indeed been circulating for years,[32] Jay-Z finally puts them to rest, in the first verse of "Smile":

> *Mama had four kids, but she's a lesbian*
> *Had to pretend so long that she's a thespian*
> *Had to hide in the closet, so she medicate*
> *Society shame and the pain too much to take*
> *Cried tears of joy when you fell in love*
> *Don't matter to me if it's him or her*
> *I just wanna see you smile through all the hate.*

The emcee flanks this stanza unveiling his mother's lesbian identity with rap verses proclaiming his success at his craft and basking in the acquisition of immense wealth: "I mastered my aesthetics / I know you often heard me wax poetic 'bout bein' in the Lexus / But trust me, that was nothin' a nigga up in the hundreds of millions, I have no ceilings." Such lyrics leave the listener questioning if this is a song about coming out or another in a long line of hip-hop boast tracks designed to remind us that "HOV" is king of the rap game.

When Gloria Carter's voice is finally heard at the close of the song, it is in a stirring monologue:

> *Living in the shadow*
> *Can you imagine what kind of life it is to live?*
> *In the shadows people see you as happy and free*
> *Because that's what you want them to see*
> *Living two lives, happy, but not free*
> *You live in the shadows for fear of someone hurting your family or*
> *the person you love.*

The monologue recalls Snorton's generative insights that the "case of blackness" disrupts understandings of the closet as dependent on the oppositional positioning of darkness and enlightenment, concealment and freedom (18). Indeed, Gloria Carter's verse underscores the fact that as a black lesbian, her closet only provided the illusion of freedom under the dark, constricting cloak of the shadows. These shadows are, as Snorton suggests, contradictory in that they are immersed in darkness, yet simultaneously transparent and revealing. Moreover, her verse puts her son's lyrics in sharper relief, suggesting that his braggadocio as a child of the Projects who bested his competitors and an industry out to exploit him actually provides shoddy cover for a man who was/is only seen as happy "because that's what you want them to see." And although Jay-Z has creatively restructured the "mama song,"[33] "Smile" also suggests that Gloria's narrative was employed to present her son as stepping out of darkness and into enlightenment. The implication is that Jay-Z is not who we thought he was because a lesbian mother was among his family secrets and that this secret has given him a particular vantage point, elevating him above the overt masculinity and bravado of hip hop. It is no coincidence that the very next track after "Smile," "Caught Their Eyes," also features an openly gay artist, Frank Ocean. In this way Jay-Z punctuates his reliance on queer culture.

The Breadwinning Wife and Black Family Formations

Just as Jay-Z envelops his mother's coming-out narrative in "Smile" within an evocation of his status as a self-made man, in the song "Family Feud" he similarly situates his role as husband and father within the context of his fortune. The recurring tenor is a message about racialized class mobility and the intergenerational transfer of wealth. In 2016, *Forbes* magazine ranked Beyoncé and Jay-Z the world's highest-paid celebrity couple. On its annual hundred top-earning celebrities list, the magazine placed Beyoncé individually at number thirty-four (she reportedly earned $54 million), with Jay-Z coming in after her at number thirty-six (with reported earnings of $53.5 million). Although Beyoncé reportedly only outearned Jay-Z by a slight margin, gossip around the couple's earnings "assume[d] that Bey would easily out-earn her husband given how dormant he's been on the music scene" (Johnson).[34] The popular assumption that his wife was outearning him puts Jay-Z's preoccupation with finances in a particular light. A tension between conventional marital roles and Beyoncé's success at accumulating immense wealth runs throughout "Family Feud." Jay-Z boasts, "What's better than one billionaire? Two," with Beyoncé chiming in to repeat, "Two." Still, elements of the song rely on conventional tropes of the male breadwinner, with the rapper at times relegating his spouse to homebound conceptions of the wife: "My wife in the crib feedin' the kids liquid gold." These tensions speak to the long-standing contradictory gender roles of black marriage; like Beyoncé, black wives have always nurtured their children *and* contributed to the household in the form of labor beyond the home.

The link that Jay-Z makes between infidelity and wealth as related themes informing the public image of his marriage touches on oppressive sociological processes that have tested black marital relationships and on racialized discourses that have demonized them. American adults widely regard infidelity as morally wrong, yet according to the statistical research that sociologist Christin L. Munsch cites, cheating is widespread (20 to 25 percent of married men, and 10 to 15 percent of married women surveyed engaged in extramarital sex) and has been linked to "a host of demographic characteristics," including "gender [. . .] race [. . .] and age," "with men, African Americans, and younger adults more likely to engage in infidelity" (469–70). Munsch finds that breadwinning husbands cheat more than breadwinning wives, and although economic dependency increases infidelity in both men and women, there is a greater correlation between dependency and cheating with husbands (469). Put colloquially, Munsch concludes that when it comes to extramarital sex, wives are damned if they do and damned if they don't earn more than their husbands.

The previous research Munsch cites is an essential component of the academic discourse that has long stigmatized black marriage and rendered black families as dysfunctional, a bias Munsch struggles to address, in part, by choosing to focus on "interpersonal dynamics as opposed to demographics" (470). Still, Munsch displays ignorance regarding how Black marriage has historically resided beyond the parameters of her data set. "[W]ives' employment has become common" (471), she writes, a conclusion blind to African American women's history of paid and unpaid labor outside the home. Even in light of recent notable treatments of black marriage (Banks; Hunter), academic analyses have fallen short of conveying the complexities of the particularly pernicious intersection of race, gender, and income in relation to black married couples.

By situating black male infidelity as an intergenerational "curse," *Lemonade* and *4:44* inextricably link extramarital sex to the notion that they have "lacked the tools" (as Jay-Z puts it) to sustain monogamous marriages, suggesting that black women have learned survival strategies to combat this masculine curse. The ways in which Jay-Z's response derives his own "womanizing" from a public housing upbringing divorces infidelity from the interpersonal dynamics Munsch stresses, wedding it instead to a racialized black family that is presented as queer by nature. For her part, Beyoncé asks her husband to hold himself accountable; after all, "Accountability" is one of her chapter titles. She also transcends the constraints of "interpersonal dynamics" by configuring family as a broader autoethnographic kinship formation.

Mama's Baby: Misnaming Beyoncé's Power

Black feminist scholarship has long confronted the sorts of tensions and incongruities at play in Beyoncé and Jay-Z's representations of their family life while also contesting damaging constructions of the black matriarch as "emasculating" the black male (Davis; Collins). Dissecting how deeply troubling logics traceable to slavery have cast the black father as absent and the black family as damaged by a matriarchal structure, Hortense Spillers's seminal essay "Mama's Baby, Papa's Maybe: An American Grammar Book" can be applied to these marital and familial representations. In particular, Spillers's charge that the lineage of slavery divorces African Americans from traditional patrilineal gender orders has special bearing on the two albums in question.

While Beyoncé comes from a middle-class upbringing, financial security (an understatement for the couple's massive fortune) is new to Jay-Z's family, a fact of which he reminds us in "Legacy," *4:44*'s final song: "Generational wealth, that's the key / My parents ain't have shit, so that shift started with me / My mom took her money, she bought me bonds / That's the sweetest thing of all time, uh." Gloria Carter's "sweet" financial gift to her son seems a meager legacy in comparison to the affluence he now stands to pass on to his children. Yet, while the verse ostensibly names Jay-Z as the originator of his family's wealth, his mother's gifts to him extend well beyond the bonds. Tellingly, the rapper's legal surname, Carter, is taken from his mother, not his father, who was named Adnis Reeves.[35] The song unfolds with Jay-Z charting a transfer of riches that centers the women in his family.

"Legacy" begins with Blue Ivy's voice asking, "Daddy, what's a will?" From here, Jay-Z outlines how he would bequeath his assets to family members, an act of patriarchal wealth distribution initiated from father to daughter, rather than from father to the son. On this song, and throughout the album, the artist's mother, daughter, and wife hold more narrative force than his absentee father. Outlining the logic of the Moynihan Report, Spillers situates her critique by unpacking patriarchal laws of inheritance, noting that traditionally, a "she" could not be designated a bastard because women did not stand to inherit their fathers' wealth (65). Although the Moynihan Report characterizes the black woman as having forced her family into a matriarchal order of inheritance, Spillers counters that the laws of slavery dictated that African Americans inherited names and social standing through the maternal line rather than from the father. She avers, "This stunning reversal of the castration thematic, displacing the Name and the Law of the Father to the territory of the Mother and Daughter, becomes an aspect of the African-American female's misnaming" (66). Having taken his mother's surname, Jay-Z goes on to center his mother, daughter, and wife in the blueprint for his legacy, in effect "misnaming" them rather than following a traditional lineage from father to son.

We must read "Legacy" not only alongside Jay-Z's rejection of his patrilineage but also as a response to the public characterization of his marriage, a treatment that hitches the pair to the very tropes of absentee father and emasculating matriarch. And while Spillers maintains that power can be found in the ungendering of African Americans that stems from these tropes, the couple's representation of their family life has, at times, been entrapped by the very logics against which Spillers writes. An example can be found in remarks Beyoncé made after the birth of Blue Ivy about her previous miscarriage. In *Life Is but a Dream*, the singer responds to rumors that Blue Ivy was born through the use of a gestational surrogate:

> *It's a stupid rumour. It's actually the most ridiculous rumour I think I've ever heard about me [. . .] to think I would be that vain [. . .]. I respect mothers and women so much and to be able to experience bringing a child into this world, if you're lucky and fortunate enough to experience that. I would never, ever take that for granted. It's the most powerful thing you can ever do in your life, especially after losing a child, the pain and trauma from that just makes it mean so much to get an opportunity to bring life into this world. (qtd. in Wilford)*

Notwithstanding the ways in which the above statement denies Single Ladies and other child-free or childless women access to "the most powerful thing you can ever do,"[36] subjecting it to Spillers's insistence that for black women, giving birth, historically, has not been equivalent to motherhood illustrates how the statement "misnames" the power of the female (66). For Spillers, African American slave women could not claim motherhood, subjecting the black family to a shadowy Law of the Mother and of the Father that was deemed pathological:

> *It seems clear, however, that "Family," as we practice and understand it "in the West"—the vertical transfer of a bloodline, of a patronymic, of titles and entitlements, of real estate and the prerogatives of "cold cash," from fathers to sons and in the*

supposedly free exchange of affectional ties between a male and a female of his choice—becomes the mythically revered privilege of a free and freed community. (74)

Put into this context, Beyoncé and Jay-Z are performing a fraught and precarious marital prototype. While in her autoethnographic kinship formation Beyoncé conjures family in a non-Western, African diasporic configuration, her husband grapples both with his contradictory denial of patrilineal name/Father Law and with his commitment to passing on patriarchal wealth in the forms of real estate and "cold cash." Amid these acrobatic renditions of kinship and marriage, both artists also point to queer family configurations. Still, it becomes clear that Jay-Z, too, falls into the trap of misnaming female power when he couches his apology for infidelity and "womaniz[ing]" as dependent on Beyoncé's ability to give birth: "Took for my child to be born, see through a woman's eyes / Took for these natural twins to believe in miracles / Took me too long to write this song, I don't deserve you." Therefore, Beyoncé has had to execute a miraculous achievement: that of overcoming miscarriage(s) to give birth to three babies over the span of two pregnancies, all while saving her marriage *and* flawlessly slaying her way, in one show-stopping performance after another, to the status of "our greatest living artist" (Raiss). Is this what one has to do to become the hardest working (black) woman in show business? We are left understanding that both Beyoncé's "power" and her husband's accountability are seated in her ability to give birth—not just to Blue Ivy, but to *twins*!—a flagrant misnaming that, as Spillers suggests, is part and parcel of what continues to dog the black family.

ONEKA LABENNETT is an associate professor of Africana studies at Cornell University. Her publications include *Racial Formation in the Twenty-First Century*, coedited with Daniel Martinez HoSang and Laura Pulido (University of California Press, 2012) and *She's Mad Real: Popular Culture and West Indian Girls in Brooklyn* (New York University Press, 2011). She is currently working on two manuscripts, "Guyanese Girl: Centering Guyana through Autoethnography" and "Daughters of the Diaspora: Reading, Writing, and Rhythm."

Notes

1   Black Twitter is a vast social network of primarily African American Twitter users whose virtual community of coordinated interactions has frequently resulted in trending topics that influence sociopolitical change.

2   I use *queer* in a number of senses, notably, to refer to the queer sexualities and solidarities upon which both Beyoncé and Jay-Z (to a lesser and more recent extent) have drawn in their performances and to analyze how their union resists heteronormative social

constructions that must be understood as racialized. Here, I follow Siobhan Somerville who, in defining *queer*, quotes Cathy Cohen to argue that heteronormativity is a racialized concept because "[racially] marginal group members, lacking power and privilege although engaged in heterosexual behavior, have often found themselves defined as outside the norms and values of the dominant society" (Somerville 206). And although Beyoncé and Jay-Z wield considerable power and privilege, the intersection of race, gender, sexuality, and class in the ways their union is represented and understood helps to expose what queer of color critique scholars have suggested about how "African American culture indexes a social heterogeneity that oversteps the boundaries of gender propriety and sexual normativity," while also underscoring what such scholars have identified as the co-constitutive production of racialized and sexualized social formations and the production of liberal capitalism (Ferguson 2).

3   My conceptualization also builds on Michael Omi and Howard Winant's seminal notion of racial formation and on their related concept of "racial project."

4   Of course, my argument engages some of the interventions of Carol Stack's landmark book, *All Our Kin: Strategies for Survival in a Black Community*. I hope to show, however, that rather than framing Beyoncé's autoethnographic kinship formation as a "survival strategy," I am situating it as an epistemological construct that challenges the very definitions of the black family.

5   *Dust Tracks on a Road* resisted truthful self-representation, prompting scholars such as Gates and Appiah to call it an

"anthropology of the self" rather than a traditional autobiography (242). For an analysis of autoethnography in *Dust Tracks on a Road* and in other works by Hurston, see Visweswaran.

6   A close reading of the growing body of scholarship on Beyoncé's work is beyond the scope of this paper. I single out Durham's research as a particularly generative example and as a jumping off point for my own analysis.

7   This article cannot exhaust all of the instances relevant to reading infidelity and kinship in Beyoncé's work, even as they relate to "ring moments." Other examples include her 2013 song "Ring Off," which includes a voice sample from her mother, Tina Knowles, and can be read as an affirmation of Tina's decision to divorce Beyoncé's father after allegations of infidelity. That so many references to removing wedding bands proliferate across Beyoncé's recordings only supports my emphasis on the centrality of "ring moments."

8   In 2009 a number of online sources reported that Jay-Z also legally changed his name to Shawn Knowles-Carter. Citing a "source" quoted in the *Daily Star*, the popular online women's magazine *Bustle* noted that no "legitimate" news outlets substantiated the rumored name change (Martin). For my purposes, it is important to note that while numerous pseudonyms exist for Jay-Z, Shawn Knowles-Carter does not emerge as common nomenclature for the rapper.

9   Beyoncé self-identified as a feminist when she quoted novelist Chimamanda Ngozi Adichie's TED talk, "We Should All Be Feminists" in her 2013 hit song "Flawless." The "ongoing debate of 'Beyoncé-as-feminist'" about which Harris

wrote referred to popular and academic dialogues that sought to reconcile the performer's evolving identification as a feminist with what some saw as artistic choices that either hypersexualized women or, as in the case of calling herself "Mrs. Carter," demonstrated a retrograde positioning of herself vis-à-vis her husband. The boiling point of this debate came when, in a panel discussion that went viral, the renowned black feminist scholar and activist bell hooks argued that Beyoncé was a "terrorist" rather than a feminist (hooks et al.). Hooks lodged her "terrorist" allegation in relation to the artist's appearance in her underwear on the cover of *Time* magazine and its potential impact on young girls. While a recap of this debate is beyond the scope of this paper, it is critical to note that the author and trans activist Janet Mock, who was also a member of the panel, disagreed with hooks and maintained that she had identified with and found strength in Beyoncé's early work, which was formative in her own sexual identity formation. The debate and the numerous thought pieces that emerged from it illustrate the degree to which Beyoncé is a lightning rod for articulating questions around feminism. See arguments within the debate in Coker; and Cooper, "Beyoncé."

10 The promotional materials, costuming, and visual aesthetic of the Mrs. Carter World Tour drew from European aristocrats such as Queen Elizabeth and Marie Antoinette, with Beyoncé appearing on the poster decked out in jewels, a tilted crown atop a Victorian updo, and a royal sash, while holding a bejeweled scepter. Although the performer retained her signature body suit—albeit heavily corseted—the apparent visual message was that "Mrs. Carter" embodied royalty and respectability.

11 The couple's alleged "lack of chemistry" surfaced repeatedly in online discussions of the tour, with rumors swirling about an imminent split amid speculations that not only was Jay-Z having multiple affairs but also that the marriage was being preserved strictly as a business venture. *Bustle* offered the headline "Jay Z & Beyoncé's Lack of Onstage Chemistry Could Be Another Reason to Worry—Except It's Not" (Griffiths), the *Los Angeles Times* published "Amid Split Rumors, Beyonce Says On the Run Was 'Best Tour of My Life'" (Saad), while *Us Weekly* offered "Beyoncé and Jay Z Were 'All Business' during Final On the Run Tour Show in U.S.: Diva Changes Lyrics to 'Resentment' Again," referring to an "eyewitness" account of Beyoncé altering the original words to her song "Resentment" from "Been ridin' with you for six years" to "twelve years," the actual duration of her relationship with Jay-Z (Lee).

12 It is difficult to reconcile Jay-Z's plural references to "stillborns" with Beyoncé's admission of only one miscarriage. Getting to the truth of how many miscarriages she suffered is, of course, beyond this paper's purview.

13 Consider that Thicke and Patton filed for divorce in October of the same year, with reports of Patton alleging that her husband had physically abused and cheated on her amid a legal battle for custody of their young son. Shelton and Lambert's marriage also ended in July of the following year after widespread rumors that both of them had committed adultery. And, although unmarried, Swift has built her career on break-up songs chronicling the demise of her numerous real-life romantic relationships (Spanos). The broken marriages, domestic discord, and relationship problems evidenced

in the lives of this audience reveal, of course, that marital dysfunction and public displays of sexual desire are not exclusive to black celebrity couples.

14   Snorton discusses rumors dating back to 2007 that Jay-Z was attracted to transgender people and had a long-term relationship with the professional football player Larry Johnson. These rumors indicate that the speculations about cheating that surfaced during the On the Run tour had, in fact, been circulating even before the couple wed in 2008 (143).

15   The choice to contest only the damaging rumors about Solange can also be read as an attempt to protect her then burgeoning career as a singer in her own right. Solange, already known as a model and performer, would later emerge as an acclaimed singer/songwriter. Her own divorce at the age of twenty-one predated her rise to commercial success.

16   The black online gossip site *Bossip* described Beyoncé's reaction as "just standing in a corner looking like a robot" ("Solange").

17   Public commentary has sometimes suggested that leaked gossip about discord in the family and in the marriage were actually public relations stunts designed to increase ticket sales and attract fan interest (Gibson). Solange and Beyoncé's father (and the latter's former manager), Mathew Knowles, has intimated much the same about the elevator scandal, in particular. If we consider that the couple pushed the boundaries of respectability and liberal sensitivities by referencing famous examples of black men who abused their wives in the "Drunk in Love" Grammy performance and then four months later, the elevator scandal broke and the outlaw-themed On the Run Tour

was launched, it is not unreasonable to see the unfolding of these events as carefully staged performances designed for the purpose of creating buzz around the tour. Still, considering the embarrassment the elevator scandal evoked destabilizes this reasoning.

18   An April 2016 post on *Bossip* argued that "the elevator moment was a tipping point" for Beyoncé and quotes a "source close to the couple" as saying, "The fact everything became so public, it was embarrassing, and the first time she had to really deal with some of the questions people were asking about her marriage. It changed things. It was a pivotal moment" ("Truth"). For her part, Beyoncé eventually explained the incident as indicative of the pressures of being super wealthy with the following lyric delivered in a remix to the song "Flawless": "We escalate, up this bitch like elevators / Of course sometimes shit go down, when it's a billion dollars on an elevator" (qtd. in Alexis).

19   Mothers of the Movement refers to a politically active group of black women who have lost children to police and/or gun violence and includes the mothers of Eric Garner, Trayvon Martin, and Michael Brown.

20   These include the work of British poet Warsan Shire, who was born in Kenya to Somali parents; appearances by French-Cuban twin sisters Naomi and Lisa-Kaindé Diaz of the group Ibeyi; and the Yoruba-inspired body paint of Nigerian artist Laolu Senbanjo.

21   Tidal is a subscription-based music streaming site, for which Jay-Z is credited as primary owner with a number of other artists, including Beyoncé, listed as co-owners.

22   Making the case that "[w]hen Jay-Z admitted that he did everything Beyoncé said he did, he affirmed that she was neither crazy nor delusional," Brittney Cooper's insightful essay on the rapper's apology makes the critical claim that his accountability for wronging his wife and other black women is a political act ("Jay-Z's").

23   Still, the one family member who remains glaringly absent from the visual text is Solange, a meaningful omission considering the highly publicized elevator scandal. Commentary on Solange's absence ranged from arguing that her influence, especially in the form of Beyoncé's reliance on indie acts to whom Solange has connections, was palpable throughout (Carlin) to speculation that her absence signaled a feud between the sisters (Norwin). We might read Carlin's argument as an extension of my elevator-as-glass-closet interpretation: Solange is relegated to behind-the-scenes labor that fuels her sister's public persona, but that will only be revealed through intense and close scrutiny. Carlin writes: "Take a closer look at the visuals, peruse the credits, and read those lyrics one more time, and you'll see that Solange's presence is felt throughout Beyoncé's most personal album to date." Beyoncé does lyrically reference her sister when she sings, "Take care of your mother / watch out for your sister," in "Daddy Lessons."

24   *Lemonade* credits Shire for "film adaptation and poetry" without specifically referencing individual poems from which the adaptation is drawn. Shire has published chapbooks including *Teaching My Mother How to Give Birth* and *Her Blue Body*, but as Hess notes, "[M]uch of her reputation was built online by publishing on Tumblr and using Twitter like an open notebook." While it is therefore difficult to point to specific publications from which every Shire adaptation is drawn, themes of infidelity and marital betrayal run throughout Shire's work.

25   Here, we should recall Hortense Spillers's arguments in her seminal essay, "Mama's Baby, Papa's Maybe":

We might choose to call this connectedness "family," or "support structure," but that is a rather different case from the moves of a dominant symbolic order, pledged to maintain the supremacy of race. It is that order that forces "family" to modify itself when it does not mean family of the "master," or dominant enclave. It is this rhetorical and symbolic move that declares primacy over any other human social claim, and in that political order of things, "kin," just as gender formation, has no decisive legal or social efficacy. (75)

While I am arguing that these forms of support are socially efficacious, Spillers's point about the oppressive systems that render such kin formations necessary is well taken. I reengage with Spillers's essay in the conclusion to this article.

26   Beyoncé released a stand-alone video for "Formation" before releasing *Lemonade*. Although the song "Formation" is included at the close of *Lemonade*, the video for that song is not part of the film.

27   DeClue argues, "Though Big Freedia does not identify as a trans person and does accept the use of the pronouns *she* and *he*, Big Freedia's gender expression can be understood as queer in that it exceeds and pushes the boundaries of imposed gender norms."

28   Elizabeth Freeman's question in her thoughtful analysis of the queering of kinship theory has relevance here: "Is queer sexuality,

then, always that which escapes
from the kinship grid (or, as Judith
Butler asks in reversed terms, is
kinship always already heterosexual)?" (296).

29   Since the couple has the Roman
     numeral IV tattooed on their ring
     fingers, one could make the case
     that Beyoncé never removed her
     more permanent wedding band.
     I discuss the significance of the
     number four in the following
     footnote.

30   The album's title, of course, speaks
     to its meaning for the couple's
     relationship. The pair has placed
     meaning on the number four,
     noting that their birthdays and
     Beyoncé's mother's birthday are
     on the fourth; they wed on April 4,
     2008, and had the Roman numeral
     IV tattooed on their ring fingers;
     and their daughter Blue Ivy's name
     also signals the number. Jay-Z
     explained the significance of the
     title thus: "4:44 is a song I wrote,
     and it's the crux of the album, just
     right in the middle of the album.
     And I woke up, literally at 4:44 in
     the morning, 4:44 AM, to write the
     song. So it became the title of the
     album and everything. It's the title
     track because it's such a powerful
     song, and I just believe one of the
     best songs I've ever written" (qtd.
     in Setaro and Espinoza).

31   I am speaking of rap battles in
     the tradition of Roxanne Shante's
     "Roxanne's Revenge" single.

32   See, for example, "Gloria Carter's
     Lesbian Life Partner Uncovered."

33   Hip hop's overt masculinity and
     misogyny have long been tem-
     pered by a devotion to mothers.
     See, for example, Gosa.

34   Although prolific during his ear-
     lier career, in which he routinely
     released a new album almost
     every year, starting in about 2009
     Jay-Z slowed down to releasing an
     album every four years.

35   A song titled "Adnis" was one
     of three bonus tracks that Jay-Z
     subsequently released to accom-
     pany *4:44*. Discussion of this song,
     and of footnotes to 4:44, can be
     found in Kennedy. Commentary
     on Jay-Z's representations of his
     estranged father can be found in
     Bristout; and Kennedy. The place-
     ment of "Adnis" as a bonus track
     separate from the *4:44* album and
     only accessible to Tidal subscrib-
     ers situates the text beyond the
     narrative thread of the album
     and supports my argument that
     4:44 positions the rapper's wife,
     mother, and daughter as central
     to his legacy. My treatment does
     not discuss Jay-Z's video material
     related to *4:44* because, unlike
     Lemonade, which was promoted
     as a visual album and meant to
     be viewed and listened to simul-
     taneously, *4:44*'s visual materials
     are more diffuse and therefore
     separable from the audio album.

36   The legions of fans who were
     brought to tears by Beyoncé's 2017
     Grammy performance—in which
     the singer appeared resplendent in a
     gold crown and exposing her belly,
     pregnant with twins, while execut-
     ing a visually stunning rendition
     of material from *Lemonade*—inter-
     preted the pregnant performance as
     still further proof of the performer's
     all-encompassing talent and power.
     Not only can Beyoncé bring twins to
     term, she *slays* while doing so. Art
     historians pointed out the perfor-
     mance's use of African, Hindu and
     Roman goddesses linked to fertility
     (Raiss).

Works Cited   Alexis, Nadeska. "Beyoncé Laughs Off That Billion Dollar Elevator Fight on 'Flawless (Remix)' with Nicki Minaj." *MTV.com* 3 Aug. 2014. http://www.mtv.com/news/1887310/beyonce-flawless-remix-elevator-fight/.

Andrews, Travis M. "Beyoncé Controversially Sampled New Orleans Culture in 'Lemonade.' Now She's Being Sued for It." *Washington Post* 8 Feb. 2017. https://www.washingtonpost.com/news/morning-mix/wp/2017/02/08/beyonce-controversially-sampled-new-orleans-culture-in-Lemonade-now-shes-being-sued-for-it/.

Bale, Miriam. "Beyoncé's 'Lemonade' Is a Revolutionary Work of Black Feminism: Critics Notebook." *Billboard.com* 25 April 2016. https://www.billboard.com/articles/news/7341839/beyonce-lemonade-black-feminism.

Banks, Ralph Richard. *Is Marriage for White People? How the African American Marriage Decline Affects Everyone.* New York: Dutton, 2011.

Beyoncé. "An Interview with Pop Superstar Beyoncé." By Oprah Winfrey. *Oprah's Next Chapter* 16 Feb. 2013. Season 2, episode 22.

——————————. *Lemonade.* Parkwood/Columbia, 2016.

——————————. *Lemonade: The Visual Album.* Dir. Kahlil Joseph, Beyoncé Knowles Carter. Film Adaptation and Poetry Warsan Shire. Good Company, Parkwood Entertainment, 2016.

Beyoncé and Jay-Z, perf. "Drunk in Love." By Beyoncé Knowles et al. 56th Annual Grammy Awards. 24 Jan. 2014. Staples Center, Los Angeles.

Bristout, Ralph. "A Brief History of Jay-Z's Strained Relationship with His Father, as Told through Lyrics." *Revolt*, 20 June 2017. https://revolt.tv/stories/2017/06/20/history-jay-zs-strained-relationship-father-told-lyrics-0600b05e44.

Bromley, Melanie. "Miranda Lambert and Blake Shelton Divorce: Signs Their Marriage May Have Been Doomed from the Start." *ENews* 21 July 2015. http://www.eonline.com/news/678230/miranda-lambert-and-blake-shelton-divorce-signs-their-marriage-may-have-been-doomed-from-the-start.

Carlin, Shannon. "Solange Is All over Beyoncé's 'Lemonade,' Even If You Don't Actually See Her." *Bustle* 28 April 2016. https://www.bustle.com/articles/156951-solange-is-all-over-beyonces-Lemonade-even-if-you-dont-actually-see-her.

Coker, Hillary Crosley. "What bell hooks Really Means When She Calls Beyoncé a 'Terrorist.'" *Jezebel.com* 5 May 2014. https://jezebel.com/what-bell-hooks-really-means-when-she-calls-beyonce-a-t-1573991834.

Collins, Patricia Hill. *Black Feminist Thought: Knowledge, Consciousness, and the Politics of Empowerment.* New York: Routledge, 2000.

Cooper, Brittney. "The Beyoncé Wars: Should She Get to Be a Feminist?" *Salon* 17 Sept. 2013. https://www.salon.com/2013/12/17/a_deeply_personal_beyonce_debate_should_she_get_to_be_a_feminist/.

——————————. "Jay-Z's Apology to Beyoncé Isn't Just Celebrity Gossip—It's a Political Act." *Cosmopolitan* 14 July 2017. http://www.cosmopolitan.com/ entertainment/music/a10307014/jay-z-444-review-beyonce-apology/.

Coscarelli, Joe. "Beyoncé Releases Surprise Album 'Lemonade' after HBO Special." *New York Times* 23 Apr. 2016. https://www.nytimes.com/2016/04/24/arts/music/beyonce-hbo-lemonade .html.

——————. "The Man behind the Music for Jay-Z's Intimate *4:44*." *New York Times* 1 July 2017. https://www.nytimes.com/2017/07/01/arts/music/jay-z-444-no-id-interview.html.

Davis, Angela. "Reflections on the Black Woman's Role in the Community of Slaves." *Black Scholar* 3.4 (1971): 3–15.

DeClue, Jennifer. "To Visualize the Queen Diva!: Toward a Black Feminist Trans Inclusivity in Beyoncé's 'Formation.'" *TSQ: Transgender Studies Quarterly* 4.2 (2017): 219–25.

Durham, Aisha S. *Home with Hip Hop Feminism: Performances in Communication and Culture*. New York: Peter Lang, 2014.

Ferguson, Roderick A. *Aberrations in Black: Toward a Queer of Color Critique*. Minneapolis: U of Minnesota P, 2004.

Freeman, Elizabeth. "Queer Belongings: Kinship Theory and Queer Theory." *A Companion to Lesbian, Gay, Bisexual, Transgender, and Queer Studies*. Ed. George E. Haggerty and Molly McGarry. Malden: Blackwell, 2008. 293–314.

Gates, Henry Louis, Jr., and Kwame Anthony Appiah, eds. *Zora Neale Hurston: Critical Perspectives Past and Present*. New York: Amistad, 1993.

Gibson, Megan. "Beyoncé's Dad Claims Infamous Elevator Fight as a PR Stunt." *Time* 29 Aug. 2014. http://time.com/3221636/beyonce-jay-z-solange-elevator-fight-stunt/.

"Gloria Carter's Lesbian Life Partner Uncovered." *Hollywood Street King* 6 Nov. 2013. https:// hollywoodstreetking.com/jay-zs-got-two-parents-and-a-father-aint-one-gloria-carters -lesbian-life-partner-uncovered/.

Gosa, Travis L. "Mama Tried: Narratives of Good and Bad Mothering in Rap Music." *Mothering in Hip-Hop Culture: Representation and Experience*. Ed. Maki Motapanyane. Bradford: Demeter, 2012. 17–27.

Griffiths, Kadeen. "Jay Z and Beyoncé's Lack of Onstage Chemistry Could Be Another Reason to Worry—Except It's Not." *Bustle* 7 Aug. 2014. https://www.bustle.com/articles/34895-jay-z -beyonces-lack-of-onstage-chemistry-could-be-another-reason-to-worry-except.

Harris, Aisha. "Who Run the World? Husbands?" *Slate* 4 Feb. 2013. http://www.slate.com /blogs/browbeat/2013/02/04/beyonc_s_mrs_carter_show_world_tour_why_use_her_married _name.html.

Hess, Amanda. "Warsan Shire, the Woman Who Gave Poetry to Beyoncé's 'Lemonade.'" *New York Times* 27 Apr. 2016. https://www.nytimes.com/2016/04/28/arts/music/warsan-shire-who -gave-poetry-to-beyonces-lemonade.html.

hooks, bell. *Ain't I a Woman: Black Women and Feminism*. Boston: South End, 1981.

hooks, bell, Janet Mock, Shola Lynch, and Marci Blackman. "Are You Still a Slave? Liberating the Black Female Body." The New School Panel Discussion. New York. 6 May 2014.

Howard, Adam. "Blame It on Beyoncé: Huckabee Slams the Obamas' Parenting Skills." *MSNBC* 13 Jan. 2015. http://www.msnbc.com/msnbc/blame-it-beyonce-huckabee-slams-the-obamas -parenting-skills.

Hunter, Tera W. *Bound in Wedlock: Slave and Free Black Marriage in the Nineteenth Century.* Cambridge, MA: Belknap, 2017.

Jay-Z. *4:44.* No I. D.'s Studio/Roc Nation, 2017.

"Jay Z Physically Attacked by Beyonce's Sister (Video)." *TMZ* 12 May 2014. http://www.tmz.com /2014/05/12/jay-z-solange-fight-elevator-video-beyonce-met-gala/.

Johnson, Tyler. "Beyoncé vs. Jay Z: Who Made More Money in 2016?" *Hollywood Gossip* 30 Nov. 2016. https://www.thehollywoodgossip.com/2016/11/beyonce-vs-jay-z-who-made-more -money-in-2016/.

Kennedy, John. "A History of Jay Z Rapping about His Dad." *Complex Music* 28 June 2017. http:// www.complex.com/music/2017/06/jay-z-rapping-about-his-dad-adnis-history/.

LaBennett, Oneka. "Beyoncé's *Lemonade*: The Aesthetics and Style of Race, Gender, and Politics." Cornell University Cinema, Ithaca. 22 Sept. 2016. Panel Discussion.

——————. "A Black History Month Lesson from Beyoncé and Jay Z." *Huffington Post* 8 Apr. 2014. http://www.huffingtonpost.com/oneka-labennett/a-black-history-month-lesson-from -beyonce-and-jay-z_b_4733404.html.

Lee, Esther. "Beyonce and Jay Z Were 'All Business' during Final On the Run Tour Show in U.S.: Diva Changes Lyrics to 'Resentment' Again." *Us Weekly* 7 Aug. 2014. http://www .usmagazine.com/celebrity-news/news/beyonce-jay-z-all-business-for-last-on-the-run-show -in-us-details-201478.

Martin, Samantha. "Did Jay Z Take Beyonce's Last Name or Is This Simply an Urban Legend?" *Bustle* 7 Aug. 2014. https://www.bustle.com/articles/34229-did-jay-z-take-beyonces-last-name -or-is-this-simply-an-urban-legend.

Morrissey, Tracie Egan. "The Top Theories about Why Solange Attacked Jay Z." *Jezebel* 12 May 2014. http://jezebel.com/the-top-theories-about-why-solange-attacked-jay-z-1575320718.

Munsch, Christin L. "Her Support, His Support: Money, Masculinity, and Marital Infidelity." *American Sociological Review* 80.3 (2015): 469–95.

Nolan, Feeney. "Jay Z, Solange and Beyoncé: 'We Have Moved Forward.'" *Time* 15 May 2014. http://time.com/101940/beyonce-jayz-solange-statement-elevator-incident/.

Norwin, Alyssa. "Solange Knowles Left Out of Beyoncé's 'Lemonade' Thank You Notes: Fight-ing?" *Hollywood Life* 28 Apr. 2016. http://hollywoodlife.com/2016/04/28/solange-knowles -beyonce-fighting-lemonade-thank-you-notes-feud/.

Omi, Michael, and Howard Winant. *Racial Formation in the United States: From the 1960s to the 1980s.* 1986. New York: Routledge, 1994.

Raiss, Liz. "3 Art History Experts Explain Beyoncé's Epic Grammys Performance: Is Beyoncé Our Greatest Living Artist? (Yes)." *MTV* 2 Feb. 2017. http://www.mtv.com/news/2983457/art -history-experts-explain-beyonce/.

Reed-Danahay, Deborah. "Autoethnography." *Oxford Bibliographies: Anthropology* 28 Feb. 2017. http://www.oxfordbibliographies.com/view/document/obo-9780199766567/obo -9780199766567-0162.xml?rskey=ZXzxSV&result=14.

Rogers, Chris. "Beyonce and Jay Z's Marriage: Tour Dancer Says There's 'Hate' on Stage." *Hol-lywood Life* 4 Aug. 2014. http://hollywoodlife.com/2014/08/04/beyonce-jay-z-hate-relationship -marriage-dancer-interview/.

Saad, Nardine. "Amid Split Rumors, Beyonce Says On the Run Was 'Best Tour of My Life.'" *Los Angeles Times* 8 Aug. 2014. http://www.latimes.com/entertainment/gossip/la-et-mg-beyonce -jay-z-on-the-run-tour-best-tour-split-rumors-20140808-story.html.

Setaro, Shawn, and Joshua Espinoza. "What Does Jay Z's '4:44' Album Title Mean?" *Complex Music* 30 June 2017. http://www.complex.com/music/2017/06/what-does-jay-z-444-mean.

Shire, Warsan. *Her Blue Body.* United Kingdom: flipped eye publishing, 2015.

—————————. *Teaching My Mother How to Give Birth.* United Kingdom: mouthpiece series, flipped eye publishing, 2011.

sleep bitch (colleenmacneil). "congratulations to Beyoncé and her husband / Or her husband who's name I forget / The one she made Lemonade about / His name is beyonces husband." 1 Feb. 2017, 3:11 p.m. Tweet.

Snorton, C. Riley. *Nobody Is Supposed to Know: Black Sexuality on the Down Low.* Minneapolis: U of Minnesota P, 2014.

"Solange Attacks Jay-Z in an Elevator (Official Footage)." *Bossip. YouTube* 12 May 2014. https:// www.youtube.com/watch?v=v9J-MHRVCI0.

Somerville, Siobhan B. "Queer." *Keywords for American Cultural Studies.* 2nd ed. Ed. Bruce Burgett and Glenn Hendler. New York: New York UP, 2014. 203–7.

Spanos, Brittany. "Ex-Factor: Taylor Swift's Best Songs about Former Boyfriends." *Rolling Stone* 16 June 2016. http://www.rollingstone.com/music/pictures/ex-factor-taylor-swifts-best -songs-about-former-boyfriends-20160616/picture-to-burn-20160616.

Spillers, Hortense. "Mama's Baby, Papa's Maybe: An American Grammar Book." *Diacritics* 17.2 (1987): 64–81.

Stack, Carol. *All Our Kin: Strategies for Survival in a Black Community.* New York: Basic Books, 1974.

"The Truth about 'Lemonade': How Close Did Bey and Hubby Hov REALLY Get to Divorce?" *Bossip* 26 Apr. 2016. https://bossip.com/1307825/the-truth-about-lemonade-how-close-did-bey -and-hubby-hov-really-get-to-divorce/.

Vargas, Ramon Antonio. "Beyoncé, Whose 'Formation' Included a Messy Mya Cameo, Is Sued by the Late Rapper's Sister." *New Orleans Advocate* 7 Feb. 2017. http://www.theadvocate.com /new_orleans/news/courts/article_cd052468-ed61-11e6-903c-1f6207a05285.html.

Visweswaran, Kamala. *Fictions of Feminist Ethnography.* Minneapolis: U of Minnesota P, 1994.

Wilford, Denette. "Beyoncé's HBO Documentary: Next Stop, World Domination?" *Huffington Post* (blog). 11 Feb. 2013. http://www.huffingtonpost.ca/denette-wilford/beyonce-hbo -documentary-life-is-but-a-dream-review_b_2662956.html.

Yahr, Emily. "Blake Shelton and Miranda Lambert Are Getting a Divorce." *Washington Post* 20 July 2015. https://www.washingtonpost.com/news/arts-and-entertainment/wp/2015/07 /20/blake-shelton-and-miranda-lambert-are-getting-a-divorce/.

Yuscavage, Chris. "Eric Benét Responds to Shot Jay Z Took at Him on '4:44.'" *Complex Music* 30 June 2017. http://www.complex.com/music/2017/06/eric-benet-responds-shot-jay-z-took-444.

Critical Commentary:
Editor's note

Almost twenty years ago, when the fight for marriage equality in the LGBT community was a crazy idea advocated by just a few gay lawyers, I started thinking: Marriage? Why marriage? Why on earth would we want to invite the state to get involved in our relationships when over a dozen states still criminalized homosexuality? Of course I also had a thorough critique of marriage as an institution that had never been very good for women. But more pressing to me was the strangeness of the idea of turning to marriage as part of a larger story of freedom and equality for a group of people that were thought of as deserving the stigma, shame and discrimination they suffered. (Franke, "Note")

Skepticism about the gay community's pursuit of marriage as a sought-after civil right and badge of citizenship led Katherine Franke, the Sulzbacher Professor of Law and Director of the Center for Gender and Sexuality Law at Columbia University, to look to the archives and the

Volume 29, Number 2   DOI 10.1215/10407391-6999830

© 2018 by Brown University and d i f f e r e n c e s : A Journal of Feminist Cultural Studies

historical experiences of another disparaged group—newly emancipated African Americans, who had been denied the legal right to marry before the Civil War—for insight into living within and without this other *peculiar institution.* What her research uncovered, she says, were untold tales of a population who celebrated their newly acquired freedom and entitlement to state-sanctioned matrimony only to find themselves "disciplined through the rules of marriage," forced by law to choose among the many partners they may have had during slavery and often "prosecuted for bigamy, adultery or fornication" when they did not comply fast enough or in a fashion sanctioned by the powers that be.

The fruit of Franke's research, *Wedlocked* deploys this nineteenth-century example of the hidden costs of marriage rights and government intervention as both a case study and a cautionary tale for gays and lesbians involved in the contemporary marriage equality movement. Hailed as a tour de force, Franke's monograph was the subject of an academic panel held at Columbia University in November 2015. Three noted social scientists and legal scholars—Patricia J. Williams, Mignon Moore, and Kendall Thomas—responded to Professor Franke's findings in equally thoughtful, probing, and provocative papers that we are honored to present here, revised and expanded—and, in Thomas's case, rewritten—for this forum.

Works Cited

Franke, Katherine. "A Note about *Wedlocked: The Perils of Marriage Equality.*" *Columbia Law School* website. http://www.law.columbia.edu/media_inquiries/news_events/2015/november2015/franke-wedlocked-book (accessed 29 Mar. 2018).

————. *Wedlocked: The Perils of Marriage Equality, How African Americans and Gays Mistakenly Thought the Right to Marry Would Set Them Free.* New York: New York UP, 2015.

Franke, Katherine, Patricia Williams, Mignon Moore, and Kendall Thomas. Panel Discussion on *Wedlocked: The Perils of Marriage Equality.* Moderated by Marianne Hirsch. Columbia University. 18 Nov. 2015. *C-SPAN.* https://www.c-span.org/video/?400857-1/wedlocked.

Intimacy and the Untouchable: Marriage and the Traumatic History of "In-law" and "Outlaw" Family

*K*atherine Franke's *Wedlocked* is an absorbing and revelatory study about the life circumstances of recently enslaved men and women who aspired to the status benefits of marriage upon emancipation. A central question raised, as per the subtitle, is that of the "perils of marriage equality," or whether the conventionalism of wedlock is a rather vexed marker of morality. Indeed, one of the most remarkable features of these interwoven stories is the culturally malleable line between intimacy and the untouchable.

Other authors in this volume will have discussed whether the institutionalization of marriage among recent ex-slaves carries all the weight one might want to assign it compared to the contemporary LGBTQ quest for marriage equality; therefore, I will narrow my reflections to a much smaller set of observations. I limit my discussion to the ways that marriage among African Americans really did affect—and I mean affect in affective ways—the institution of marriage among whites.

As Franke notes in several of the case histories she examines, the recognition of African American agency was, as ever, slow in coming during the postbellum period. This meant that significant numbers of marriages in

Volume 29, Number 2   DOI 10.1215/10407391-6999844

© 2018 by Brown University and **d i f f e r e n c e s** : **A Journal of Feminist Cultural Studies**

the 1860s were still overseen within the hierarchies of plantation politics. One dimension of that legacy was the power white people frequently had to grant "permission" to marry. This was a kind of intercession that came about most particularly through the civilizing, uplifting, ever-so-self-interested ministrations of the white wives of former owners and recent slaveholders. That white prompting of unions between African Americans to some degree operated like any other social dynamic around the ritual of marriage: it made public an exclusivity of intimacy. To some degree it eliminated the dangerousness, as well as the perversions, of unbounded sexuality. But marriage among African Americans, from the Civil War until the Loving case in 1967, was a double-edged thing: purifying, respectability-making, but also underscoring the dangerous untouchability of sexualized black bodies—particularly when it came to white women.

Marriage in this era and context was a ritual performed against the backdrop of breeding farms, of "mysteriously" light-skinned house servants, and of unnamable acts of incest—all disguised as production of salable inventory rather than as progeniture, to say nothing of primogeniture. Toni Morrison, in her book *The Origin of Others*, describes the meticulous journal-keeping of one Thomas Thistlewood, a slaveholder in the mid-1700s: "Among the intimate marks of his exhaustive note-taking are details of his sexual life on the plantation [. . .]. He noted the time of the encounter, its level of satisfaction, the frequency of the act, and, especially, where it took place. Other than the obvious pleasure were the ease and comfort of control. There was no need for seduction or even conversation—just a mere notation among others about the price of sugarcane or a successful negotiation for flour" (8). Thus, postbellum marriage was a ritual prompted perhaps most particularly, and justified most poignantly, as a way of formally corralling white male control and inhibiting perceptions of the unregulated jouissance of black sex, of sex with black bodies.

So marriage between black men and women is remarkable not only as a manifestation of autonomy, love, property exchange, and full citizenship; it is also noteworthy as a kind of formal genuflection toward the repair of threatened white families. Reading white women's histories of the time, there is something to be said about how, if marriage left African Americans freed but not free, it did something of the same thing for the gender politics of slaveholding families: it had at least as much to do with reinforcing not just the legal but also the moral status of terrified white wives.

Such sexual anxieties have only recently begun to be excavated, from Annette Gordon-Reed's history of Thomas Jefferson's fathering children by his slave Sally Hemings all the way through to the backlash from a recent Cheerios advertisement featuring an adorable little girl urging the heart-healthy benefits of oat cereal to her black father and white mother. (It was a blowback so hateful that Cheerios had to take down its website.)

This is a traumatic history of family "in-law" and of unmarriage-able or "outlaw" family. Even so, the salutary and sanctifying properties of marriage as institutional uplift were applied to a cultural landscape torn, scarred, and upended by the unspeakable. And so marriage operated—continues to operate—in this double sense: as the pathway to salvation but also as a sealant against the leakage of miscegenation.

This affective dimension is accompanied by all the dodges and feints marked in the words we use and don't use when it comes to race and coupling, even to this day. In today's world, the benefit of marriage and the status it confers are very peculiarly configured when it comes to African Americans—not so much when they marry others deemed African American, but very much so particularly when they marry "outside the race" or transgress what is perceived as a racial boundary.

Just think about the use of the word *biracial*. First of all, the term is a biologically incoherent designation, implying that there is such a thing as racial purity—a singular pure white race and a separate pure black race, so that a child born of such a pairing would come out fifty-fifty or "bi." Putting biology aside, however, the term is also flawed as a cultural matter: *biracialism* is used in a way that grants a certain exceptionalism of descent to children born of a modern or contemporary marriage between one parent deemed white and one deemed nonwhite. This is a false hierarchy and is not accorded to those who are "merely" descendants of, or the "products" of, being tossed around in the back of slave cabins. In other words, *biracialism* denotes not children of racially mixed lineage, but only children of recent racially mixed marriages. No matter how light skinned, a child born of two parents, both of whom are descended from slaves and slaveholders, is nearly always referred to as "black" and not *biracial*. Thus, *biracial* confers a seemingly unconscious legitimacy or emphasis on the lineage of the white parent that is not otherwise marked as a historical matter.

This diction was perhaps most noticeable when then-senator Barack Obama first appeared on the national political scene. His being "biracial" marked him as "different," particularly to many white observers. After all, as so many media pundits enthused, he had a white mother and he loved her; thus it was presumed he would never be a nudge about race like Al Sharpton or Jesse Jackson. But, of course, as Obama was normalized over time—and by that I mean, as he was swallowed by older American racial tropes, as he was familiarly stereotyped and made unexceptional—he became just another black man, particularly among those who didn't like him.

In this way, marriage among or with African Americans has an extra burden of operating to simultaneously proclaim and deny the rambunctiousness of our recent lineage. The language by which we assign the benefits of marriage uses racial category to narrow or expand our perception of who is more like whom; it tells us who can be considered marriageable or untouchable. Our habit of burying the relentlessly polyglot nature of our American identity renders us blind to how intimately we are tied as kin, as family, and as intimates.

Consider Essie Mae Washington-Williams, the daughter U.S. Senator Strom Thurmond had by his family's black teenage maid. She lived her life as a "Negro," then as an "African American," and attended an "all-black" college. But in her seventies, when Thurmond's paternity became publicized, she was suddenly redesignated "biracial." Or take Tiger Woods and Kimora Lee Simmons, who are alternatively thought of as African American or biracial but rarely as Asian American.

If this is often unspoken, there is nevertheless something gestural and indicative about the consuming power of African descent and its dangers in American society. This kind of layered signification nods to both desire and taboo—the sight, the smell of black bodies, the aesthetics of beauty and desire. Marriage is only one site where one can track this anxiety; the affective nature of racial boundary and its constructed "perverse" transgressions are all about sympathy and sympathizers and associational contagion.

As Franke describes so eloquently in *Wedlocked*, cruel retribution was rained down on the left-behind wives and children of freed black soldiers who left the plantation and joined the Union army, and it was a retribution that extended not only to them but to any white person deemed sympathetic as well. This was an assault on the emotion of sympathy itself, and its traces endure even now—from the use of the term *nigger lovers* during the Civil Rights Movement to some of the very dehumanizing locutions used to describe the marriage between New York City's white mayor Bill de Blasio and his black wife; to the attacks not just on the football player Colin Kaepernick's kneeling protest but also the bitter denigration of his white mother's marriage to his black father; to the demonizing of those who ally themselves or empathize with the Black Lives Matter movement.

Elizabeth Roudinesco describes perversion thus: "It uses the speech of the subject, but only to mimic the nature from which it has been extirpated so as to parody it all the more. That is why perverse discourse is always based upon a Manicheaism that appears to exclude the dark side to which it owes its existence" (5). This nimbly parodic, eternally reversible tension is what the American history of gender, race, sexuality, and ethnicity so often challenges us to overcome as "perverse." It is a national paradox whose tangled intractability, yet quicksilver plasticity, bedevils all the cases in Franke's wonderful and intriguing book.

PATRICIA J. WILLIAMS is the James L. Dohr Professor of Law at Columbia Law School. A MacArthur fellow from 2000 to 2005, she is one of the foremost legal scholars and critical race theorists in the nation and the author of several important, award-winning books on gender, race, law, and cultural theory, including *The Alchemy of Race and Rights* (Harvard University Press, 1991), *The Rooster's Egg* (Harvard University Press, 1995), *Seeing a Color-Blind Future: The Paradox of Race* (Farrar, Straus and Giroux, 1998), and *Open House: On Family, Food, Piano Lessons, and the Search for a Room of My Own* (Farrar, Straus and Giroux, 2004). She also writes a monthly column in the *Nation*, "Diary of a Mad Law Professor."

Works Cited   Franke, Katherine. *Wedlocked: The Perils of Marriage Equality*. New York: New York UP, 2015.

Morrison, Toni. *The Origin of Others*. Cambridge, MA: Harvard UP, 2017.

Roudinesco, Elizabeth. *Our Dark Side: A History of Perversion*. Trans. David Macey. Malden: Polity, 2009.

Marriage Equality and the African American Case: Intersections of Race and LGBT Sexuality

*A*s has been stated thus far in different ways, Katherine Franke's book, *Wedlocked: The Perils of Marriage Equality: How African Americans and Gays Mistakenly Thought the Right to Marry Would Set Them Free* (2015), looks at the role of marriage in liberation movements for formerly enslaved people and for same-sex couples. It asks what kind of freedom and what kind of equality the capacity to marry mobilizes. The principal argument here is that gaining rights can bring about disadvantages in other ways, particularly when the group in question does not have full equality: "A close look at the history of marriage among African Americans and the newly won rights of same-sex couples illuminates how gaining marriage rights can come at the price of stigmatizing other groups and ways of life on marriage's outside" (207). The book compares the historical case of African Americans and their experience of gaining the right to marry with the contemporary case of marriage equality for lesbians and gay men.

As a family sociologist who focuses on African American households, I was particularly interested in thinking about how the ideas in *Wedlocked* relate to actual people's lives, particularly those of sexual minorities

Volume 29, Number 2 DOI 10.1215/10407391-6999858

who are experiencing the aftereffects of the marriage equality movement. Sociologists like to talk to people, ask questions, and use this "data" as one basis for evaluating information, so I ask: what, if anything, do we gain by using marriage as the platform for reducing the stigma associated with same-sex desire? I would like to consider this question as it relates to a population that stands at the juncture of the two seemingly disparate groups Franke uses in her arguments: sexual minorities who are black. I find that throughout the text, the persistent overlap between the categories of white and gay versus African American and deviant subtly strengthens race and class inequities because each dimension of inequality is lent legitimacy by its alignment with the other. I will respond to some of the arguments in *Wedlocked* by considering the analyses that were not presented—the experiences of African American LGBT people and intraracial relationships among blacks as they relate to the marriage equality campaign.

For the past fifteen years I have been focused on the intersections of race, class, gender, and LGBT sexuality, looking at concepts such as identity, parenthood, race consciousness, racial group commitments, and other aspects of life and meaning-making among black same-gender-loving people. Elsewhere I argue that marriage equality is a public issue that has provided a vehicle through which sexual minorities who also have a membership in a racial, ethnic, or cultural category can develop a conversation about their sexual orientation with family members and others in their communities (Moore, "Articulating"). The use of marriage equality as the platform for LGBT rights has helped move homosexuality from the private sphere, as a behavior that individuals act out in secret and under a cover of shame or as a secondary status, to one that initiates a public openness about who members of these identity groups are as African American people who also have or desire same-sex partners. It has provided a means for lesbians and gay men to have a voice around multiple identity statuses.

One might ask why marriage equality should be the impetus for these discussions and for this move. There are certainly other issues important to sexual minority populations. For example, Wilson et al. discuss the unique challenges faced by LGBT homeless and foster youth. Tilcsik's work on employment discrimination of openly gay men shows the relevance of this issue as it relates to LGBT equality. And access to reliable health care is an important issue, particularly for transgender people and sexual minority elders, as Mayer et al. and Dahlhamer et al. note. So we must ask what if anything is gained by selecting marriage as the site of contestation.

Wedlocked argues that in the minds of larger society, "Marriage has been and largely remains a kind of test that the African American community is seen as failing" (202). In my first reading of the book, I was somewhat put off by this and similar statements argued in its chapters because this type of framing does a disservice to those couples who have and are succeeding at marriage. It ignores the advantages blacks who marry actually gain in society or the special status married people of *any* race or ethnicity receive, and it removes any agency or self-empowerment from African Americans by only presenting the ways some groups pathologize all blacks, regardless of marital status. This was most likely not the intention of the work. I believe the intention was to call awareness to the structural racism that vilifies African Americans, a vilification they cannot elude, despite behavior that might reveal alternative realities.

Nevertheless, the topic of marriage is *particularly* relevant as a point of entry into discussions of LGBT identity and acceptance for African Americans in that it serves as a *physical response* to the stigma that is often associated with the wider range of family structures among blacks: the stereotypes of black men who fail to hold up their responsibilities as fathers and partners and the stereotypes of black women as sexually permissive beings who immorally choose single-motherhood over the stability of a martial union. Weddings in black communities symbolize the attempt of the couple to conform to notions of respectability and show to their families, members of their racial communities, and others in society that they defy the negative stereotypes of black people and of gay people and that they can create and sustain stable families. In *Private Lives, Proper Relations*, Candice Jenkins maintains that intimacy has political significance for African Americans because they possess a particularly complex relationship to the exposure of intimacy. The book reasons that there is a "doubled vulnerability" associated with *black* intimacy as a result of the ways black sexuality has historically been understood in society (5), and this is a central part of the black cultural imaginary. African American attempts at respectability are based in historical tensions and suppressions surrounding black erotic and domestic behavior.

Marriage offers a conventional, and some might say conformist, presentation of self, an antithesis to the images of gay counterculture. But because of the racialized contexts in which same-sex marriage among African Americans is taking place, I contend that it is experienced by those in the community as a radical and transformative act (Moore, "Articulating"). In *Invisible Families* I found that some same-sex couples wed in part to remove the ability of their parents to engage in "don't ask don't tell" with themselves and their partners. By drawing a line in the sand, they are risking rejection and disappointment from parents, adult siblings, or a favorite uncle. A wedding lets the pastor in the church they grew up in know affirmatively that yes, they have taken on this "lifestyle" and are going to openly live with a mate. And many who have a religious wedding service actually want their God to recognize and bless their same-sex union. Anyone who has knowledge of traditional black religious communities can see the radical nature of this supposedly conformist behavior.

I am not trying to take away from the persuasive arguments that *Wedlocked* makes regarding the critical view of marriage as a force in social movements that are about liberation. I am saying that it is precisely *because* marriage holds such an important ideological position in the minds and experiences of so many different identity groups that it is an important and serviceable frontier. The marriage equality movement is functional in a way that is separate from the question of the kind of *equality* the capacity to marry might mobilize.

Wedlocked also critiques contemporary LGBT social movements for the overwhelming "whiteness" that has characterized their political campaigns, particularly during the 2008 political debates around marriage for same-sex couples. But between the 2008 election and the 2015 Supreme Court decision, there was a noticeable shift in the way LGBT organizations tried to "sell" the country on marriage equality. For example, in 2012 I began to follow the Freedom to Marry Campaign, founded by Evan Wolfson, and there I saw a genuine effort to expand the representation of same-sex couples in the public eye. There were images of older couples, couples from the South, Midwest, and Mountain regions of the country, Latina women, African American men, even some conservative religious couples. Through these images the movement recognized and tried to rectify some of its prior mistakes. The photos were used not just by LGBT organizations but by other groups and outlets in support of marriage equality as *Obergefell v. Hodges* moved forward.

Wedlocked argues that marriage for same-sex couples "both reflects and then reproduces a new form of respectability so yearned for in many sectors of the gay community" (201). It says, "Removing the marriage ban removes the 'badge of inferiority' for whites in a way that it does not/cannot do for blacks because of race" (200). While I agree, I also see important class differences in the extent to which blacks experience this disadvantage. In some ways, the argument in *Wedlocked* goes too far when it depicts marriage as only "a site of failure and dysfunction for many African Americans" (198).

Middle- and upper-middle-class African Americans are able to benefit from many of the advantages and legitimacy marriage brings. Their class status grants them certain privileges, and this is true even in religious communities. In my ongoing research on religion and LGBT identity, I interviewed Raheem (pseudonym), an African American gay man who lives in a large southern city with his husband and their two adopted children. He was raised in the conservative Holiness Pentecostal faith. Raheem has a graduate degree and works for a biotech company. His husband Glen is a pastor of a church that keeps traditional Pentecostal beliefs but is welcoming to everyone, including LGBT people. They live in a grand house and together bring in a high six-figure income. When I asked how he and his family were faring in this conservative state in the South, he told me he has experienced only an enormous amount of love and support, even from those who "might not support the [LGBT] community." He said that when he walked around with his daughter in a baby carrier, even when he was with his husband, black people have said to him that rarely have they seen black men so actively involved in raising their young children. They say that is not the norm in their experience with men.

In this example, the comparison group for the racial community has not been a heterosexual couple ("Are the children worse off being raised by gay men instead of a married man and woman?"), but absent black fathers ("Look at these men, they are very present and involved in their children's lives, and that is a good thing. And they appear well off, and isn't that great for the children as well?"). So this is one area where the racial context, and the community's experience around black men in families, sets up a dynamic that may not have been considered in debates and discussions about male couples who marry and raise children.

It was also clear that Raheem's household income was able to "buy" his family out of many of the negative experiences less advantaged African Americans and sexual minorities of different racial backgrounds report. Although *Wedlocked* argues that African Americans have not been able to use marriage to "rebrand blackness in the way that sanitized racist stereotypes," this black gay couple has been able to silence or protect themselves from the harm affiliated by those stereotypes. There are heterosexual black couples similarly situated who have also used income, education, and social status to shield themselves in important ways, however institutional racism rears its head from time to time to interject itself into their lives. I suspect this truth is at the heart of *Wedlocked*'s argument. But the drag of two subordinated statuses based in race and sexual orientation do not seem to affect the lives of advantaged African American sexual minority couples on a daily basis.

What do black LGBT communities say about marriage equality as a vehicle to liberation for sexual minority people? I see two primary responses. In the spring of 2015, I participated on a panel organized by the Columbia University Institute for Research in African American Studies on the relationships African Americans have to organized religion. Darnell Moore shared about his childhood experiences ("No Ashes"). In his family, women generally did not marry. They raised children with the help of their mothers and sisters, and the relationships they had with men were, for different reasons, fleeting or short-term. Many times they were worried about daily acts of survival, like trying to maintain a roof over their heads or protecting their children from dangerous situations. Marriage was not a priority for the women and men in his family, and this has influenced his own lukewarm feelings about marriage. He said there were many other pressing needs that the LGBT populations he works with are focused on, such as obtaining safe places to live, increasing employment opportunities, fostering kind and nurturing relationships.

From his remarks, I suggest that the focus on marriage equality may not be as useful to those who are unpartnered or socioeconomically disadvantaged. So in this sense, *Wedlocked*'s argument is right, even for the intraracial case, in that marriage equality cannot be the only story the movement brings to disenfranchised communities. LGBT leaders have to also show that they care about and realize the importance of other issues those communities are fighting for, what political observer Jasmyne Cannick calls the "bread and butter" issues of black communities: poverty, unemployment, racial profiling, inferior grocery stores, inadequate services.

Other black LGBT leaders have looked beyond the specific example of marriage equality and used it as a tool to promote greater understanding and acceptance intraracially. The dominant concern for these activists is how to maintain and build relationships within the racial community, how to stand proud and openly express a gay identity that is simultaneous with a racial identity. One articulated goal black leaders of the LGBT movement have is for this work to challenge and conquer their own homophobia. In addition to working to change the minds and hearts of the racial group, black LGBT political work is expressly meant to build the group's self-acceptance of their own sexual orientation by destigmatizing and transforming the meaning of gay sexuality (Moore, "Articulating").

I see the potential for marriage among same-sex couples to radicalize marriage because of the lack of sex differences between partners and the greater equality that comes from it. Distinctions in gender presentation that may exist between partners do not translate into the gender inequality a century of sociological literature has found in heterosexual relationships through men's advantages in the labor force and other societal institutions. Simply put, some women may dress in a boyish fashion, but they lack men's *institutional* power and do not assume a hegemonic masculinity. Instead, couples are making decisions on how to lead their lives based on factors other than sex, and the power distribution in these relationships is not based on gender or purely on who has the greater economic resources (Moore, "Gendered"). I see the potential for these relationships to create something different within the state of marriage. I say this even while agreeing with *Wedlock*'s assertion that the institution of marriage "was and still is structured around gender roles and inequalities" (207).

MIGNON R. MOORE is the chair of the department of sociology at Barnard College. She is the author of *Invisible Families: Gay Identities, Relationships, and Motherhood among Black Women* (2011) and numerous scholarly articles on LGBTQ families, LGBTQ people of color, and intersections of race, gender, and sexuality. She has received funding from the National Institutes of Health and National Institute on Aging for her research on sexual minority seniors. Her current book project is a social history of black LGBT older populations, tentatively titled "In the Shadow of Sexuality: Social Histories of African American LGBT Elders."

Works Cited

Dahlhamer, James M., et al. "Barriers to Health Care among Adults Identifying as Sexual Minorities: A U.S. National Study." *American Journal of Public Health* 106.6 (2016): 1116–22.

Franke, Katherine. *Wedlocked: The Perils of Marriage Equality.* New York: New York UP, 2015.

Jenkins, Candice M. *Private Lives, Proper Relations: Regulating Black Intimacy.* Minneapolis: U of Minnesota P, 2007.

Mayer, Kenneth H., et al. "Sexual and Gender Minority Health: What We Know and What Needs to Be Done." *American Journal of Public Health* 98.6 (2008): 989–95.

Moore, Darnell L. *No Ashes in the Fire: Coming of Age Black and Free in America.* New York: Nation, 2018.

Moore, Mignon R. "Articulating a Politics of (Multiple) Identities: Sexuality and Inclusion in Black Community Life." *Du Bois Review: Social Science Research on Race* 7.2 (2010): 1–20.

——————. "Gendered Power Relations among Women: A Study of Household Decision-Making in Lesbian Stepfamilies." *American Sociological Review* 73.2 (2008): 335–56.

——————. *Invisible Families: Gay Identities, Relationships, and Motherhood among Black Women.* Berkeley: U of California P, 2011.

Tilcsik, András. "Pride and Prejudice: Employment Discrimination against Openly Gay Men in the United States." *American Journal of Sociology* 117.2 (2011): 586–626.

Wilson, Bianca D. M., et al. "Sexual and Gender Minority Youth in Los Angeles Foster Care: Assessing Disproportionality and Disparities in Los Angeles." Los Angeles: The Williams Institute, UCLA School of Law, 2014. https://williamsinstitute.law.ucla.edu/wp-content/uploads/LAFYS_report_final-aug-2014.pdf (accessed 23 Mar. 2018).

Is Black Marriage Queer?

*I*n the opening pages of the introduction to *Wedlocked*: *The Perils of Marriage Equality*, Katherine Franke proposes to stage a "queer" encounter between and exploration of "the experiences of freedom of newly emancipated people in the immediate post–Civil War period and [those] of lesbians and gay men today" (7). The goal, writes Franke, is to "better understand how the gay rights movement today has collapsed into a marriage rights movement" and what some of the "costs" of that movement strategy might be by looking back at "an earlier time when marriage rights intersected with the rights of freedom, equality, and dignity" of another "marginalized population: newly emancipated people in the mid-nineteenth century."

My thoughts in these pages on the "queer" potential and possibilities of "black marriage" respond to a provocation in Franke's final introductory paragraph, which announces the "central question" (21) with which *Wedlocked* wrestles. Readers who are familiar with the book may recall that this question is prompted by an observation (which I believe to be entirely correct) that while their successful campaign for marriage rights

Volume 29, Number 2   DOI 10.1215/10407391-6999872

"[elevated] the civil status of gay people" in the United States, the institution of marriage has emphatically not "played the same role" in the lives of Americans of African descent (21). In Franke's blunt terms, "marriage has by and large served as a test" that African Americans have been and "are doomed to fail." "Through these failures," she continues, the "*stain of race*—as much moral as biologized—has been *written and rewritten* on black bodies" (19; my emphasis). For Franke, the central question then becomes: "how does a right to marry help us better understand the stubborn, *even indelible*, nature of racial stigma, particularly when compared with the stigma of being gay?" (21; my emphasis).

Note the shift here in accent and emphasis. Within the course of a few pages, *Wedlocked* moves from its initial stated preoccupation with what the *postbellum* experience of a formerly enslaved and unmarriageable people in the American conjugal order can teach today's gay and lesbian community about "the perils of a politics of equality and freedom made real through marriage rights" (Franke 19) to a very different field of investigation. Inverting the terms and reversing the pedagogical relationship with which it began, this second narrative of marriage in America looks to the lessons we should draw from today's gay and lesbian movement and the success of the "freedom to marry" campaign regarding the history and present pertinence of the "stubborn, even *indelible*" racial "stigma" whose *longue durée* has denied, and continues to deny, African American people the "dignity of self-definition" that allowed lesbian and gay Americans "to redefine what it *means* to be gay" (21; my emphasis).

What accounts for this redefinitional divide? *Wedlocked* offers two separate explanations, each of which gestures in different theoretical directions. The first, more explicit and sustained line of interpretation tells an "economic" story centered on the idea-image of "racial capital." In an intriguing formulation, Franke contends that the divergent fates of lesbigay and black experience in the American conjugal order stem in part from the "social reputation" that the marriage equality and gay and lesbian movements "enjoy as white" (198). Put another way, because the public face of the gay and lesbian marriage equality movement has been imaged and imagined as white, the campaign has benefited from American society's "possessive investment in whiteness" (Lipsitz 2) and the "racial endowment" effects (Franke 13) connected to the reputational asset that Cheryl I. Harris has incisively denominated "whiteness as property" (1713). The racial privileges and dividends of this reputational "capital in whiteness" (Franke 198) are assets that the gay and lesbian marriage movement could put to productive, transformative use. By contrast, the straight African American community has yet to accumulate comparable "sexual capital" from the "social reputation" it "enjoys as heterosexual" (Franke 198). Indeed, argues Franke, "the same-sex marriage movement is itself racialized" in ways that have not only benefited it but also contributed to and reinforced "the ongoing subordination of people of color" of every sexual orientation, while simultaneously diminishing and constraining the sexual and reproductive rights of American women (12).

I cannot possibly do justice to the dense, complexly plaited historical, conceptual, and normative arguments *Wedlocked* advances to support the story it tells about (white) lesbian and gay success and (heterosexual) African American failure. Let me confine myself, then, to a cursory comment or two about the "curious" (Franke 51) assumptive architecture that subtends Franke's account of race, sexuality, "sexual race," and the meanings of "black marriage" in American conjugal politics. My interest is in how and why the book's "queer pairing" (6) of the experiences of formerly enslaved black people in the period after the Civil War and of formerly criminalized gay men and lesbians after marriage equality is nested in a "logical space" (to use Richard Rorty's term, 13) whose vision of what black marriage is or might become is, in fact, curiously *unqueer*.

Let me explain what I mean by returning to the thought train with which Franke ends the book's introduction. I noted earlier that *Wedlocked* offers two distinct explanations for the persistent inability of straight African Americans to use marriage and marriage rights to "rebrand blackness in a way that sanitized racist stereotypes and coercive forms of racialized discipline" (61). I have already mentioned Franke's racial capital narrative, which attributes the Freedom to Marry campaign's successful sexual rebranding strategy to the social reputation it enjoyed as a movement made up of, and led by, white people. Although it is less fully developed than her economic interpretation, Franke argues that there is a second reason straight African Americans have failed to leverage marital ideology and institutions or their social reputation as heterosexuals to craft a revised conception of race in general, and of blackness in particular. We might describe this second explanation as a "semiotic" story, since it presses focus on the idea-image of "racial meaning" and representation.

In my remaining pages, I want briefly to tease out the theory of racial representation and meaning that is advanced—or perhaps less advanced than simply *assumed*—in the final sentence of the introduction to *Wedlocked*. What, Franke asks, is it about black marriage that makes it (in contrast to lesbigay marriage) such an ineffective vehicle for "elevating the status" (21) of African Americans? She traces the source of the problem to the "definitional indignity" that has historically denied African Americans access to the means of individual and collective self-representation. Unlike sexuality, she suggests, "the signature of race is a mark that African American people have had little hand in writing or rewriting" (22).

An air of ambiguity about the nature of the discursive disenfranchisement that makes it difficult if not impossible for African Americans to "re-represent" race and racial meaning attends this and related passages. Is the central claim here a *historical* claim that African Americans have "never been allowed" to participate in the public discourse of making race and black marriage *mean* (Franke 202)? This would seem to be the thrust of such qualified claims as the assertion that "for the most part marriage for African Americans has been a vehicle for reinforcing their inferiority and for eliciting familiar responses that assign a badge of inferiority" or the contention that "marriage has been and largely remains a kind of test that the African American community is seen as failing" (202). In contrast, other passages in *Wedlocked* suggest a less historical and more *categorical* line of argument, which attributes the discursive inability of African Americans successfully to refigure the meaning of race and black marriage to qualities that inhere in the very idea-image of race—or more precisely, of blackness—*as such*. How else is one to understand Franke's insistence that the right to marry reveals the "stubborn, *even indelible*, nature of racial stigma" or the thesis that the "signature" of race "is not one written by black people, but its mark is truly 'theirs' in the sense of belonging to them, *as being a property of their blackness*?" (21, 200; my emphases).

At stake here are not merely two very different conceptions of the meanings of race and racism in America. Depending on how one reads it, *Wedlocked* may be said to advance two distinct, contradictory visions of the prospects and potential uses of black marriage as a venue and vehicle for empowering black agency and enabling intimate relational resistance to the u.s. racial state and civil society. The notion that racial stigma is "indelible" or that the signature of race is a "property" of black bodies implies a theory of racial meaning that is only one step to the side of the semiotic view that construes race as an "unpassable symbolic frontier" (Hall 131) and an eternal, unchanging same. Put another way, to lose sight of the "writtenness" of race and racial meaning is to risk forgetting something we all by now surely know: race is a "discursive construct" and a "sliding signifier" (Hall 32) whose meanings can be *unwritten* and, indeed, *rewritten* to produce countermeanings and counterdiscourses. The world of race, "like all worlds of meaning," is a world where discourse "can never be finally fixed," a world in which racial signs and signifiers are "open to an infinite sliding," to "crossing," contamination, disruption, and destabilization by other signs and "other signifiers—[for instance,] of class, gender and sexuality" (Hall 171). To be faithful to its aspirations, then, a queer critical theory of black marriage must refuse to restrict its field of vision to what black marriage was in the nineteenth-century past, or even to what it is in our twenty-first-century present; it must also be willing to reflect speculatively on what black marriage might become in a twenty-second-century future. Similarly, in taking up the question of how black intimate alliance and the black intimate imagination can be mobilized to forge new, more democratic forms of sexual and racial citizenship, a critically queer engagement with the politics of black marriage must declare its independence from the ideological terms and institutional terrain of "law and rights-based advocacy" (Franke 61).

One potentially productive site for the speculative, queer, Afro-futurist reflection on black marriage I am urging here can be found in the domain of culture and the arts where, as Stuart Hall once noted, "things get said in ways in which they can't get said in any other domain" (Hall and Schwarz 153). Consider in this connection the extraordinary body of work that African American filmmakers have produced in the last few years on black intimacy in America. Narrative films such as *Mudbound*, *Fences*, *Birth of a Nation*, *Fruitvale Station*, and *Moonlight*, to name a few, tell stories and paint portraits of black love, sex, gender and sexuality, marriage, family, and kinship that imagine and represent, figurally, the hopes and fears and dreams and desires and dangers and delights of African American erotic and intimate life *beyond* the binary boundaries of normative whiteness and nonnormative blackness, of white supremacy and black inferiority that center the account of black marriage in *Wedlocked*.

To my mind, one of the more interesting aspects of these recent cinematic figurations of African American eros and intimacy is the way even the most conventional of these films manage to create aesthetic and imaginal space that positions black lives in the marital narrative with unexpected and even "queer" effects. Take the case of the Disney blockbuster *Black Panther*, in which director Ryan Coogler brings the Marvel comic book world of an imaginary African nation called Wakanda to three-dimensional life. *Black Panther* tells the story of Prince T'Challa, who becomes the king of Wakanda and superhero Black Panther after his father is murdered while giving a speech at the United Nations. T'Challa's nemesis is Prince N'Jadaka, a former u.s. black-ops soldier and the bastard son of T'Challa's late uncle, who was conceived in the late twentieth century when his father was assigned to Oakland, California, as a secret agent.

Thematically, *Black Panther* is an allegory about the epic struggle within the Black Atlantic between two warring visions of the politics of belonging: the nativist, nationalist, ethnic identity of T'Challa and the globalist, diasporic, racial identity of N'Jadaka. Narratively, the film is a domestic family drama of the struggle to the death of two brothers and those brothers' sons. Some gay and lesbian press coverage has faulted the movie version of *Black Panther* for not including a subplot in the comic series that recounts the romance between two members of King T'Challa's all-female personal guard. However, commentary on the film has overlooked one decidedly queer feature of the world of Wakanda as the filmmakers imagine and represent it. One insistent motif in *Black Panther* is the question of identity that, by tradition, Wakandans put to one another when they meet: "Who are you?" During the course of the film, the denizens of Wakanda address one another by many names: Mother, Father, King, Queen, Prince, Princess, Sister, Brother, Aunt, Uncle, Cousin, Son, Daughter. There are two names, however, by which no Wakandan is called or calls another: Husband and Wife. Indeed, by the end of *Black Panther*, the viewer comes to realize that the institution of marriage may not even exist in Wakanda; the film's scrupulous silence on this score is deafening.

Black Panther conjures the queer possibilities of black intimacy and the nonidentity of intimacy and conjugality in the romance between two lover-warriors, the heterosexual couple Okoye and W'Kabi. Throughout the film, W'Kabi and Okoye call one another "my love," a phrase that figures black intimacy at one and the same time as a mode of address (my *love*) and as a self-interpellative affective signature (*my* love) whose terms resist the identification and institutionalization of marital discourse. In *Black Panther*, the relationship between Okoye and W'Kabi becomes a cinematic point of departure for envisioning black heterosexuality beyond the boundaries of conjugality's constricted codes and conventions. The film invites its viewers to imaginatively enter the *mode de vie* (Foucault et al. 136) of Okoye and W'Kabi's queer, black heterosexual friendship. The story of these two lovers highlights the fluid, fecund possibilities of an amatory amicability "that might be and become just about anything" (Roach 45). The heady mix of mutual attraction and shared estrangement is brilliantly captured in the charged scene toward the end of *Black Panther* when Okoye and W'Kabi find themselves on opposite sides of a pitched battle. Okoye, spear in hand, commands W'Kabi to stop fighting and throw down his weapon or risk annihilation. W'Kabi asks her, "Would you kill me, my love?" Okoye replies, "For Wakanda? No question."

The fictional lifeworld of *Black Panther* is, of course, an imaginary domain. Okoye, W'Kabi, and the other citizens of Wakanda inhabit a fairy-tale realm that is far removed from the real, historical world of black marriage on which *Wedlocked* focuses. The imagined queer place from which the film's alternative vision of black intimacy springs exists only within the four corners of the theater screens on which that vision is projected. Nonetheless, the remarkable reception *Black Panther* has garnered since its release suggests that the racial fantasy it gives us of an "as yet unimagined [form] of individual and collective [black] existence" (Love 181) speaks to a deep yearning to "re-vision" race—or more precisely and in this context, blackness—as something *other* than, in Franke's words, a "curse" (12) or a "stain" (19) or a "badge of inferiority" (199) or a "mark" that African Americans ought or ought to want to "cleave" out of race in the same way that she says homosexuals have been able successfully to "cleave the sex out of homosexuality" (6). The sheer taken-for-grantedness of the film's "unapologetic blackness" has, in the words of one commentator, opened "a door into a radical blackness on the screen" (O'Brien). The power and the pleasures of *Black Panther* lie precisely in its flagrantly fantastical refusal to linger too closely or too long in the world of "actually existing race."

Black Panther may be a fiction, but as an *event* the film tells us a lot about the work that culture and cultural representation are doing at this vexed moment in the political history of race. First, *Black Panther* reminds us that the brute force and continuing social power that keep Americans of African descent "tethered to an identity that explains and justifies the many forms of inequality they endure" (Franke 62) always travel through the symbolic circuits of culture and the culture industry. Second, the film's account of the intersecting national and global dynamics that subtend contemporary race and racism raises hard questions about how people of African descent in the u.s. and elsewhere can effectively forge new black subjectivities and produce "new black subjects" (Hall 293) to interpret and interrupt the cultural and signifying economy within which the racial is imagined and fantasized and "written" in today's networked world. Third, and finally, *Black Panther* underscores the importance of art and culture for the urgent "imaginal" (Bottici 54) project of seeking and sustaining new, more open modes for engaging and living with cultural difference (Hall and Schwarz 148) in an age of resurgent racial and ethnic conflict.

These large and complicated issues raise questions to which I have no ready answers. Of this, however, I am certain. A queer, critical theory of race must eschew the white mythology of a closed "Americanist" narrative that always and only figures blackness as accreted stain, lack, failure, inferiority, stigma, mark, or curse. This means, in the first place, thinking the question of the Black American and the Black Atlantic *together* in a way that situates questions of race and racial discourse in a broader diasporic frame. In contrast to *Wedlocked*'s *nationalist* focus on black and lesbigay marriage in America, *Black Panther* suggests a different, *transnational* agenda for queer and race critical comparative research on black marriage. The chief questions that a transnational comparative study of black marriage would pose and try to answer are whether, why, and how bisexual, heterosexual, gay, and lesbian black people around the world experiment with conjugality by crafting spaces *within* marriage that engage and include intimate relational possibilities *outside* it. The transnational turn urged here recognizes that what we call "race" operates as a mobile modality in which *other* identities and categories—such as class, religion, gender, sexuality, ethnicity, nationality, region, and language—are lived, governed, and regulated; it understands, too, that race and racism do what they do at different times and in different places through complex, labile articulations that produce unpredictable consequences and unstable, uncanny, and even "queer" effects. This opening up of race—and with it, of gender and sexuality *inter alia*—beyond the "national signifier" (Hall 159) is one of the most urgent tasks for a queer, race critical project that aims to understand not only what black marriage has been or is but also what black marriage might *become*.

KENDALL THOMAS is the Nash Professor of Law and cofounder and director of the Center for the Study of Law and Culture at Columbia Law School. He is the coeditor, with Judith Butler and John Guillory, of *What's Left of Theory?* (Routledge, 2000), of *Critical Race Theory: The Key Writings That Formed the Movement* (New Press, 1995) with Kimberlé Williams Crenshaw, Neil Gotanda, and Gary Peller, and of *Legge, Razza e Diritti: La Critical Race Theory negli Stati Uniti* with Gianfrancesco Zanetti (Diabasis, 2005). He has published numerous articles, essays, and book chapters on constitutional law, feminist legal theory, critical race theory, human rights, and law and sexuality. An activist educator, Thomas is a past chair of the jurisprudence and law and humanities sections of the Association of American Law Schools and a founding member of the Majority Action Caucus of the AIDS Coalition to Unleash Power, Sex Panic!, and of the AIDS Prevention Action League.

Works Cited   *Black Panther.* Dir. Ryan Coogler. Marvel Studios, Walt Disney Pictures, 2018.

Bottici, Chiara. *Imaginal Politics: Images beyond Imagination and the Imaginary.* New York: Columbia UP, 2014.

Foucault, Michel, René Ceccaty, Jean Danet, and Jean Le Bitoux. "De l'amitié comme mode de vie." *Gai pied* 25 (1981): 38–39.

Franke, Katherine. *Wedlocked: The Perils of Marriage Equality.* New York: New York UP, 2015.

Hall, Stuart. *The Fateful Triangle: Race, Ethnicity, Nation.* Cambridge, MA: Harvard UP, 2017.

Hall, Stuart, and Bill Schwarz. "Living with Difference: Stuart Hall in Conversation with Bill Schwarz." *Soundings* 37 (2008): 148–58.

Harris, Cheryl. "Whiteness as Property." *Harvard Law Review* 106 (1993): 1709–91.

Lipsitz, George. *The Possessive Investment in Whiteness: How White People Profit from Identity Politics.* Philadelphia: Temple UP, 2006.

Love, Heather. "Queers ____ This." *After Sex? On Writing since Queer Theory.* Ed. Janet Halley and Andrew Parker. Durham: Duke UP, 2011. 180–91.

O'Brien, Brandon. "'Who are you?' *Black Panther* and the Politics of Belonging." *Tor.com* 26 Feb. 2018. https://www.tor.com/2018/02/26/who-are-you-black-panther-and-the-politics-of -belonging/.

Roach, Tom. *Friendship as a Way of Life: Foucault,* AIDS, *and the Politics of Shared Estrangement.* Albany: SUNY P, 2012.

Rorty, Richard. "Philosophy as Science, Metaphor, and Politics." *Essays on Heidegger and Others: Philosophical Papers.* Vol. 2. Cambridge: Cambridge UP, 1991. 9–49.